Standing at the Crossroads

Standing at the Crossroads

SOUTHERN LIFE SINCE 1900

Pete Daniel

Consulting editor: Eric Foner
American Century Series

Hill and Wang / New York
A division of Farrar, Straus and Giroux

Copyright © 1986 by Pete Daniel
All rights reserved
Printed in the United States of America
Published simultaneously in Canada by
Collins Publishers, Toronto
Second printing, 1988
Designed by Constance Ftera
Library of Congress Cataloging-in-Publication Data
Daniel, Pete.
  Standing at the crossroads.
  (American century series)
  Bibliography:
  Includes index.
  1. Southern States—Social conditions.   2. Southern
States—History—20th century.   I. Foner, Eric.
II. Title.   III. Series.
HN79.A13D36   1986   306'.0975   86–215
ISBN 0–8090–8821–5
ISBN 0–8090–0167–5 (pbk.)

For Nicholas

Preface

THROUGHOUT THE TWENTIETH CENTURY, THE SOUTH STOOD AT the crossroads. Would it continue along the road of segregation or move toward equal opportunity; would it continue with a labor-intensive sharecropping system or turn toward mechanization; would it dissolve the grid of violence or persist with lynching, peonage, and intimidation; would it mythologize the past or construct a better society; would it linger as a creative backwater or offer new music and literature; would it lose its distinctive accent or cling to it; and, finally, would it continue as the South or become a replica of the North?

Such questions crisscross the Southern historical experience during the century. Although most major changes in Southern society came during and after World War II, the seeds were planted and growing years earlier. Still, Southerners were ambivalent about giving up old ways, whether it was labor-intensive agriculture, old-time religion, or customary patterns of speech and life. I have weighted the book with Southerners who have not always been considered an integral part of Southern history. To my mind, farmers, mill-workers, miners, sawmill hands, musicians, and writers are important in understanding the contradictions that have made Southern history so inviting as a field of research.

The idea for this book was suggested by Arthur Wang and Eric Foner, and they have offered invaluable advice in its conception and writing. Louis R. Harlan, James P. Kelly, Jr., and Nancy D. Bercaw have read drafts of the manuscript and have made numerous suggestions, and I have received encouragement from Arthur Molella at the National Museum of American History. I owe a special debt to my parents, Stella Hunt and Peter Edward Daniel, and to the people of Spring Hope, North Carolina, who taught me about work, responsibility, and the Southern way of life. My grandparents, Annie Sykes and Robert Calvin Hunt, taught me about farm life, and some of my earliest memories are of sitting at the crossroads store at Seven Paths among farmers. There are debts to teachers and colleagues too numerous to recount.

P.D.

Washington, D.C.

Contents

Standing at the Crossroads

1 / Southern Cultures in Conflict

As the South entered the twentieth century, it carried the burdens of its history—defeat in war, a race and class system, poverty, and the recent failure of the Populist movement. Its poverty, undeveloped economy, and great mineral wealth in many ways resembled that of countries in Africa and Latin America. Just as imperialistic countries opened doors, created spheres of influence, and annexed land on other continents, the capitalists of the Northern United States regarded the South as their colony. Lacking capital, Southerners became foremen and workers for Northern masters, and farmers were even further removed from the lines of power and wealth.

Although Southerners did not understand the exact relationship they had to Northern capital, they had a vague idea of how they were linked to it. Testifying before the Industrial Commission in 1899, Georgian J. Pope Brown told the story of a sawmill owner. Every Saturday night before his workers showed up for pay, he would go to a neighbor's house to get money. "He would go to the man and take off his hat and ask for a little money, and said he thought to himself if he got in that man's place he would not have to do that." But a few days later he was in Macon "and he saw that fellow up in Macon bowing and scraping and asking for money, and he said, 'I heard them say that the Macon fellow went up to New York and just beat everybody bowing and scraping.' "

The Southern colony, the twelve Southern states south of the Potomac River and west to Texas, in 1900 contained some 11.2 million whites and 6.9 million blacks. Only eighteen percent of these people lived in urban areas, whereas the nation at large had an urban population of 39.7 percent. It would take the South until World War II to bring its urban population past forty percent. In most respects, Southern rural life was typical of the region, and farmers and their retainers rarely looked beyond the community, only occasionally showing interest in state and national politics and the issues of the wider world. In many people's minds, the outside world seemed threatening, full of ideas that could jeopardize their way of life.

Rural Culture

Within the South, there were two primary cultures—black and white. One of the reasons that whites insisted on segregation was their lack of understanding of black culture. Black religion, leisure, and family relations and a different view of work and capital accumulation presented a riddle to white Southerners. The response of blacks to Emancipation provided a case in point. Like emancipated people elsewhere, Southern blacks did not initially desire wealth but instead wanted land for subsistence and independence. When this dream was not fulfilled, black workers struggled to attain the best conditions possible under the sharecropping system. They also established their own churches and their own way of life as best they could. The wall of laws that proscribed blacks shut them off from competing on equal terms with whites. Yet laws did not allow them simply to subsist, as many desired, but instead forced them to work within the system of commercial agriculture. Instead of accepting the differences and allowing blacks to progress along ways amenable to their culture, whites segregated them, deprived them of the vote, and used violence to enforce color lines. Most whites pointed to differences in black culture as marks of inferiority.

Yet, in many ways, black and white Southerners shared a common way of life. All farmers moved in harmony with the seasonal demands of crops, often lived in run-down houses, complained about interest rates, and worshipped on Sunday. Increasingly, the economic situation of whites deteriorated, and many lost their land and became, for all purposes, equals to black sharecroppers.

But the South proved far more diverse than these two cultures. Mountain people were proudly different from low-country people, more likely to accept a subsistence existence and shun outside economic forces—until timber barons, mining companies, and cotton mills ushered them into the national economy. Louisiana Cajuns, descendants of exiled French Canadians, established a separate culture complete with French language. Like mountaineers, Cajuns largely ignored worldly goods and lived by hunting, fishing, trapping, and raising subsistence crops, including rice. They settled along the southwest Louisiana network of bayous, which they used for transportation. These diverse rural people differed from their urban cousins. They had made the best they could of their limited opportunities, but their confining existence exacted its toll.

Not only did the South consist of separate cultures, but each commodity dictated the seasonal work routine. Most rural Southerners were tied to King Cotton and its exacting cultivation. Cotton farmers worked in spurts, plowing the land in the spring, planting, chopping weeds, and finally ending cultivation in midsummer, laying the crop by, as the term went. Children often stayed out of school for the autumn harvest and spring planting. Cotton farming was a family enterprise. The year's work ended in late autumn when the farmer settled up. For a tenant or sharecropper, this meant watching the planter or merchant consult ledger books and pronounce the verdict, seldom more than a few dollars' credit or debit. A family, depending on its size, could till only some ten to twenty acres. The implements used throughout the cotton South were primitive and consisted of plows and a farm wagon and mules to pull them, mechanical seeders, hoes, cotton sacks, and a scale to weigh the cotton. By the turn of the century, on-farm mule-driven gins gave way to commercial steam gins located in towns. Each community had a cotton gin, usually owned by a planter or merchant, that separated lint from seeds. After ginning, a compress packed the lint into bales; the seed fed the growing cotton-seed industry, which manufactured vegetable oil and other by-products. Customarily, in autumn, farmers got cash for their seed—seed money—and it was the first money they received for the work they had been doing since January. Later they or their creditors sold the cotton to local buyers.

The South produced several varieties of tobacco; burley, which dominated Kentucky and the mountains of Tennessee and North Carolina; fire-cured in western Kentucky and Tennessee; and the flourishing flue-cured weed in Virginia, the Carolinas, and by the 1920s in Georgia and Florida. The cultivation of these various tobaccos was similar. Seed grew in plant beds till the seedlings were ready for transplanting in freshly plowed fields. The entire family chopped out the weeds, plowed, and later broke off suckers and tops and crushed worms. Burley farmers cut the entire stalk in the autumn, and then they hung it in barns, allowing the air to dry the leaves before stripping them and tying them for market. The harvest routine for flue-cured tobacco was highly labor-intensive, for the leaves were pulled from the stalks three or four at a time as they ripened and then tied to sticks that were hung in a barn for curing. The routine of daily harvest for flue-cured tobacco farmers proved exhausting, but the yearly routine never ended, unlike that of cotton farmers, who had a lay-by season and other periods of leisure. After the crop had been harvested and cured, each leaf was graded and then tied into hands, bundles of some twenty-five to thirty leaves. Both burley and flue-cured farmers sold their crops at auction in large warehouses. A line of buyers from tobacco companies trailed behind an auctioneer and bid on each farmer's crop. It took only a few moments for the incomprehensible pageant to pass by the farmer, who then took his sales tag to the warehouse pay window and, after charges had been deducted, had his reward for the year's work. He then returned home and began cutting firewood for the next summer's curing.

These commodity cultures (the annual routines of plowing, cultivating, harvesting, and marketing crops) turned on annual credit.

Around Christmastime, a farmer made arrangements for the next year. A tenant who could afford cash rent simply arranged to farm a certain acreage; he owned his own work stock and tools and in most cases resided in a house on the farm as part of the bargain. Farmers who owned work stock and implements agreed to pay a certain amount of rent in kind, a specified number of cotton bales or pounds of tobacco, and were called standing renters. They usually ran the farms, with no supervision from the landowner. Many farmers worked for wages year round, while other laborers only entered agriculture as seasonal workers. Although their number steadily decreased, many black and white Southern farmers owned their farms. In 1910, of the 847,907 black farmers, 195,432 owned 15.7 million acres of land. There were 1.6 million white farmers.

Sharecropping became customary. The idea of sharing the crop between landlord and tenant evolved from the Reconstruction era, when landowners struck deals with former slaves to work on shares. Ultimately, lien laws put sharecroppers at the mercy of their creditors, who had a lien on the growing crop in exchange for a unit of land that fit the size of the sharecropper's family. The shares varied, but usually the landlord and the cropper split the cash crops fifty-fifty. The law in most Southern states defined a cropper as a wage laborer. Increasingly in the years after the Civil War, white yeoman farmers were sucked into commercial farming, lost their land, and became sharecroppers. In such an arrangement, the landlord or merchant had tremendous power. He dictated the rations the family received, the acreage planted, the mix of crops, and the ledger books. At settlement time, many farmers believed, in some cases correctly, that they did not receive a fair share of money. Over time, sharecroppers moved from farm to farm, usually within the same community, always searching for a good parcel of land and a fair landlord. Annual agreements between owner and worker relied on oral contracts and varied from area to area, from farm to farm.

Southern farmers organized their lives around crop cycles, community stores, and churches, and they paid more attention to almanacs than to scientific notions of farming. The community patronized crossroads stores or small towns as centers for exchanging news about crops and local politics—and trading stock. Farmers needed plowlines, plows, harnesses, and other supplies, as well as credit, for which they were charged exorbitant rates, from twenty-five to seventy percent in most cases. Farmers would gather around a stove or on the front gallery of these small stores to talk. Such men hunted and fished together to supplement their meager diets, and let their stock roam the unfenced land. Such privileges went with the way of life and sometimes crossed class and race boundaries. Blacks and whites, careful about the peculiar lines of deference, shared talk, hunting, and work.

On Sundays most rural Southerners went to church. The preaching service, picnics, and revivals became an integral part of life, and for many farm women the church offered the only escape from the exhausting round of chores. Most Southerners were Fundamentalists; they took the Bible literally and attended Baptist and Methodist churches. Whether in black or white churches, Southerners believed that sin was identifiable and would be punished by a just God, although blacks had a quite different regard for the devil. While whites saw the devil as evil incarnate (with horns and a forked tail), blacks regarded him more as a trickster. For both, the Bible promised a better life in the hereafter for the poor and oppressed. The Lord made the sun shine and the rains fall, and He also brought the hail and wind that could destroy crops.

Even as the pace of life quickened and broadened in many sections of the country, most Southern rural people stayed close to home and cared little for organized recreation. Schoolchildren played baseball and basketball, and families enjoyed fairs, tent shows, and an occasional movie. In 1925 a North Carolina rural economist concluded: "The farm people of the South are suspicious of what we call play and recreation." If children were having a good time, he observed, "their fathers and mothers are apt to think that they are in a state of mortal sin. A common saying in our country regions is 'An idle brain and a playground are the devil's workshop.'" He suggested that rural people should change their "psychology."

In one sense, Southerners were imprisoned in the past. Most farmers cared less for modern notions of farming than for owning good work stock and fertile land. Of course, they hoped for high commodity prices, yet returns rarely allowed bottom-rung farmers a surplus after the usurious interest rates on overpriced merchandise. Dependence on outside sources of supply put farmers at the mercy of the corporations that manufactured them. They instinctively understood, as the Populist analysis of the economy showed, that they were being exploited by trusts. The failure of the Populist movement left them not only at the mercy of such trusts but still divided by race.

The pre-Civil War insistence on separation of blacks and whites continued after Emancipation. Despite experiments in school integration, the participation of blacks in politics, and an easing of color barriers in transportation, blacks and whites often moved along different roads in work and recreation. After freedom, blacks established their own churches and found familiar routines of family life and creativity that were outside white traditions. In the late 1880s, however, a radical mood in politics led to efforts to deprive blacks of the vote and remove them from social contact with whites. Disenfranchisement and segregation had a greater effect than putting blacks aside; it stunted black aspirations and stamped blacks as inferior.

Wherever blacks moved in the South, they encountered barriers. They could not eat in white restaurants or ride in first-class sections of public transportation. Their schools were not only separate but unequal, and, increasingly, residential areas became segregated in towns and cities. Laws included stiff penalties for petty offenses. Stealing a pig, shooting across a public road, or not fulfilling a contract could mean a heavy fine and a long prison term. There was little appeal from such punishment, for juries were, by law or custom, all white. Labor laws as well as those pertaining to other crimes grew more restrictive as the radical mood increased in the 1890s. When in 1908 Alonzo Bailey, a rural wage laborer in Alabama, left his employer, he had the choice of returning to work or going to the chain gang. The law specified that simply leaving his job without paying back his advance was evidence of his intent to defraud his employer, and a rule of evidence prevented his testifying as to his intentions. In 1911 the U.S. Supreme Court ruled that Bailey had been a victim of peonage, that the Alabama labor law coerced him to work out a debt.

The laws that took away the vote and segregated blacks had

other effects. Traditional occupations such as carpentry, masonry, and barbering became white occupations. Textile mills, from the beginning, were largely white enclaves. On the other hand, blacks became miners and industrial workers. Black women, anxious to shed one element of slavery, had left the fields after the Civil War, but in many cases economic hardship had driven them back. To earn money to keep the family intact, many black women took in washing and ironing or worked as maids for whites.

The system of segregation solidified in the first years of the twentieth century. Most contacts between the races were formalized, and blacks affected a certain style of address, of clothing, and of speech. They learned through experimentation how to approach whites and minimize friction, and whites came to assume that blacks were what they appeared. Yet blacks joked about whites and in their segregated communities had a distinct culture. In essence, both cultures grew further apart at most levels, and despite contacts in field and factory, in towns and along roads, color barriers inhibited the exchange of ideas and opinions. Not even laws and customs could prevent all exchange, however, for people interacted, sharing speech, music, stories, and, in many cases, a culture of poverty.

Until recently historians have regarded the rural South from Reconstruction until the New Deal as a static unit. Despite the burden of defeat, the harsh sharecropping system, racism, and the failure of Populism, new opportunities appeared in the most unlikely places. In the 1880s a land-promotion scheme in southwestern Louisiana attracted Midwestern wheat farmers who were losing a battle against grasshoppers and debt. Railroads and land promoters urged migration, and thousands of farmers went into the Louisiana prairie. At first, they were alienated, disturbed by the Cajuns, who seemed content to fish, trap, and grow their small stands of rice, which relied on rainfall—Providence—for water. Prairie settlers discovered that they could grow rice successfully by relying on Providence and using adapted grain binders from the wheat area to cut it and steam threshers to prepare it for market. Quickly, the prairie filled with a new farming population and Northern implements.

The expansion of prairie rice proved fortuitous, for even as the Louisiana rice culture boomed, the old Carolina rice areas fell into disarray due to labor problems and hurricane damage. By the turn of the century, Louisiana and Texas had supplanted the Carolinas and Georgia as the country's largest producers of rice. By 1908, farmers in the Arkansas prairie adopted the same methods and created a thriving rice culture there. Prairie rice farmers personified modern notions of farming, for they used binders, steam tractors, and threshers and irrigated their fields.

At harvest time the farmer hired a crew to drive the binders and shock the rice. A few weeks later, after the rice had dried in shocks, the crew loaded it on wagons and hauled it to a thresher. The harvest proved the most labor-intensive time of the year for rice farmers. Otherwise, one man and his family and perhaps a hired hand could tend several hundred acres of rice. Women did no field-work as they did in tobacco and cotton cultivation. In almost every way—labor requirements, implements, annual work cycle, and profits—the rice culture differed from cotton and tobacco. The rice frontier not only illustrated the opportunities left in the rural South but also pointed toward the use of machines in agriculture.

As different as rice was from tobacco and cotton, when it came to marketing, all three kinds of farmers shared a distrust of those who bought their crops. At first, prairie rice farmers sold through brokers from New Orleans mills who handled river rice. Enterprising prairie businessmen quickly built mills and challenged city domination. Yet, no matter where the farmers sold their produce, they complained of low prices. Cajuns were drawn into the mechanized rice culture, and Midwestern immigrants and Cajuns blended their radically different cultures. Some blacks owned or worked on rice farms year round. Farm laborers from nearby cotton or sugar areas arrived at harvest time to work for wages, even as other Southern farmers took odd jobs at sawmills, cotton gins, oil mills, factories, and mines to supplement their incomes.

As rice and tobacco cultures expanded, cotton farmers watched helplessly as an insect, the boll weevil, destroyed their crops. From 1890 to 1920, the boll weevil had eaten its way from south Texas to Georgia, and it had left a wider track of devastation than had Sherman's army. Like pestilence, flood, and drought throughout history, the boll-weevil devastations altered the direction of people's lives. The weevil bored into the young cotton bud and laid eggs, and these small weevils then ate the developing lint, leaving the bolls empty. All attempts to halt the insect's advance had failed, for state governments refused to quarantine infested areas, and the federal government proved loath to interfere with interstate commerce, even the possible ruin of it. Some farmers turned to other crops, and laborers fled to new locations ahead of or behind the insect's advance. The impact was not uniform, for in the Mississippi Delta the weevil did little harm, while in the Black Belt of Alabama and Georgia its destructiveness proved enormous.

The significance of the boll weevil lay not only in the overt destruction that it wrought but in the role of the federal government in fighting it and in the shift of cotton acreage to the West. For the first time since the Civil War, Southerners welcomed federal agents. Government entomologists failed to discover ways to kill the weevil effectively, so agriculturists taught cultural methods of dealing with it. Late planting, picking up infested squares (young buds) that fell from the plant, plowing under the stalks after picking, and, ultimately, chemicals could, if not kill off, at least discourage the insect. To teach this to farmers, the federal government set up a system of demonstration farms under the direction of Seaman A. Knapp, who had taught, farmed, edited a farm journal, and been a university president before moving to the Louisiana prairie to sell land and encourage the rice culture. Allied with land-grant universities and depending on local committees for backing and financing, Southern demonstration farms evolved into the Federal Extension Service, formalized by the Smith–Lever Act of 1914. The American Farm Bureau Federation grew from local committees and by 1920 became a lobbying arm of commercial farmers.

From its beginning, the Federal Extension Service relied on the leading farmers in a community, and it taught those who could best help themselves. Its main purpose was to war on the weevil, but it also strongly advocated diversification and mechanization. Different crops, of course, meant different machinery, and quickly Extension Service county agents became disseminators of new technical and mechanical knowledge. Obviously, the gospel was aimed at landlords—not tenants; few sharecroppers could diversify, since they were under the control of a landlord, and just as few could buy implements.

The Extension Service in the South followed class lines, since the ideal the agents offered was one that generated middle-class farmers. Leery of education and unable to buy implements, sharecroppers clung to the old and often stultifying ways. They studied the weevil and fought it with calcium arsenate dust, but they could not diversify or purchase modern implements. Thus, two types of farming emerged in the South. More wealthy farmers bought machinery and diversified, and they paid attention to new farming methods taught through county agents, agriculture schools, and farm magazines. Sharecroppers continued in the old ways, but their cost of production rose, actual production decreased, and their already sparse earnings fell.

Farmers in the Mississippi Delta and in the new lands opened in Oklahoma and Texas grew more cotton, tilting cotton production to the west. By World War I, a vast shift in cotton production had occurred, a trend that would increase through the century as the culture entered California and New Mexico. Production from new growing areas drove prices down further, and the international collapse of cotton prices in 1919 sounded a death rattle throughout the old cotton-growing states. Attempts to organize collectives and cut back production failed, and by 1930 many farmers in the old growing areas prayed for a miracle to free them from their oppression, even as floods and drought put them more and more in debt. The Southern states were as much colonies as ever and lacked the resources to regenerate the old agricultural system.

Despite the dynamic expansion of the tobacco and rice cultures and the migration of cotton westward, by 1930 most Southern farmers were desperate. Prices had fallen far below the cost of production, and all efforts to halt the slide had failed. By 1930, there were 336,817 white and 384,541 black sharecroppers; in the 1920s, the number of white tenants increased by 200,000. A heritage of independence that had thrived in rural areas of the South dissipated before the forces of depression. Many farmers, their wills broken, were ready for a savior.

Mountain Culture ————————————————————

In the late nineteenth century, travelers and reporters set in print a tangled notion of Appalachian mountain people. Because mountaineers were independent and self-sufficient, outsiders labeled them backward, judging the traditional culture as an anachronism, a throwback. A superficial trip through a few settlements often served as the basis for pronouncements on mountain people as primitive, romantic, violent, and retarded. Indeed, many Americans seemed fascinated by a people who had largely repudiated the American dream of progress, mechanization, and consumer goods. Like the Amish today, mountain people seemed strange to a country indoctrinated with a notion of progress tied to industrialism and accumulation of capital.

From one perspective, mountain families preserved the Jeffersonian dream of a small farm, distant neighbors, a school, church, and a nearby gristmill as the basis for community. From another view, they were underprivileged, uneducated, and forced to live in poverty. Whether isolation had been thrust upon mountaineers or they had sought it, that such an existence could be fulfilling and complete puzzled not only Northerners but also other Southerners. Mountain people had remained loyal to the Union during the Civil War, for they did not share the dream of a slaveholders' empire. The divisive class distinctions that characterized most of the South and North seemed unnecessary to people living in compact hill communities. They characteristically owned small farms in a valley, and the family operated the farm, with little need for outside contact. Most farms had work stock, pigs, chickens, cows, a few plows, a stout house, and a barn. Usually a nearby gristmill powered by a fast-running stream ground corn. Sheep furnished wool that was spun and woven on the farm. The rough terrain and a subsistence economy militated against improved roads that could handle commercial traffic. What did move across the roads and trails were herds of cattle, hogs, and sheep headed for the flat country on either side of the mountains.

In Avery County, North Carolina, for example, farmers raised cattle and corn, and they also had apple orchards. Every autumn, caravans of wagons laden with apples filed out of the county and descended to the surrounding towns—Johnson City, Bristol, Marion, and Asheville. The people would camp out near the towns for several days and sell apples. At night they built fires, cooked, talked, shared stories, and argued. When they had sold off their apples, they would shop for hardware, leather, shoes, and some candy for the children. They then headed back to the mountains. This was pretty much the annual involvement in the commercial world for these families. During the remainder of the year, they lived at home, grew their food, tended their stock, occasionally took a bag of corn to the mill to be ground into meal, and visited nearby towns for court days. Many mountaineers, as did their flatland cousins, distilled corn into liquor.

Cade's Cove in the Great Smoky Mountain National Park preserves the material elements of the old mountain culture. Small isolated cabins nestle on the flanks of the cove floor, and churches and a gristmill and general store serve as the community locus. Beehives, barns, pastures, and cleared fields provided the honey, shelter for stock and crops, grazing land, and fields for growing corn, wheat, hay, and vegetables. It takes little imagination to reconstruct the dynamics of the Cade's Cove community from these restored objects.

Students of material culture can also see the way that inhabitants used wood for houses, barns, and fences. Women carded wool, spun it, and wove it into garments, and occasionally quilting bees would produce colorful bed covers. The family served as the primary social unit for mountain people, whose independence created strong nuclear families. Religion was a unifying experience, and once or twice a month circuit riders brought not only the Gospel but also news from other settlements.

Like rural people elsewhere, men and women divided their tasks and took pride in their separate spheres. While men tended crops, cattle, and orchards, women did household chores and also spun and then wove. They toted water from a spring, washed in black iron pots, made soap, milked cows, did chores, and chopped in the fields. It was a full life. A family prided itself on its size, its brawn, its musical ability, its faith, and its role in the community. It celebrated marriages, mourned deaths, rejoiced in baptisms, and shared work with other families. The neighborly spirit reflected in barn raisings and corn shuckings welded a powerful communal force.

Those who castigated mountaineers for their backwardness missed the role of family and land in organizing mountain life. The plot of land played a sacred role; it was the place of life, the locus for eating, sleeping, earning a living, birth, and death, and it passed from generation to generation, providing continuity and order. Mountain people opted for a way of life outside the mainstream of industrialism and commercial farming. In a sense, they preserved the Jeffersonian dream in an age when Hamiltonian manufacturing and banking conquered most of the country.

The Appalachians presented great opportunities for commercial development. Travelers who passed through the area saw incongruity in what they perceived as poor and illiterate people and the vast timber and coal resources around them. Such views stimulated missionary zeal that justified the exploitation which leveled mountains for coal and denuded forests for timber. Such intrusion found ready justification in the American ethic of progress. The forces that entered the mountains in the late nineteenth century envisioned a new mountain culture, one tied not to subsistence, family and community but to business. Just as the failure of the Populist movement and the rise of the Extension Service in farming regions of the South opened agriculture to commercialism, the investors who arrived in the mountains at the turn of the century signaled the end of the old culture.

Most development capital came from the North, and profits returned there, although enterprising natives who had the foresight to buy up mineral rights and land and then sell or lease them to Northern firms also prospered. Lawyers discovered flaws in land titles and purchased valuable tracts for a few cents an acre as confused residents fought back as best they could. Agents toured the mountains searching for coal and other ore deposits. Having located a promising ridge, the agent would find the owner, usually receive a hearty welcome, and then offer either to buy the land outright or to lease the mineral rights. No doubt, many farmers thought they had skinned another flatlander—until railroads and miners appeared with the legal power to alter and ruin the land.

The great change in life in the mountains could be gauged from the change from the small subsistence farms to company towns in the mining and timbering regions. Mountain people had not been conditioned to industrial life, and at first they would work only enough to get money to live out the month. They would also leave work for fishing, funerals, or to keep up the farm. Mining bosses wanted regular workers. The routine and environment that dominated life in the coal fields bore little resemblance to farming, except that both required brawn and endurance. Like farmers, miners rose early, and after breakfast they walked to the mines. Once inside, they worked in dim lamplight.

After working all day in the mines, they retraced their steps home, to eat, enjoy their family, and sleep. The company often owned the houses and seldom furnished running water or sanitary facilities, except outhouses shared by three or four families. The company store provided rations on credit and deducted the charges from the paycheck or issued scrip. There was little recreation, although some owners offered movies, bowling alleys, pool halls, and organized baseball teams. Saloons and gambling dens sometimes became the center of company towns. Churches and schools grew along with the seamier areas. Crowded housing, confining work, temptations, and low pay contrasted starkly with the small farms that had earlier characterized the region.

Not all the mountain wealth lay underground, for vast forests covered the land. With the coming of railroads into the mountains, these stands were no longer safe from the saw. By the turn of the century, timber companies, most financed by outside capital, invaded the Southern mountains to harvest the resources aboveground, just as miners bored into the hillsides to take the underground wealth. In both cases, mountaineers underestimated the impact of this exploitation. Timber and coal interests merged into one great operation that used rails for transport.

It was like a huge pincer operation as the men first cut at the fringes of the forests, and as rails pushed farther, they surrounded the heart of the old mountain forests. Logging companies did not replant behind them but instead left the denuded hillsides to erode. The industry employed mountaineers, but after World War I much of the virgin timber had been cut; by the beginning of the Great

Depression, the timber industry languished throughout the South. Since subsistence agriculture had been disrupted by the shift to mining and lumbering, mountain people found it difficult to return to traditional life.

Lumbering was a rough life, as was mining, but by its very nature it existed at the frontier of settlement. Both mining towns and lumber camps contained an element of wildness that contrasted with the culture that had been left behind. Both occupations strained family life and consigned women to the home, instead of allowing them to share the concerns and work of a farm. Other industries also changed the nature of mountain work. Families moved from the hills to towns and cities where mills manufactured textiles, furniture, rayon, and tannin, a derivative of chestnut and oak bark used in leather production. While some towns thrived and provided steady jobs, others served as a base for lumbering or mining, boomed, and then disappeared.

A missionary impulse inspired teachers who decided that mountain people needed aid in combating the forces of change. In 1902, Katherine Pettit and May Stone, two women from the Kentucky Bluegrass area, set up a settlement school at Hindman in Knott County. No one could doubt the sincerity of these women in forsaking middle-class comfort for the isolation of the mountains. The teachers taught not only the basics but also crafts and manners. To an outsider, the old culture seemed static, fixed in time, unchanging. As historian David Whisnant has pointed out, however, mountain culture was "characterized by both continuity and discontinuity, stability and change, indigenous and borrowed elements . . . It was old quilt patterns cut from new store-bought goods; old (and new) songs played on mail-order instruments; new realities (coal mines and coal camps and post offices) cast in old ballad meter or parlor song style." Whisnant concluded: "In sum, much of the indigenous culture of the area was being intentionally replaced by genteel turn-of-the-century mass culture: light bread, pump organs, 'socials,' Fletcherized food, and napkins on the left, please."

Whisnant took as a symbol of this subtle change the Hindman attitude toward Christmas. Mountain people customarily celebrated the Christmas season, not a single day, and the festivities stretched from December 25 to Old Christmas on January 6. On December 25 the younger people had a boisterous party, while on January 6 the elders held a quieter celebration. The settlement teachers taught that a Victorian Christmas, celebrated on December 25 with a tree, stockings, and carols, was proper.

Intrusion into the mountains came from both capitalists and the bearers of middle-class culture. Both introduced some positive aspects, and both extracted wealth in different forms. Such attitudes encouraged both the romanticizing of mountaineers for their old culture and the denigrating of them for being fit to work just in mines or to cut trees. Historians have only recently begun to whittle away at the myths and misunderstandings of mountain culture.

The Music of Exiles

Even as the sprawling agricultural areas and the isolated mountains faced the challenge of the twentieth century, new types of Southern music spread across the country. The South gave license to musical genius, and by the turn of the century, spirituals, blues, jazz, Cajun, mountain, and barrelhouse music emerged from the experiences of people who in many cases had lost nearly everything but hope and pride. In many ways the greatest contribution of the South in this century can be found in its music—and in its literature. Both musicians and writers chronicled the travail of lost or tormented souls, whose resilience was constantly reiterated in song and story.

The origins of this music have been traced to Africa, Europe, and England; it evolved in slavery, in exile, and in the aching life of sharecroppers. The music of black Americans originated in travail that started in the seventeenth century as Africans were taken slaves, separated from home and kin, and transported across the Atlantic Ocean. Hymns of suffering related the perplexing experience of slavery and later the disillusionment of freedom. Blacks used fiddles and banjos to accompany work songs and chants that expressed their feelings and sometimes, through symbolism, messages about freedom, flight, and the nature of white folks.

The same experiences shaped the music that accompanied worship. Denied their African gods, blacks seized the Old and New Testaments and altered them to their circumstances. They sang of Moses leading the Israelites out of bondage, of crossing the Jordan, of sweet Jesus, of heaven and of hell, and of chariots swinging low to transport the chosen to heaven. Blues became the devil's music, and spirituals became the Lord's music, although the roots of both were inextricably tangled. The blues came out of the fields and entered the dance halls (juke joints) of the rural and small-town South, while spirituals flourished in churches. The two musical forms became the expressions of the preterites and the elect, the damned and the chosen.

Most Americans, of course, heard the Lord's music. After the Civil War, Northerners recognized the beauty and distinctiveness of spirituals, and by the turn of the century a number of black colleges regularly sent their choirs north to loosen the purse strings of well-meaning whites. Some blacks loathed such a hat-in-hand approach to fund-raising, and others complained that whites came away from such concerts with black stereotypes reinforced. Although W. E. B. Du Bois is best known for his scholarly writing and his activism as a leader of the National Association for the Advancement of Colored People (NAACP), he had a keen ear and a deep understanding of black music. In *The Souls of Black Folk,* in 1903, he commented on the nature and origin of religious music. "The music of Negro religion is that plaintive rhythmic melody, with its touching minor cadences, which, despite caricature and defilement, still remains the most original and beautiful expression of human life and longing yet born on American soil." He traced its origins to the African forests; in the New World, "it was adapted, changed, and intensified by the tragic soul-life of the slave, until, under the stress of law and whip, it became the one true expression of a people's sorrow, despair, and hope."

Even as Du Bois was explaining the origin of black religious music, the blues was developing in the Mississippi Delta. The blues was not the sound of hope but of despair and suffering, and it grew out of the experiences of rural workers, mostly sharecroppers. Early in the twentieth century, travelers through the Delta reported hearing a kind of music that resembled a field holler or the repetitive song that accompanied gang labor. In 1907, federal agent Michele Berardinelli left a Delta plantation after secretly investigating a peonage case. He observed a black woman plowing in a cotton field that was "flat and equal like the sandy expanse of the desert." She was singing, and "the notes of her song went high in the ether of fire, and then were stopped abruptly with a guttural modulation that sounded like the lamentation of a creature in great distress and desolation." It made Berardinelli "feel as if I were travelling through an African region and had just been to visit a Colony of prisoners in confinement."

Berardinelli's account was highly significant, for it described not only the music but also its context. As music critic Robert Palmer has made clear, music that came out of the Delta at the turn of the century was "created not just by black people but by the poorest, most marginal black people. Most of the men and women who sang and played it could neither read nor write. They owned almost nothing and lived in virtual serfdom." Many of those who played blues, however, managed to escape from the sharecropping system by playing music in dance halls and on street corners of small Delta towns.

As far as Palmer could discover, the blues began in the heart of the Mississippi Delta in the 1890s. Using the career of Charley Patton, Palmer traced the family's move in the 1890s to the Dockery Plantation, Patton's development as a guitarist under the spell of Henry Sloan (who later moved to Chicago, as did many Delta bluesmen), and how the blues, with guitar work that was fretted with a knife or bottle neck, became the music of choice at the Saturday-night dances that broke up the weekly Delta work routine. The blues spread from one musician to another, each adding verses or stamping a particular style on the songs.

By the 1920s, Charley Patton, Son House, and Tommy Johnson personified the blues. Variations of this music ultimately had a profound influence on the development of rock 'n' roll, but that was after Robert Johnson had left his unique stamp on the evolution of blues. Born in Mississippi in 1911, Johnson apprenticed himself to Son House, Willie Brown, and Charley Patton, but his talent showed little promise. Then he disappeared for months. When he returned, his old mentors yielded him the stage when they took a break. What they heard amazed and disturbed them, for Johnson had somehow not only mastered their blues but transcended them. "He sold his soul to the devil to get to play like that," Son House murmured. The idea persisted, not only because Johnson never denied it or because his lyrics overflow with references to Satan, but also because some people claimed they could locate the exact Delta spot where he made the bargain, and that inspired his "Crossroads Blues."

Johnson, then, personified the bargain with the devil that led to evil music. "Unlike gospel," Greil Marcus observed, "blues was not a music of transcendence; its equivalent to God's Grace was sex and love. Blues made the terrors of the world easier to endure, but blues also made those terrors more real." And Robert Johnson could make evil incredibly real and chilling. His songs were of the devil, of women, of frustration, and of a force driving him on, ever restless. "There's a hellhound on my trail," he reiterated again and again. By the mid-1930s, Johnson was recording some of his songs, but he was still a backcountry musician who sang in the roadhouses and bars of the Delta. In 1938 in Greenwood, he got drunk, made a pass at the bar owner's wife, and was poisoned. He was dead at twenty-seven. Yet his music lived on, influencing his contemporaries and ultimately the Rolling Stones, Eric Clapton, and many others.

Five years after Johnson died, McKinley Morganfield, who had picked up the nickname Muddy Waters, quit his tractor-driving job on the Stovall plantation and took the train to Chicago. There was already a large community of Delta exiles in the city, including many musicians, and Muddy Waters started playing for rent parties and at neighborhood bars. In 1944 he bought an electric guitar, and with his band helped transform Delta blues into popular music that attracted a large black following, and European interest, and inspired emerging rhythm and blues musicians. Records, the radio, and the constant mobility of blues musicians spread the music across the country, but until the early 1950s it was largely unknown outside black communities.

Another type of music evolved at the same time as the blues. In the logging camps of Texas and Louisiana, solitary blues performers accompanied by guitar were often drowned out by the roaring crowds in barrelhouses, shacks where liquor was sold from barrels. As in other areas of the country, Saturday night provided the opportunity to forget work and release frustrations and celebrate. In these hinterland lumber camps emerged a new piano style that could cut through the cacophonous din—barrelhouse piano. The strong, rhythmic, almost drumlike beat of barrelhouse piano evolved into boogie-woogie and ultimately influenced jazz. Both blues and barrelhouse musicians worked in dangerous environments and often sat near doors or windows in case the dance hall exploded into violence. As one musician who played the barrelhouse circuit explained: "Some of them died real young—and some lived to be thirty-five or forty."

It was fitting that jazz, the most cosmopolitan musical form, emerged in New Orleans at the turn of the century. In law and in custom, the city bore heavy Spanish and French influences, and although it was racially segregated, its easygoing ways lessened its harshness. Among longtime black residents, brass bands were popular and were heard at dances, picnics, concerts, and funerals. Eventually, the march structure fractured as musicians improvised with blues sounds, jazz sounds. Such music emerged from the influences present in New Orleans. Buddy Bolden personified the transition from the traditional brass band motif to jazz. Born during Reconstruction, he learned to play the cornet and in the 1890s organized a band. Like many blues musicians, Bolden could not read music, and so the band improvised. Quickly, Bolden became the leading cornet player in the area. Tragically, in 1907 he went mad while playing in a street parade and spent his last twenty-four years in a state mental institution.

By the turn of the century, jazz became a sound in search of a home. As fortune would have it, New Orleans tolerated Storyville, an area filled with houses of prostitution, bars, and strip shows. In this setting, jazz musicians became established, earned money, and popularized the new sound. Like their blues and barrelhouse counterparts, these musicians traveled widely. Riverboats hired jazz bands, and the sound reached Memphis and St. Louis. By the beginning of World War I (when, incidentally, the Navy Department closed down Storyville), jazz had become established throughout the country.

These musical forms—spirituals, blues, barrelhouse, and jazz—were derived from Africa and filtered through the slave experience and later the experiences of poor people who were increasingly considered to be inferior. As whites made Progressive reforms and boasted of white supremacy, black musicians set a backfire of musical innovation that would ultimately become universally recognized as one of the great creative forces of the century.

Another form of music migrated south. The French residents of Canada played music that had originated in sixteenth-century France, and when they were expelled from Canada in the mid-eighteenth century, their music also migrated, as did the French language. Cajuns were sociable people, and they often gathered in homes for dinner; later the elders played cards and the young people danced to Cajun music. The accordion player took the lead, supported by fiddlers and a triangle player. The waltzes and Cajun two-step were irresistible. Blacks in the area learned Cajun music and eventually gave it a Caribbean beat; they called it Zydeco. The origins of Zydeco are lost in the double isolation of blacks in Cajun country, all of whom were adrift from the mainstream of American music and culture.

Far from the Deep South, mountain people continued an English musical tradition that withstood centuries of isolation. Even as travelers roamed the mountain vastness searching for the English roots of ballads early in the twentieth century, musicians were responding to new influences. Mail-order instruments and later recordings and the radio influenced traditional mountain music. In time, such music found its center in Nashville.

As the music moved out of the homes in the hills into the bars of towns and cities, the notes and lyrics reflected the loss of place, the alienation of working-class life. As more proper Southerners searched, largely in vain, for high culture to answer Northern criticism, other Southerners generated a series of musical forms that are commonly accepted as the driving creative musical force of the century.

By the end of World War I, all these musical forms were mature and dynamic. Recording machines were making music available to consumers, and soon the radio would spread it across the country. The blues moved upriver, uptown, and finally into the suburbs to intrigue whites. The other forms became progressive, found new expression in film and fiction, or lingered as a reminder of the agrarian past. The musicians always sought new inspiration, whether it came from a church service, the radio, or a juke joint.

The rural South in the first quarter of the century was complex and dynamic. Low prices and high production costs in some commodities offset expansion in others; wealth came from the mountains and at the same time created poverty, whose destructive impact should have eviscerated people's spirits but instead produced innovative music. The South defied stereotyping, for it harbored great contradictions. Yet there were harbingers of change in the emphasis on commercial agriculture and the use of machines and new methods as well as in the extraction of natural resources. Northern investors did not care for old traditions or distinctiveness; they preferred to routinize Southerners and tame them as dependable workers in field and in factory.

2 / Politics and Urban Growth

DURING THE YEARS OF RECONSTRUCTION AND REDEMPTION, AS Southern whites used violence and fraud to regain political power from Republicans, they nervously glanced over their shoulders to gauge Northern reaction. Defeat at arms and chafing submission had created wariness about provoking federal intrusion. In the waning years of the nineteenth century, however, the old abolitionist spirit ebbed, and Southerners less often tested the reaction of Northerners. Free from the influences that had hounded them for a generation, in the 1890s Southern white politicians boldly restructured politics. In one sense, the new system would be a measure of how responsible Southerners could be if they were left alone. This political license manifested itself in diverse ways, reiterating geographical, racial, and demographic distinctions in the region. Urban growth and the development of business and industry, on the other hand, pointed the South in a direction that would eventually merge with the North.

The Minnows of Progress _____

In a sense, the new structure was a reflection of the old. From the earliest days of settlement, colonies along the Atlantic Coast contained factions (usually the frontier against the settled areas), and arguments between slaveholders in the East (and later in the Black Belt and the Delta) and small farmers of the Piedmont and hills often defined politics. Looked at another way, the planter-dominated areas ran along the Atlantic tidewater, curved in a crescent tracing the Georgia–Alabama Black Belt, and embraced the Mississippi Delta. Within this cordon, planters dominated life and labor, and the ripples of their power spread throughout other areas of the South. After the Civil War, Southern whites ended the political experiment that combined blacks, Northerners, and their white allies. Using violence, fraud, and the legacy of the Lost Cause, whites, according to their interpretation, redeemed the South, and then they set up conservative state governments.

While political quarrels between large and small farmers persisted into the twentieth century, developments in agriculture and in manufacturing introduced new issues and new divisions. The emergent steel industry around Birmingham, Alabama, for example, challenged the power of Black Belt planters. The proliferation of mill towns in the Carolina Piedmont likewise threatened the power of low-country planters. Each state contained such political divisions.

The emergent conservative politicians, called Bourbons since they represented a return to power of former leaders (who, like their French namesakes, had learned nothing and forgotten nothing), retrenched into parsimony and were largely indifferent to demands for government services. In the 1890s, the Populist crusade generated an awareness of state-government responsibility and offered a host of demands that would bring government—both state and federal—into a more responsible relation to human needs. The Populist demand for economic reforms—nationalization of railroads and telegraphs, anti-trust laws, cooperatives, and agricultural reform—frightened conservatives. At the turn of the century, after Populism disintegrated, the Progressive movement emerged as a distinct program. A variation of its national counterpart, Southern

Progressivism owed some of its agenda to rural-reform sentiment, but it also reflected the needs of the business elite and the middle class. Issues such as education, rural poverty, the convict-lease system, peonage, city management, child labor, and prohibition became political causes. Each Southern state approached this agenda in a way that reflected its political peculiarities and its leadership, and each discovered that the race issue could be an effective tool. By the 1890s a Southern politician had to take a stand on the race issue if he entertained serious thoughts of a political career.

Southern politics changed significantly at the turn of the century, primarily because white supremacy reemerged as a campaign weapon. The election of blacks to public office, which had been possible until 1900 in some areas of the South, ended until the emergence of the civil-rights movement over a half century later. Even if blacks could register, which meant overcoming the disenfranchising provisions written into state laws, their Republican votes hardly mattered, for the Democrats were ascendant after 1900. The Democratic Party became a white man's party, at least until women secured the vote. But for white politicians it was not enough to strip most blacks of their vote and consign the others to a party that could not win office; in addition, many politicians denounced blacks as dishonest, ignorant, and a threat to white womanhood.

The racial rhetoric that came to epitomize Southern politics emerged a decade before the turn of the century as Civil War and Reconstruction patriarchs began yielding power to the younger generation—and as the first generation of blacks born outside slavery matured. Historian Joel Williamson has labeled as radical this faction of white politicians, distinguishing them from conservatives or Bourbons. Radicals charged that, without the discipline of slavery, younger blacks were reverting to savagery (the history of African civilization had not made inroads into Southern academies), and the prime manifestation of bestiality was the raping of white women. Whereas interracial rape had not previously been worthy of comment, suddenly whites struck out at blacks by lynching them. "The sudden and dramatic rise in the lynching of black men in and after 1889 stands out like some giant volcanic eruption on the landscape of Southern race relations," Williamson concluded. State after state fell into step with laws that stripped blacks of political power, segregated them from whites, and denied them equal opportunity.

The Mississippi legislature led the way in writing blacks out of power; it embodied the radical spirit. Small farmers of the hills and herders and lumbermen of the piney woods united against conservative Delta planters, who had maintained political control by manipulating the convention system. In 1902, Mississippi replaced this elite-dominated system with a primary. Blacks could not belong to the Democratic Party, nor could whites who failed to meet registration requirements. Yet whites who could register had a voice in the election of officials which had been denied them under the convention system, and this meant that politicians had to canvas voters in earnest. Since the plantation-dominated Delta counties had proportionately fewer whites, their ability to offer candidates for state-wide and federal offices was lessened. The primary brought candidates face to face with voters and often with each other. Rural folk flocked to the county seats for the spectacle.

The rise of such politicians as James K. Vardaman and Theodore Bilbo and the use of white supremacy as the central issue in Southern politics signaled a change in political tone, if not direction, and this new breed of politicians challenged the power of such Delta families as the Percys of Greenville. They did what they had to do to regain political power during Reconstruction, William Alexander Percy remembered, and though there was violence and dishonesty during balloting, they were convinced that political power had returned to hands that could best wield it. This coalition of conservative Democrats rode out the Populist challenge in the 1890s but were alarmed at Vardaman and the new style of campaign introduced by the primary-campaign law. Previously, it seemed appropriate to Percy and his friends that decisions on political leadership could best be made behind closed doors, where the best men could cut deals.

James K. Vardaman personified the new political style in Mississippi. Tall, dressed in a white suit, cowboy boots, and a Stetson hat, his long black hair falling to his shoulders, Vardaman strode across the stage of Mississippi politics boasting a Populist bag of anti-trust sentiment, education and prison reform, and public ownership of railroads. He also traded on race. He observed, for example, that blacks paid little in the way of taxes but benefited from schools nevertheless, and he proposed dividing state school funds not by the number of potential pupils but by the amount of taxes paid by each race. He also advocated repealing the Thirteenth and Fourteenth Amendments to the U.S. Constitution. Viciously, he charged that blacks were immoral, lazy, deceitful, and a threat to white women. The race issue became Vardaman's trademark.

In the gubernatorial election of 1903, Vardaman drew large crowds and left them spellbound with his oratory, alternating reform and the race issue. Though the state press supported his more conservative opponents, Vardaman appealed to the masses, and with the new primary law that allowed political participation on a larger scale, he carried the election.

Vardaman had an ambiguous impact on racial tension. Despite his fiery speeches, lynching did not increase during his terms as governor from 1902 to 1906. Indeed, he called out the militia to prevent lynchings and received national praise for his stand. He also employed agents to investigate incidents of whitecapping, the intimidation of property-owning blacks. According to his friends, he was kindly disposed to blacks with whom he came into contact. Vardaman, like other Southerners, realized that the race issue paid high political dividends; it was nothing personal. Unlike more recent politicians who speak in code words and cloak their sentiments behind budget cuts, Vardaman campaigned as an open racist.

More important, with the exception of his stand on racial issues, Vardaman combined the heritage of Populism and the crusade of Progressivism. He advocated and obtained the end of convict leasing and an increase in school funds and teachers' salaries, set up a state textbook commission, and regulated banks, insurance companies, railroads, utilities, manufacturers, and trusts. He advocated but failed to obtain laws that would have reduced interest rates, established a state highway commission, given aid to handicapped people, prohibited child labor, and constructed a school for the deaf. Bills that would favor corporations brought forth his veto.

Three years after leaving the governor's chair, Vardaman saw a golden opportunity to seek a U.S. Senate seat. In 1909, shortly before Christmas, the death of U.S. Senator Anselm J. McLaurin also gave the conservative Percy forces an opportunity once again to operate in hotel lobbies and backrooms, for a Democratic caucus would select McLaurin's successor. On February 22, 1910, after fifty-seven votes, charges of corruption and vote buying, a break for Mardi Gras, and many smoke-filled rooms, the Democratic caucus picked LeRoy Percy as its senatorial nominee.

The conflict between LeRoy Percy and James K. Vardaman personified not only the political geography of Mississippi but class divisions in the state. Percy came from the Delta, that rich crescent of land that curved away from the Mississippi River just below Memphis and traced the rising hills outward for sixty miles before meeting the river near Vicksburg. Planters who settled along the river cleared the land and set up large cotton-farming operations that relied on black labor, mostly sharecroppers. The rich soil had been built up over millions of years as the river overflowed its banks and deposited layers of nutrients. Delta planters fought the river with levees and tried as well to preserve their way of life, which relied on black labor. The Percys were perhaps the cream of this society, models of community and Delta responsibility. Yet they never understood the price their black laborers paid for their lords' wealth and position, nor did they understand the people who lived in the less fertile and mostly white-populated hills.

Hill people looked upon the Delta as a place dominated by rich planters living in columned mansions waited on by black servants and made wealthy by the labor of black sharecroppers. They supported Populism and desired to reform the system that kept them poverty-ridden. When the Populist movement failed, they looked to James K. Vardaman and later to Theodore Bilbo as their champions. Both politicians understood the deep resentment that flowed from the hills, and they directed it not only against Delta planters but also against their black laborers. In 1911, when Percy ran to retain his Senate seat, Bilbo campaigned against him even though he was running for lieutenant governor and Vardaman was the senatorial candidate.

William Alexander Percy, who recounted his view of the planters' world in *Lanterns on the Levee* (1941), described a typical crowd.

In Percy's eyes, it was an "ill-dressed, surly audience, unintelligent and slinking." It was not moved by LeRoy Percy's explanation of the Panama tolls or the tariff, or by a plea for fair treatment of blacks. "They were the sort of people that lynch Negroes, that mistake hoodlumism for wit, and cunning for intelligence, that attend revivals and fight and fornicate in the bushes afterwards," Percy wrote with distaste. "They were undiluted Anglo-Saxons. They were the sovereign voter. It was so horrible it seemed unreal." After defeat in the senatorial election, LeRoy Percy returned to Greenville, fought to control the Mississippi River, practiced law, and no doubt retold the stories of the first redemption of Mississippi after the Civil War. Both he and his son regarded the advent of Vardaman and Bilbo as the end of an era. It was an end—as well as a beginning.

Vardaman's charisma brought him success in politics, but his stand on World War I ended his political career. Although in 1912 he won overwhelmingly in the U.S. Senate race, his opposition to United States participation in the war offset even his great popularity. Not even the race issue could garner him many votes in 1918. Lacking the vision to forge a plan that cut across racial boundaries, he poisoned relations between the races while trying to reform society at large.

If James K. Vardaman personified the contradiction inherent in pressing for social reform while stirring racial passions, Governor Charles Brantley Aycock of North Carolina turned the equation upside down. A railroad lawyer and conservative Democrat, Aycock launched a white-supremacy campaign, for lack of any substantial issue. He supported an amendment to the state constitution that would, among other restrictions, disenfranchise many voters with a literacy requirement. The North Carolina Populist Party had made significant inroads in state politics and joined with Republicans in 1896 to elect a governor. Capitalizing on the 1898 Wilmington riot, conservative Democrats used the race issue to end the Populist–Republican threat. In Mississippi, Vardaman translated Populist ideas into progressive reform, but in North Carolina the conservative Democratic Party used radical racism to consolidate its political power but left a paltry progressive record. In the eastern part of the state, where most of the black population resided, Aycock denounced black officeholders, lauded white supremacy, and boasted that few blacks could even register. Such attacks had no relevance in the western counties, where the only people who would be disenfranchised by the amendment's literacy requirement were white. There, almost as an afterthought, Aycock offered education as his platform, for a good educational system would make it possible for all citizens to become educated when the literacy provision took effect for voters in 1908.

Aycock did not clarify whether or not he supported schools for blacks, but he blurred the issue with a fortunate (for him) term—universal education. His campaign, offering white supremacy to the east and education to the west, succeeded, as did the constitutional amendment. His administration, and through public relations his educational reform and Progressivism, made him famous. However, except for a child-labor law passed in 1903, there was no other progressive legislation.

Georgia politics at the turn of the century boasted elite and modest reform for whites only. Such progressive reforms as a railroad commission, a child-labor law (which was not enforced), a compulsory school-attendance law (which if enforced would have crowded the schools), and abolition of the convict-lease system were enacted at the same time that race relations deteriorated. In the early years of the century, Georgia laws, like those in other Southern states, segregated eating places, bars, fairs, zoos, places of entertainment, prisons, and streetcars. Outraged at these laws, blacks protested having to sit in the back of streetcars in Atlanta, Augusta, Rome, and Savannah, but their boycotts failed. When facilities such as swimming pools and libraries could not be segregated to suit white tastes, they were closed to blacks altogether.

In 1898, Georgia replaced its Democratic Party nominating convention with a primary, and two years later it became a white-only party. Prospective Georgia voters also faced a host of requirements, beginning with a poll tax, in effect since 1877, and a white primary and literacy test. Military veterans, literate or not, and their descendants, could vote, as could property owners and people securing testimonials of good character. Restricting the vote to respectable and literate white men proved another dubious element of Progressivism.

Hoke Smith personified the spirit of Georgia Progressivism. He arrived as a teenager in Atlanta in 1872; later he read law, practiced mostly against corporations, bought the Atlanta *Journal* in 1887, and dabbled in politics. In 1892, he vigorously supported Grover Cleveland for President and became his Secretary of the Interior. Smith returned to Atlanta in 1897 and for ten years shunned politics. In 1906, he successfully campaigned for governor, calling for disenfranchisement of blacks, railroad regulation, and better schools for whites. Most of all, he called for white supremacy and the disenfranchisement amendment. Smith's legacy as Georgia's leading Progressive rests less upon his legislative achievements in the state than upon his sponsorship of the Smith–Lever and Smith–Hughes acts while in the U.S. Senate. These laws institutionalized the Federal Extension Service and secondary agricultural education and were intended to educate farmers to utilize science and machines in their husbandry.

In state after state, variations on the themes played out in Mississippi, North Carolina, and Georgia emerged. It took ten years for South Carolina to find a voice that spoke for the masses, but by 1910 Coleman Livingston Blease attracted poor farmers and millworkers and served two terms in the governor's mansion. In Florida, from 1904 to 1908, the flamboyant Governor Napoleon Bonaparte Broward championed the common man and condemned railroads, pushed through a child-labor law, a pure food and drugs act, a reorganization of the higher education system, and regulation of public utilities. Virginia's Andrew Jackson Montague, elected governor in 1901, pushed through similar progressive reforms. In Tennessee, the mountains harbored a strong Republican Party (the heritage of Unionist convictions during the Civil War), and in 1910 a Democratic factional struggle opened the way for the election of a Republican governor. Tennesseans seemed more interested in Prohibition than in other progressive concerns, although the legislature enacted child-labor, education, and health laws. Feuding in the faction-ridden Kentucky Democratic Party led to the assassination of governor-elect William Goebel, the champion of anti-trust sentiment in the state.

West of the Mississippi River, Arkansas produced Jeff Davis, a genuine post-Populist leader. As attorney general, Davis attacked insurance companies and other corporations. Elected governor in 1900, he served three terms before moving to the U.S. Senate. Texas, the cradle of the Populist movement, attempted unsuccessfully to control the emerging power of the oil industry, but Progressive legislation did ease the state's entry into the urban and commercial world.

Both the Populist and the progressive movements largely by-passed Louisiana. Neither rural reformers nor urban Progressives could gain political power. The state's politics revolved around interests in New Orleans, the southwestern prairie (shared by sugar and rice growers and Cajuns), and the small farming area in the northern part of the state. No leader emerged who could unite these interests, yet the legislature managed to pass a few token reform laws. Many observers have commented on the state's tolerance of corruption, and T. Harry Williams, Huey Long's biographer, commented that some sages "have ascribed it to the state's Latin-French background. Some have gone so far as to suggest that Louisiana is not really an American state but a 'banana republic,' a Latin enclave of immorality set down in a country of Anglo-Saxon righteousness." The Populist flame burned brightest in the northern part of the state, where in 1893 Huey Long was born in the town of Winnfield. His formative years were spent listening to the frustrated dreams of Populists and the bland promises of Progressives. He seemed instinctively to know that the reform vacuum had to be filled.

Progressivism as a Southern movement transcended politics and moved through other levels of society. The Reverend Edgar Gardner Murphy personified the spirit of Progressivism in the South. After holding pastorates in Texas, Ohio, and New York, Murphy settled in Montgomery, Alabama, where he championed education, in-dustrialization, and better race relations. After the Montgomery Race Conference of 1900 failed to improve race relations, Murphy turned to the issue of child labor and in 1901 became chairman of the Alabama Child Labor Committee. Three years later, he founded the National Child Labor Committee, but in 1907 he resigned when his states'-rights scruples prevented him from backing a federal law.

Murphy regarded blacks as inferior and subservient to whites but adrift outside slavery and its system of control, for Emancipation had interfered with the gradual uplift of blacks before they had completely absorbed white values. Booker T. Washington, with his emphasis on a practical and industrial education for blacks and his careful attention to Southern customs, was a natural ally. In 1903, Murphy became the first executive secretary of the Southern Education Board, hoping that education would help solve the race problem. He aided black schools, but he was hesitant to challenge white supremacists. Although he believed that the fate of Southern blacks and whites was intertwined, he advocated a separate and unequal path of development that would keep blacks subservient. "Few whites in his age could claim his sincerity, his compassion, or rival his ingenious drive to harness the historic racial feeling of the South for humane ends," historian Jack Temple Kirby concluded.

Middle-class Southern women offered a unique contribution to Progressivism. By 1900, many Southern white women rejected the notion that they belonged on a pedestal, and, like women throughout the country, organized to secure the ballot and, in a larger sense, equal rights. Middle- and upper-class women did not dwell on militance. "Drawn from the social and political elite," historian Marjorie Spruill Wheeler wrote, "the leaders of the suffrage movement were proud of the image of the Southern Lady, and emphatically denied that they were untrue to their heritage in seeking the vote." Despite their syrupy words, some women compared themselves to slaves and argued for the right to dispose of property, to move into the business world, and to break down barriers to professional and legal schools. They also wanted equal pay for equal work. "Despite their economically privileged position, these women seemed to have a strong sense of sex solidarity and a genuine concern for the women 'beneath the pedestal,' " Wheeler wrote.

They received little encouragement from men. When Belle Kearney, a Mississippi temperance and suffragist leader, revealed her ambition to become a lawyer, her father warned: "No woman had ever attempted such an absurdity, and any effort on my part in that line would subject me to ridicule and ostracism." She was willing to pay the price to escape from what she considered a useless life on a plantation. When Sue Shelton White, a court reporter in Tennessee, revealed that she wanted to become a lawyer, she was called impractical. Men suggested that it was about time she got married. She was in her thirties before she completed law school by going to night classes. "She received her degree in 1923," Wheeler wrote, "the same year she helped Alice Paul draft the Equal Rights Amendment." Many men romanticized the image of women to their advantage. "Last year at the Capitol," Virginian Mary Johnston stated, "I heard more talk in one day about chivalry from the lawyer in the pay of the knitting mills who were under indictment from overworking women and children than you could perhaps have heard from Bayard or Sir Philip Sidney in a year."

While Southern women sometimes shared the same Progressive goals as men, they often moved along a different tactical path. Still, instead of shyly waiting for chivalry to bring them equality, women aggressively fought for their rights. "In conclusion," Wheeler wrote, "the so-called woman suffrage movement in the South was a fullfledged women's rights movement seeking, in Laura Clay's words, 'absolute equality with men in the right to free enjoyment of every opportunity that . . . civilization, long the work of both sexes, offers for the development of individual capacity.' "

In essence, Southern states under Progressives were restructuring society after redeeming it from the threat of Populism. Many Populists were disenfranchised, and though a few of their planks were enacted, Progressives coopted the more radical movement and passed a few cosmetic but ineffectual laws. A veneer of progress hid the racism, peonage, lynching, race riots, illiteracy, disease, and other ills that characterized the region.

Although racial radicals continued to hold office through the war era, the frenzy that they stirred up subsided. "By about 1915 Radicalism as a whole operating system had, indeed, died," Joel Williamson judged, "and Conservatism emerged from its strongholds to control a new set in race relations. In the new set the black as beast was lost to sight, and the black as child was very much to the fore."

If one cast a net into the waters of Southern Progressivism, the catch would not be impressive. Although Southern states enacted primary laws, they also disenfranchised blacks. Emphasis on up-grading backward educational systems floundered on the issue of according black children equal treatment. Child-labor laws were often weak and seldom enforced, and while the end of the convict-lease system showed a responsible retreat from human abuse and corporate favoritism, most Southern states ignored peonage and left prosecution to often inept federal officials. There were, of course, constructive efforts to realize change—railroad rate commissions, court reform, compulsory school attendance, municipal reform, em-phasis on health care—but many of these issues were either skim-mings from the Populist pot or middle-class reform that aided the emerging business structure. To some extent at least, every Southern state supported Prohibition, yet in many cases the impetus came not from the desire to ban strong drink for whites but rather to keep it out of the hands of allegedly dangerous blacks.

The minnows that came up in the Progressive net did not reflect the nature of life in the South. The constant emphasis on black shortcomings, real or imagined, did not address the sources of conflict along the black-white interface. Child-labor laws did not challenge the mill towns, company stores, and low wages that characterized the textile industry. Railroad-rate commissions seldom challenged "all the traffic would bear" rates; they certainly did not reflect the Populist demand for public ownership. In one sense, Progressive legislation coopted certain Populist ideas and diluted them; in an-other, the reforms supported emerging urban and business concerns. Agriculture, the way of life of most Southerners, seldom concerned Progressives, except in tightening the net around rural workers with more restrictive laws. Southern Progressivism ended the more rad-ical Populist reform threat, rallied whites around the race issue, and encouraged business to set in motion changes that in time would create a South that, except for the race issue, would more resemble the rest of the country. Ironically, the most earnest Progressive reforms came from the most virulent racist, James K. Vardaman. He made the race issue central to politics, but Southerners in effect ignored and fled from it.

Southern politicians still glanced over their shoulders, but in-creasingly they were gauging how to replicate Northern customs.

While resenting federal intrusion, the legacy of Reconstruction, Southerners of the Progressive stripe opened the gates to Northern and foreign capital. Finally, they boasted that the South no longer had a race problem. Such boasts, spoken despite so many obvious contradictions, were the essence of whistling Dixie.

Centers of Trade

While Southern farmers adjusted to the boll weevil and to new demands for commodities, while mountaineers watched their heritage unravel, and while politicians capitalized on race and class, urban areas expanded rapidly to lead the South more in the direction of the country at large. Prior to the Civil War, a few Southern cities served as the centers of the cotton trade, but New Orleans, Mobile, Savannah, Atlanta, and Charleston, among other urban areas, suffered from the ravages of the Civil War. After the war, cotton marketing shifted from such cities to towns located along rail lines, where farmers sold their cotton directly to local brokers, who shipped it North. Southern towns and cities, no matter how fast they grew, still retained a rustic and rural character. "The rural condition, whatever it was—poverty, filth, disease, individualism, fatalism— became the urban condition," historian David Goldfield has observed.

By 1900 the population of Atlanta grew to almost 90,000, and by 1920 over 200,000 residents had joined with the spirit of enterprise that epitomized the city. Durham, under the iron hand of the Dukes and the American Tobacco Company, grew from a town of 6,000 to 22,000 over the same years, while in Winston the R. J. Reynolds tobacco factories and the Haynes knitting mills surrounded the Moravian village of Salem. The textile industry in the Carolina Piedmont swelled Greensboro, and its population of 10,000 doubled in twenty years, as did both Greenville and Spartanburg, South Carolina. Such growth characterized the South in the first two decades of the century, and the old pattern of coastal cities and a few inland towns of consequence altered as throughout the South small towns expanded rapidly along railroad tracks and crossroads.

Tobacco towns such as Oxford, Wilson, and Rocky Mount, North Carolina, grew from villages to thriving towns as farmers crowded into the mammoth warehouses to sell their tobacco at auction. Old seaports woke up and thrived. Savannah increased its 54,000 residents at the turn of the century by 30,000 in twenty years, while New Orleans grew from a quarter of a million to 387,000. Norfolk grew fastest, increasing its 19,000 residents in 1900 to 115,000 by 1920. Natchez and Vicksburg, lazy towns along the Mississippi River which formerly thrived on the cotton trade, remained nearly static.

Most Southern cities grew far more rapidly than their ability to provide services or paved streets. Towns were bogged down in mud when rain was heavy. At night a pedestrian off the main street wandered in pitch dark and, given the lackadaisical law enforcement, ran a grave risk of being robbed or assaulted, with little recourse. Southern cities boasted a higher homicide rate than other areas of the country. New arrivals from the countryside brought their penchant for violence with them; in many ways the South outdid Wild West towns in the frequency of shootouts and general gunplay. Indeed, urbanization and adjustments to new routines throughout the country seemed to breed violence. Health problems also threatened urban dwellers, for city fathers paid scant attention to sewage disposal or pure drinking water. New Orleans and Memphis suffered from yellow-fever epidemics, and other towns also faced health problems engendered by squalor and unsanitary conditions. Despite such problems, many Southern cities ran streetcar lines far into the surrounding countryside and then annexed even more land. It was part of the booster spirit; growth became an obsession, a yardstick to measure progress and encourage even more expansion.

From 1891 to 1906, state laws and municipal ordinances segregated streetcars. As August Meier and Elliott Rudwick have indicated, blacks boycotted streetcars in at least twenty-seven Southern towns and cities. None of the boycotts was successful in the long run, but in several localities the decline in riders drove transit owners to side with blacks, primarily because they realized it was good for business. In Savannah, for example, the city council, reacting to pressure from blacks and the streetcar company, rejected a segregation ordinance in 1901, but five years later the temper of the times forced approval of segregation.

In some cases boycotts succeeded for a time in keeping all black riders off the cars. The black clergy often took a leadership role, and black hackmen and draymen reduced their fares for blacks and sometimes refused to carry whites. In Nashville black citizens attempted to organize their own bus system, and in Florida sought legal redress, but these attempts failed to end segregation on streetcars. Some boycotts lasted weeks, while a few continued for several years. "The remarkable thing is not that the boycotts failed," Meier and Rudwick concluded, "but that they happened in so many places and lasted as long as they often did." There is an inviting parallel between these turn-of-the-century boycotts and the Montgomery bus boycott of 1955 and 1956.

Southern cities sometimes showed surprising initiative in reacting to the modern world. Even as the president of the Savannah Electric Company complained that the streetcar boycott had resulted in a $50,000 loss, the city fathers approved a plan to organize international automobile races through the streets. Organized automobile racing, a staple of present Southern popular culture, traces its roots to Vanderbilt Cup races in Savannah. In 1908, Savannah won support from the state house, used troops to patrol the track, employed chain-gang labor to bank curves and smooth the roads, and even had streetcar operation suspended. The Savannah races in some respects resemble present-day street races such as those held at Long Beach, Detroit, Miami, and Monaco.

Ironically, the proliferation of automobiles and urban demands ended the races. Despite worldwide publicity and the superb race organization, inconvenience to residents, especially motorists who wanted free use of the roads, led to criticism and ultimately ended races through Savannah's streets. Racing took to back streets, pastures, and rural lanes before emerging first on dirt tracks and finally on superspeedways and twisting road courses.

Since there had been little planning in the growth, many towns and cities lacked parks and recreation areas. By 1900, led largely by women's groups, cities began clearing areas for parks and gar-

dens. After the flush of growth, many cities paused to survey the
dingy environment and belatedly applied an aesthetic touch, at least
in the more prosperous areas. Prior to the twentieth century, many
towns had a poorly defined color line, and blacks often lived ad-
jacent to whites. By the turn of the century, however, residential
segregation became the law, and blacks lived separately, usually in
the poorest sections of town.

The Business South

While some of the South's urban growth relied on ocean trade
or railroads, other towns and cities thrived on local factories and
businesses. The South fought the Civil War in part to preserve an
agrarian way of life, but, ironically, New South boosters looked
enviously at Northern factories. The South had its tempting lures—
laborers suspicious of unions and willing to work for low wages,
small towns with free factory sites, and low tax assessments. After
Southern entrepreneurs showed the way, bigger fish, especially flag-
ging textile companies of the Northeast, took the lures. Cotton
mills spread across the South from the 1880s onward and evolved
from small, locally owned, water-driven operations into mammoth
multinational corporations. In the process, absentee ownership, more
efficient machinery, and scientific management changed factory work.

Southern millworkers often came from surrounding farms and
represented a cross section of rural white workers. Blacks were
seldom hired and then only at the lowest job level. Many millworkers were women—widows, single women, and young girls who
could be spared from the farm work force. In some cases entire
families would move to the village and work together in factories
as they had on the farm. Workers often managed to split their work,
moving to the mill villages in the winter and then back to the farms
in the spring and summer. Other workers brought their mules, cows,
chickens, and hogs to town, and many grew vegetable gardens. All
too frequently, millowners or superintendents acted much as had
rural landlords. They inquired after the family, encouraged church
attendance, discouraged drinking, and deducted purchases made at
the company store. Villages became communities, and people learned

to get along in the often cramped homes. People helped each other in towns as they had in the country, and in the days before worker compensation, this eased hardship for many families. When doctors were not available, people turned to folk cures, and midwives usually helped with birthing. People visited, attended church, drank, and listened to local bands on Saturday nights, and in general adjusted their lives to the factory's demands.

There was the routine in the community, and there was the routine in the mill. In the factories rural people learned that work differed radically from the seasonal imperatives of farming. They became, in some respects, the slaves of machines, and instead of the seasonal hard work on farms, they daily attended loud, dirty, complex textile machinery. Foremen often shouted at workers, cursed them, and at times manhandled children. Before the turn of the century, workers would appeal directly to millowners for relief from overzealous foremen, much as slaves had appealed directly to masters for relief from oppressive overseers. With foremen who came from the workers' ranks, ties of family and kin frequently militated against harshness.

Most mills ran off a central source of power which was transmitted through drive belts. When one machine broke, an entire line had to be halted; when one task was completed, there might be time for a break. Factory work, before management found ways to keep workers at machines full-time, ran at a haphazard pace. Although machinery ruled their lives in some respects, workers seldom performed to management's expectations. Eventually, management's obsession with efficiency and production changed mill organization and put new demands on workers.

Prior to World War I, there were few strikes in Southern mills. The Knights of Labor had some presence in the South in the 1880s, and at the turn of the century the National Union of Textile Workers appeared. A scattering of strikes at the turn of the century did little to aid workers and was met with hostility by factory owners. Yet workers did not bear grievances lightly. Millworkers moved around from mill to mill, much as sharecroppers had moved about in their rural communities. If they disliked a foreman or a new policy, or objected to working or living conditions, they moved to another mill. Southern workers were restless, whether they toiled on farms or in factories. In some instances families worked at several mills before settling down. Such mobility allowed families to move easily from place to place, for they had kin and friends throughout the mill network. The profusion of new mills made mobility easy, but it upset millowners, who were forced to pay higher wages to keep workers, or to raid competitors.

As the Progressive era unfolded, textile owners sought to rationalize their operations through cooperation. In 1907 they formed the Southern Textile Association and opened membership to management, mechanics, and engineers. To win workers' support, they instituted social services in the villages. Owners hoped to weaken some of the bonds of community and dampen the urge to wander, and by encouraging workers to turn to the mill for support, management lessened some of the community's strength. Clubs, organized baseball, musical performances, and insurance programs tied workers closer to the mills; by popularizing consumer items, management-sponsored organizations encouraged workers to labor steadily to afford furniture, clothes, and appliances. In one sense such creature comforts helped workers, but they also pushed them into the consumer society and into debt. Many workers realized that such programs had the tendency to tie them closer to the mills and refused to participate. By the 1920s such programs had withered.

While New England looked askance at the rising Southern textile industry, the steel magnates of Pennsylvania and the Great Lakes region warily watched Birmingham, Alabama, which emerged after 1870. Much of the capital that flowed into the production of pig iron, as well as the rails that carried the ore and processed steel, came from outside the South. The political needs of the mills, mining, and smelting areas of the South set in motion new political alliances. Progressivism, in this sense, served the needs of the emerging urban and business interests.

Progressivism encouraged business, and the burgeoning industries enjoyed political support. They received local subsidies and state favor, and their destruction of the environment was tolerated. After surface copper had been mined and shipped away, the mine owners of Polk County, Tennessee, for example, discovered that, to survive, they had to purify the copper on location. This imperative set in motion a ludicrous train of circumstances, a classic case of New South business blackmail. The copper ore was roasted to burn off impurities, and the heat came from wood. As local people worked in the mines, their cousins cut timber to feed the fires. Meanwhile, the sulphur dioxide from the fires irritated eyes and noses; it also destroyed vegetation and wildlife for miles around. The half-million-dollar payroll gave the mineowners immunity from surrounding irate farmers and timbermen, who, year after year, watched forests recede and farmland become less fertile. Tennessee courts refused to halt the ecological nightmare, and, downwind, Georgia timidly complained but feared putting some of its citizens out of work. Even a Supreme Court decision in 1906 failed to halt the deadly fallout, and attempts at arbitration did not pacify farmers and timbermen. The companies continued to spread the deadly mist over the area into the 1970s, and by that time the barren earth would not even support a kudzu plant. The jobs gave the area some security, and since the copper companies were viewed as good corporate citizens, they were above reproach. It was New South blackmail: do our bidding or we will leave and take our payroll elsewhere.

The machine age grew and with it the demand for lubricants and lighting and finally for gasoline to burn in internal-combustion engines; the oil industry boomed. Even as Rockefeller control of oil production in Pennsylvania and neighboring states tightened, the gusher at Spindletop near Houston, Texas, in 1901 shifted the balance of power in the industry. Quickly, Texas and Louisiana became boom areas as derricks shared pastures with cattle and rice. The oil industry with its gambling, roughnecks, and quick fortunes fitted well into the Southern temperament.

The most Southern-dominated major industry to emerge after the Civil War was developed by enterprising tobacco men in Durham, North Carolina. Washington Duke returned from the Civil War nearly broke, but he had a supply of tobacco that he packaged under the label Pro Bono Publico, and he sold it to Union troops as they marched by on their way home. From this modest start, Duke and his son, James Buchanan ("Buck") Duke, drummed trade throughout the area, and eventually in 1874 built a factory. James A. Bonsack, a Virginian, invented a mechanical cigarette-rolling machine, and the business of packaged cigarettes began. To supply the addicted masses, tobacco farmers along the border of Virginia and North Carolina imperialistically spread the bright tobacco culture south—into South Carolina, Georgia, and Florida. Julian S. Carr had risen to prominence marketing his Bull Durham line of tobacco, and he merged his fortune with that of the Dukes and other firms to form the American Tobacco Company. Their hold on the tobacco industry lasted from 1890 to 1911, when the Supreme Court dissolved the empire that by that time controlled plug, snuff, cigarettes, and, to some extent, cigars.

Southern railroads, which had been expanded to carry new products manufactured in the South, were eventually absorbed into national networks dominated by Northern capital. During the depression in the early and mid-1890s, Drexel, Morgan and Company created the Southern Railroad out of its holdings. Other Northern capitalists owned the Chesapeake and Ohio, the Norfolk and Western, the Baltimore and Ohio, and the Louisville and Nashville railroads. Henry Flagler used his oil wealth to extend his railroad down the east coast of Florida and on to Key West and to build hotels along the way. Finding it difficult to obtain laborers to work in the shallow water and hot climate along the right of way, the company lured Northern immigrants to "the land where it never snows," and in some cases held them in peonage on the isolated keys.

Although most Southern blacks labored at agriculture or manual jobs both in rural and in urban areas, there was an emerging black capitalist class. Recognizing this, in 1900 Booker T. Washington (picking up on an idea of W. E. B. Du Bois) founded the National Negro Business League. The character of black business in these early years of the century shifted from catering to whites to firms that took advantage of segregation and discrimination. Savings banks, undertaking establishments, insurance companies, and barbers no longer cutting white heads emerged throughout the South. Still, if white Southerners were in some respects the servants of Northern capital, black businessmen were lackeys of the servants. Against tremendous odds, some blacks entered real estate, retailing, insurance, and professional fields, and succeeded.

Perhaps the most notable success was in Durham, where three men, John Merrick, C. C. Spaulding, and Dr. A. M. Moore, founded the North Carolina Mutual Life Insurance Company. The business grew partly from the tradition in black communities of providing insurance for burial and from the refusal of old-line life-insurance companies to cover blacks. Such associations existed in some areas of the North and the South before the Civil War, and after Emancipation the idea spread across the South. Such societies not only provided burial services but also held picnics, excursions, and parades; some Southern towns still feature such festivities. In Durham the original stockholders were representative of the emerging black middle class—a real-estate owner, a physician, a teacher, an attorney, and a pharmacist. Each pledged fifty dollars, and they applied for a state charter. With the blessing of Buck Duke, the company started selling the customary nickel-and-dime policies, the usual rate per week for coverage.

The three men who headed the company came from diverse backgrounds, and they typified the way aggressive blacks rose in the segregated South. John Merrick was born a slave, and in 1871 his mother left the plantation and moved to Chapel Hill. Merrick worked as a brickmason, then learned the barbering trade, and in 1880 opened a shop in Durham. By 1898 he owned six shops in the city, plus some real estate, and used his status as Buck Duke's private barber to travel north in the shadow of the tobacco baron and observe the magic of capitalism. Like many blacks in this era of segregation and deference to race lines, Merrick could, as historian Walter Weare wrote, "with great poise, tip his hat to the white man and at the same time call him a son of a bitch under his breath." Dr. A. M. Moore sprang from yeoman stock and in 1888 became Durham's first black physician. An intensely religious man, Moore treated the poor without charge and encouraged education. C. C. Spaulding came from Columbus County and had black and Pembroke Indian ancestry. His father had been a county sheriff during Reconstruction. In 1894, Spaulding left the farm for Durham, finished high school, and worked as a dishwasher, bellhop, waiter, office boy, and manager of a black cooperative grocery store before turning to life insurance in 1898.

By 1906 the company moved into a new office and set up a more businesslike method of operation than the guesswork that had characterized the early years. It became a haven for middle-class blacks, the Talented Tenth, as W. E. B. Du Bois called them. When John Merrick died in 1919, Moore took over the company, and after his death four years later, C. C. Spaulding took charge. The company by this time had expanded into most Southern states and into the District of Columbia and Maryland.

The company also created a political base for blacks. Long before the voter-registration drives of the 1960s, Durham blacks had the franchise. By 1939 black voters in Durham County comprised thirteen percent of the county's registered voters. The culmination of the company's growth came in 1966 when it moved into a new high-rise building that dominated Durham's stunted skyline, and welcomed Vice President Hubert Humphrey as the speaker of the day. The company and its impressive building stand as a monument to the triumvirate of former slaves and spirited businessmen who set it in motion at the turn of the century.

Southerners looked at the emerging business world with ambivalence. On the one hand, they realized that industry and factories provided opportunities that agriculture could not offer, especially as land concentrated in the hands of merchants, mortgage companies, and large planters. While many preferred husbandry, factory jobs or mines offered higher pay and an opportunity to break out of the cycle of dispossession and sharecropping. Life in the mill villages, however, often proved as debilitating as farm life, since debt dominated both groups. Some Southerners did rise to managerial positions, and these Horatio Algers served as models for many aspiring young workers.

No other historian has matched C. Vann Woodward's succinct, accurate, and enduring analysis of the South's colonial position at the turn of the century: "The Morgans, Mellons, and Rockefellers sent their agents to take charge of the region's railroads, mines, furnaces, and financial corporations, and eventually of many of its distributive institutions." Though the South produced businessmen, it did not spawn the likes of Northern financial giants. Instead, Southerners "acted as agents, retainers, and executives—rarely as principals. The economy over which they presided was increasingly coming to be one of branch plants, branch banks, captive mines, and chain stores."

What happened to the South resembled the fate of emerging countries around the world where men founded timber, mineral, and plantation empires. From the vantage point of a New York boardroom, Southern resources and labor were ciphers to be manipulated. Investment and earnings in the South were reckoned as they were in other areas of the country, and in the world. Many Southerners welcomed the intrusion of the business world, but the gears of industry, the puffing farm machines, and the county agents drumming them represented forces that would gradually erase Southern distinctiveness.

3 / The Grid of Violence

DURING THE LAST DECADE OF THE NINETEENTH AND THE FIRST decade of the twentieth century, black and white Southerners learned conflicting premises about life. Despite feelings of goodwill which occasionally emerged, whites were far more often taught to scorn blacks and treat them as inferior. Whites could engage in good-natured joking, show a certain deference to elderly blacks, and accept black children as playmates, but the place prescribed for blacks in society was clearly defined. Segregation found justification in pseudo-science and half-truths that became the conventional wisdom of the white South. Eventually, all Southerners—black and white—either accepted the color line and worked around it or left the South. Black children learned the etiquette of survival, of deference, of burying their aspirations and dreams and to some extent their personalities inside a shell. As Richard Wright observed, "disfranchisement had to be supplemented by a whole panoply of rules, taboos, and penalties designed not only to insure peace (complete submission), but to guarantee that no real threat would ever arise." The difficulty, he stressed, came because this struggle "took place between people who were neighbors, whose homes adjoined, whose farms had common boundaries."

A great deal has been written about Southern violence, about the frontier, Indian wars, duels, and the violence that accompanied slavery. Violence, it seems, is deeply implanted in the human species, yet some cultures yield to it more easily than others. Over the years, Southerners have killed, beaten, and maimed each other in proportions that have amazed people in other areas of the country. Southern society gave license to violence. Much of the fighting, cutting, shooting, and threatening in the twentieth century was among neighbors, even friends, and did not involve race, although racial incidents were generally the most brutal and inexplicable.

Certain manifestations of Southern behavior became ritualized by 1900, and while eccentricities were tolerated or even encouraged, even minor violations of customs could elicit rage. Black Southerners lived in a world of uncertainty, bound to careful behavior that still did not guarantee safety. Planters seldom hesitated to strike black workers long after the end of slavery, and blacks had little recourse; resistance was suicidal. Ultimately, this volatile grid covered the South, and at any point, at any time, in any town, crossroads, house, or field, a short circuit in racial customs could spark violence.

Nearly every Southerner, black or white, man or woman, knew how to kill. The daily and seasonal routine of rural life spun around the life cycles of farm animals, especially poultry and swine. Women casually wrung a chicken's neck or cut it off with a hatchet, and children watched, fascinated, as the chicken with its head cut off danced and jerked across the yard before falling dead. At hog-killing time each winter, the entire family dressed the pork. First the hogs were killed, either by rifle or by slitting their throats. Nearly every farmer had a gun or rifle that hung over the door or mantelpiece. In most cases, these weapons were turned against game—birds, rabbits, squirrels, deer, or possum. Men hunted together and generally knew the skills each possessed with a weapon. Southerners not only knew how to use knives and guns, but these implements were close at hand.

Violence could explode from any number of causes, but in many cases it came from arguments over women, debts, grudges, or simple frustration. In the Southern rural environment there were few strangers and, for most residents, little mobility outside the community. Even highly mobile sharecroppers seldom moved outside a county or community. Fights, beatings, and murder were most often visited upon intended victims; violence was seldom random.

Southern people knew each other, and they often passed their leisure time at a country store or at the courthouse square; they visited and worshipped together. People measured each other, probed weaknesses, joked, and swapped tall tales. They gossiped and drank and gambled and hunted and worked. These cycles took on a rhythm, a cadence, that was familiar. Southern ears were tuned to this beat, and dissonance produced tension. With little in the way of earthly goods to defend, Southerners paid close attention to their pride and to keeping it intact. Jokes were accepted and given in kind, but few Southerners, black or white, accepted insult without redress. Southern literature and history are filled with incidents of insult and retribution.

In William Faulkner's *The Hamlet*, for example, Mink Snopes kills his neighbor Jack Houston over a dispute about Snopes's cow grazing in Houston's pasture and the ensuing court case. Joe Christmas, in *Light in August*, kills his adopted father and then alternately denies and embraces the doubtful trace of black blood in his veins. After murdering his white abolitionist mistress, he is in turn murdered and mutilated by a racist National Guardsman, acting out the ritual of the Puritan slaying a black devil. In this fictional instance, and in most interracial violence, blacks paid with their lives. In many episodes of violence there were simply no community checks to prevent it. Violence is so deeply buried in the human psyche that fiction is often as good a guide as history and formal analysis.

History sometimes produces bizarre and instructive incidents that rival fiction. On September 11, 1916, the Sparks Circus conducted its afternoon performance in Kingsport, Tennessee, and eager hill people filled most of the five thousand seats under the big top. The show's star elephant, Mary, advertisements embellished, was "The Largest Living Land Animal on Earth," three inches taller than

Barnum's Jumbo. It was not just Mary's bulk that was important but also her skill; she could play a series of horns, hit baseballs at a .400 average, and even argue with the umpire. Only two days earlier Walter Eldridge, a young man from nearby St. Paul, Virginia, had joined the circus and was assigned to handle the elephant, and as the show progressed, he proudly straddled the world's largest land animal.

At some point in the performance, things went suddenly wrong when the inexperienced mahout hit Mary to correct her course. Mary smashed Eldridge to the ground, gored him, and then tossed his remains into the crowd amid screams, panic, and a scattering of pistol shots aimed at the pachyderm by alarmed spectators. The bullets, the press reported, did not take effect. The Kingsport city fathers decided that Mary had to pay for this crime with her life, and after rejecting further gunplay and poison, they agreed to hang Mary from the Clinchfield and Ohio Railroad crane located in nearby Erwin. On September 13 there were five thousand people waiting in Erwin for the execution, as many as had attended the circus and watched Eldridge's death. Before her burial, a doctor helped saw off her tusks and noticed several abscessed teeth, and he speculated that Eldridge's blow to her head may have hit the sore teeth and provoked her rampage.

On first glance, the hanging of Mary seems so bizarre as to preclude analysis; yet there are elements that provide insight into Southern psychology. Obviously, a number of spectators attended the circus armed, and one can only speculate why they carried pistols into a circus tent for an afternoon performance or why they felt compelled to fire their weapons at Mary even though the tent was crowded with women and children. Mary's death sentence came from the eye-for-an-eye sense of justice that pervaded the South, but the decision to hang Mary instead of shooting her was more puzzling. Fourteen years earlier, the police chief of Valdosta, Georgia, killed Gypsy, another circus elephant, with his rifle when she trampled her keeper to death and ran wild through the streets. (A photograph shows chief of police Calvin Dampier sitting atop the slain elephant, with his rifle prominently displayed.) The argument that a rifle would be ineffective on Mary seemed lame among a people who were descendants of Daniel Boone. No doubt the prospect of a hanging intrigued the Kingsport city fathers; it would be a spectacle far more gripping than a firing squad or death by poison. The incident shows that Southerners not only were armed and ready for violence but insisted that murder be punished, after, of course, a trial of sorts. It also indicates that, given the opportunity, Southerners opted for spectacle.

Night Riders

In addition to the everyday violence that permeated Southern communities, there were categories of violence such as whitecapping, lynching, race riots, and the often violent relations between landlords and tenants. Whitecapping was a form of vigilantism that flourished in the South roughly from the late 1880s into the first decade of the twentieth century. To drive blacks off their land, night riders intimidated, beat, and sometimes murdered their victims. Historian William F. Holmes counted 239 episodes of whitecapping throughout the nation during these years. The term originated in the 1880s in Harrison and Crawford counties, Indiana, where night riders wore white caps as part of their disguises. By the 1890s such violence erupted in Georgia, Tennessee, Alabama, and Mississippi.

During the 1890s whitecaps rode through southern Mississippi intimidating black farmers, and complained that merchants foreclosed on white farmers, displaced them, and hired black sharecroppers. Other attacks were aimed at black property owners. This wave of violence quickly passed, but in 1902 whitecapping emerged again, this time springing from the fear that white merchants and their black laborers were monopolizing land in the area. In Amite, Lincoln, and Franklin counties, Mississippi, concerned white farmers organized secret associations to protect themselves from further displacement and from increasing merchant control over land and labor. Whites realized that for some time their economic condition had been deteriorating as many lost their land and were forced to sharecrop, thus falling to the same status as black agricultural workers.

Small groups of night riders from the larger organizations posted notices warning blacks to leave, administered beatings, and fired shots into houses. Businessmen convinced Governor Andrew Houston Longino that the situation was serious, and he offered rewards for information leading to convictions. A series of trials in 1903 discouraged night riders in Lincoln and Amite counties.

After James K. Vardaman became governor—and perhaps because of his racist campaign—whitecapping broke out again in Franklin and Lincoln counties. Two black landowners in Lincoln County were murdered by whitecaps, and beatings, shootings, and intimidation were widespread in both counties. Violence in these counties drove off some black workers, and an influx of labor agents encouraging more to leave complicated the situation. When blacks hesitated to leave for new jobs outside the community, some labor agents posed as whitecaps, sent threatening notes, or even raided homes to encourage migration.

Although Vardaman's rhetoric had encouraged violence against blacks, bankers' threats to curtail loans in the area and the potential flight of merchants and black workers stirred him into action. He hired Pinkerton detective A. J. Hoyt to investigate the lawlessness in Lincoln County. Hoyt's investigations of whitecapping in Mississippi and of peonage throughout the South show that he had considerable talent. Early in 1904 he appeared in Lincoln County, collected evidence, enlisted the support of the business community, ignored local law-enforcement officials, and helped form a local law-and-order committee. At first, Hoyt thought that labor agents were responsible for all the violence, but in July two informants described the inner workings of the secret leagues. They eventually revealed the entire membership of the organization in Lincoln County, identified the night riders, and named the murderers. This led to the trial and conviction of several men for murder and for posting whitecap notices. Having the names of all members, the judge encouraged them to rely on the mercy of the court, and three hundred men heard a stern warning to abandon the secret organization or face charges. With Hoyt's evidence, organized whitecapping ended in Mississippi. The state government, aided to some extent by the federal charges in Franklin County, stamped out whitecapping.

A significant episode of night riding swept through the dark-fired-tobacco area of western Kentucky. Farmers complained that tobacco prices were too low, that the tobacco trust was robbing them, and in 1906 started cooperatives to hold tobacco off the market and force up prices. When some farmers refused to join, members resorted to coercion and violence. Threats, beatings, pillaged plant beds, and shootings spread through the area. In 1907 and 1908, when their initial efforts to control prices failed, night riders burned storage warehouses to destroy the crop. Robert Penn Warren in his novel *Night Rider* described the desperation of the farmers, and the factors that motivated them to resort to violence. Eventually, a series of trials and convictions ended the effort to control the marketing of the tobacco crop.

Lynching

From 1882 to 1901, the number of lynchings throughout the country did not fall below a hundred a year (in each of three years, it rose above two hundred), and the figures did not fall below fifty until 1923 and stayed at double figures until 1932. There was at least one person lynched each year until 1951. The wave of lynchings directed against blacks after 1889 contrasted with former white violence. During slavery, planters customarily whipped slaves, and during Reconstruction, assaults, whippings, and murder abounded. By the late 1880s, however, the generation of whites and blacks born after slavery matured. Suddenly the cry of rape and the punishment of lynching swept the South.

Most lynchings took place in poor counties with overwhelmingly rural and ill-educated populations. Williamson argued that lynching "tended to occur in areas undergoing rapid economic changes or in counties where murders had been frequent and murderers rarely punished." In many cases law officers either passively acquiesced to the mobs or participated in the murders, nor did ministers step between mob and victim. The list of causes ran from suspected rape to murder, insult to mistaken identity, plundering graves to a bad reputation.

There were blacks who never accepted either the form or the

content of Jim Crow, the wall of segregation laws that surrounded them. They challenged the system and frightened the white community. In the white fantasy, black men could revert to savagery, transmogrify from a dozing Uncle Tom to an avenging Nat Turner. Bigger Thomas, the central character in Richard Wright's novel *Native Son,* who personified this fantasy, evolved from memories of rough and rebellious black men whom the author had known both in the South and in the North. Such a man, Wright explained, "had become estranged from the religion and the folk culture of his race." At the same time, his personality "was trying to react to and answer the call of the dominant civilization whose glitter came to him through the newspapers, magazines, radios, movies, and the mere imposing sight and sound of daily American life." Bigger Thomases were the only blacks who violated Jim Crow taboos and even for a short time got away with it. "Eventually, the whites who restricted their lives made them pay a terrible price. They were shot, hanged, maimed, lynched, and generally hounded until they were either dead or their spirits broken." By lynching, the white community reaffirmed its control over all blacks.

Despite the fact that fewer than a quarter of the lynchings were triggered by rape or allegations of it, relations between the sexes were at the core of such violence. In the white fantasy, black men were threats to white womanhood, and there was an almost universal consensus among white men and women that any threat to white women should be punished by lynching. Such fears grew beyond protectiveness into an obsession. White women were portrayed not only as frail and helpless but also as the repositories of white virtue. Since lineage was traced through the mother, white men placed white women on a pedestal, inviolate. White men, on the other hand, felt free to have relations with black women and then refuse to acknowledge their children as heirs, a practice that did not end with Emancipation. As Lillian Smith put it in *Killers of the Dream:* "The more trails the white man made to back-yard cabins, the higher he raised his white wife on her pedestal when he returned to the big house." Thus, the threat of rape also controlled white women and limited their sphere of activity. By 1930, when white women began organizing to prevent lynching, they were irrationally accused of desiring relations with black men, a charge designed to keep them on the pedestal. In another sense, any relationship outside wedlock threatened the idea that a husband had a property investment in his wife. "The ritual of lynching, then," historian Jacquelyn Hall explains, "served as a dramatization of hierarchical power relationships based both on gender and on race."

Given the number of lynchings, the disparate locations, the different cultural variations in the South, and the provoking causes, there was no "typical lynching." In some incidents, whites retaliated against blacks who fought back, who defended black women from attack, or who argued about farm accounts. In other cases, it all happened so quickly that there was little fanfare and no publicity. But sometimes an entire community became obsessed and demanded immediate retribution.

The threat of lynching and other violence served to create fear among blacks, demean labor, and increase insecurity. Black aspirations were blunted by whitecapping, untoward behavior was punished by beatings or night riders, and lynching served as the ultimate reminder of white power. Blacks retreated into their own world and sought, as much as possible, to avoid contact with unreasoning and dangerous whites. In most cases, lynch mobs acted with impunity. In the first thirty years of the century, only twelve lynchings led to convictions. No federal law applied to lynching, for it was basically murder by mob, a state infraction. Local law officers buckled under the pressure of mobs, and governors seldom acted to prevent lynchings even when they were advertised in newspapers.

Publicizing lynching, and writing about the horror of it, had no effect on spontaneous lynchings, which continued. In the early 1900s, the NAACP began a national crusade to bring lynching to the awareness of the country. It sent investigators into communities to discover the facts of the incidents and then publicized them in its journal, *Crisis*, edited by W. E. B. Du Bois. In 1919 the anti-lynching campaign succeeded in getting a bill introduced into Congress and passed by the House, but it was filibustered to death in the Senate. Subsequent efforts to obtain federal legislation also failed.

Race Riots

The Atlanta riot on September 22, 1906, epitomized how irresponsible newspapers, politics, and, in this case, even a play, could contribute to violence. In 1905, Thomas Dixon's novel *The Clansman* was dramatized on an Atlanta stage and rekindled myths of the Reconstruction era. In August 1906, Hoke Smith ended his gubernatorial campaign, which stressed the race issue. At that time, Atlanta's three newspapers were battling for circulation by featuring stories of black crime and warnings that blacks sought social equality. On the afternoon of September 22, sensational stories about black men attacking white women appeared in the Atlanta *Evening News* and the Atlanta *Journal.* When the newspapers reached Decatur Street, the center of vice and prostitution, a mob quickly formed and began beating blacks and securing arms. By ten o'clock, there were ten thousand armed whites roaming the streets, beating and in some cases murdering blacks, and destroying black businesses. Blacks armed and fought back.

Walter White, who later became executive secretary of the NAACP, was thirteen years old at the time, and in his autobiography, *A Man Called White,* he vividly recalls the riot. His father was a mail collector and drove a horse-drawn cart about the city from three in the afternoon until eleven at night. His father often let Walter drive the team. Both father and son were light-skinned; indeed, years later, when he investigated racial violence for the NAACP, Walter White often posed as white. As they tried to avoid the mob, the elder White saved a black cook from a group closing in on her.

The day of rest, Sunday, did not see a slaking of the mob's thirst for violence. On Sunday night the black section of Atlanta (called Darktown) was tense and expected an attack. For the first time in his memory, Walter White saw his father bring firearms into the house. While his mother and sisters waited in the back of the house, father and son pointed their weapons toward the front gate. "Son, don't shoot until the first man puts his foot on the lawn and then— don't you miss!" his father instructed him. When the mob appeared, its leaders shouted that the mail carrier's house should be burned: "It's too nice for a nigger to live in." As the mob surged toward the house, the teenager experienced a disturbing insight. "I was a Negro, a human being with an invisible pigmentation which marked me a person to be hunted, hanged, abused, discriminated against, kept in poverty and ignorance, in order that those whose skin was white would have readily at hand a proof of their superiority." The mob hesitated before the Whites' gate, then some neighbors fired; a second volley sent them down the street in retreat.

On Monday law officers entered the black residential area and started searching for weapons and arresting blacks. Black snipers ambushed the officers, and one died and others were wounded. On Tuesday the police returned, arrested residents, and filled three wagons with confiscated weapons. Three hundred prisoners were marched through the streets, and the police wantonly killed four people during the search. The riot, according to official statistics, had claimed twenty-five black lives and one white police officer, but blacks argued that the count on both sides was much higher. In some ways the riot reflected prejudice among recently urbanized whites, but the racist Hoke Smith campaign and the lurid newspaper accounts built up an atmosphere of fear and hate. The politicians, the police, and the newspaper editors shared the blame with the white mob. In 1906, Atlanta was not too busy to hate.

Racial incidents on and around military bases dated to at least the Civil War era. Jim Crow followed black troops west during the Indian Wars, and in Florida interracial fights broke out between troops about to embark for Cuba during the Spanish-American War. Southern communities resented black troops, and townspeople usually grew hostile when black soldiers were stationed nearby. It did not matter that the black troops had served their country, or that whites were in control of the troops. The very uniform, the lack of servility, the pride, and, no doubt, the weapons blacks carried gave the white community pause. Having black soldiers in a Southern white community could challenge too many black stereotypes. Such strains emerged when in 1906 black troops arrived in Brownsville, Texas.

Around midnight on August 13, 1906, gunfire broke out in Brownsville; a bartender was killed and a police officer wounded. At that time the 25th Infantry (Colored) was stationed at Fort

Brown, near where the shooting occurred. In the two and a half weeks since they had arrived in the Texas border town, the black soldiers, veterans of Indian wars, the Cuban campaign, and Philippine duty, were subjected to discrimination, insults, and even violence. On the night of the shooting, all troops were under an eight-o'clock curfew because of an incident the day before. Even as the shooting continued in town, the troops on base fell in, and except for two men who were on twenty-four-hour leave and were later accounted for, every soldier answered to his name. They were then deployed in a skirmish line facing the town. Later they marched into town, only to confront an armed mob that blamed them for the incident.

When no black soldier came forward to admit guilt or give evidence, the War Department concluded that a conspiracy of silence had served to protect the guilty. The case came before President Theodore Roosevelt, who dismissed 167 black soldiers from the three companies—without honor, without trial. The abruptness led the Senate Committee on Military Affairs to hold a hearing two years later. Senator Joseph B. Foraker raised serious doubts about the soldiers' guilt in the shooting, but the committee concurred with the President's decision.

It was not until 1970, when historian John D. Weaver published his definitive *The Brownsville Raid* proving that no blacks were involved, that the Secretary of the Army ruled that the soldiers dismissed be given honorable discharges. By that time nearly all of the men had died. They had been framed by elements of the community who shot up the town, planted evidence, and achieved their purpose of getting the black soldiers moved from Brownsville.

A decade after the Brownsville raid, a similar crisis developed in Houston, Texas. When the 3rd Battalion, 24th Infantry, consisting of four companies (seven white officers and 645 enlisted men), arrived in Houston on July 28, 1917, they received the usual icy reception that white Southerners reserved for black men in uniform. Quickly, a list of grievances accumulated on both sides as blacks challenged the segregation barriers (tossing Jim Crow signs off streetcars, for example), and whites retaliated. Early on the morning of August 23, two white policemen, Lee Sparks and Rufe Daniel, broke up a crap game in an alley near San Felipe Street and arrested a black woman dressed in a housecoat. A black soldier, along with some thirty neighborhood friends, attempted to rescue her, but patrolman Sparks pistol-whipped the soldier "until he got his heart right," and arrested him.

Rumors spread quickly, and the black soldiers at camp did not know how badly their comrade was hurt. To clear up the matter, Corporal Charles W. Baltimoore, a black military policeman (armed only with a nightstick), approached the two arresting officers in what he later described as a respectful manner. Lee Sparks's version insisted that Baltimoore "rushed up to me and nearly rubbed his belly into mine" and demanded to know what had happened. When Sparks retorted, "I don't report to no niggers," Baltimoore said, "By god, I will know about it." Sparks then took out his pistol and struck Baltimoore; he fell but quickly got up and started running. Sparks then fired three shots that narrowly missed the fleeing corporal. He chased Baltimoore into a house, assaulted him again, and arrested him. By early afternoon the rumor spread on base that Baltimoore, an extremely popular soldier, had been shot in the streets. The reaction was immediate; the soldiers decided that they would march into town that night, and as one soldier said, "we are going down there and shoot that force up." By the time Baltimoore showed up with a bandaged head, there was a plan to march on Houston at dark.

At eight o'clock that evening, Major Kneeland S. Snow, a white officer who had been in command of the fort only a few days, discovered troops breaking into the supply tent and getting weapons and ammunition. As darkness fell, the camp streets were filled with excited men running about with their weapons. "They are coming," someone shouted, and in the confusion soldiers lay down and began firing wildly, aiming at lights in neighboring houses. In these early volleys, three whites and one black soldier were fatally wounded. Then Sergeant Vida Henry, who only a few minutes earlier had warned Major Snow of trouble, commanded Company I to fall in. Troops from other companies followed. Henry left his eighteen-year unblemished service record behind as he marched his company down the road to Houston. Once outside the camp gate, there was no turning back. He knew the consequences of his action: "I'm not going back—I didn't come out to go back."

Despite the tension in Houston, whites were completely surprised by the riot. It was simply beyond their imagination to expect black retaliation. For the next few hours, a wave of terror swept the city, and seventeen whites and four blacks were killed. Eventually the column reached the street where the two policemen had beaten the two soldiers, and they found and killed Rufe Daniel. Lee Sparks had been temporarily suspended from the force for his excesses earlier in the day. After the confrontation in the middle of the black section of town, the soldiers began to melt away into the dark, some returning to camp and others hiding under houses. Sergeant Henry was wounded and later took his own life. By daylight, all was quiet and order returned to the camp and community. Not since Nat Turner revolted in 1831 had Southern whites seen such fury from blacks.

Only a protest from the black press, the NAACP, and other black leaders slowed down the hasty justice and won a review of the riot. Whites in Houston blamed women and liquor and lax discipline at the camp. In the courts-martial, however, it became obvious that the continual abuse from whites and especially the treatment by the white police triggered the riot. On December 11, 1917, thirteen black soldiers were hanged, and later six more were executed.

These riots were part of a continuum, and two years later another flurry followed the world war. Later still, in the 1930s, during the Second World War, and in the 1960s, race riots spread across the land. Increasingly, such riots consumed Northern cities, a reflection both of black migration and of the tensions generated by urbanization, especially competition for jobs and housing.

The Banishment of Ideas

Although some people protested against racial violence, white Southerners were impatient with any hint of change. The racial climate of the early twentieth century served to mute even moderate discussion of racial violence or the host of laws that operated to keep blacks as second-class citizens. This atmosphere of repression is evident in two cases in which university professors wrote articles that asked for a discussion of the race issue. In the July 1902 issue of *The Atlantic Monthly*, Emory College professor Andrew Sledd wrote a reasoned article, "The Negro: Another View," accepting the conventional wisdom that blacks were lower in the scale of evolution than whites but also calling for an end to lynching and for fair treatment for blacks. Evidently most Georgians would have ignored the piece had not Rebecca Latimer Felton written a letter to the Atlanta *Constitution* condemning it. A former schoolteacher, the wife of a former congressman, and a prominent feminist and advocate of prohibition, Felton often wrote letters to newspapers to champion her causes. She had long been an outspoken opponent of blacks and in this respect differed from many other women of the era, who included anti-lynching as part of their reform program. A few years earlier she bluntly stated: "If it requires lynching to protect women's dearest possession from ravening, drunken human beasts, then I say lynch a thousand negroes a week, if it is necessary."

Felton's vitriolic letter, which demanded that the professor (she did not mention him by name) be run out of the South, started a wave of interest in the article which ultimately led Sledd to resign his position. The issue of academic freedom was lost in the furor over race. He left the South and continued his graduate work at Yale University, complaining that he felt "cramped and stunted by the atmosphere that prevails." He had only meant to bring the issue of race before thinking people, but, he concluded, "the people and the College will have none of it."

A year later, in 1903, John Spencer Bassett, a native Tarheel and a professor at Trinity College (now Duke University) in Durham, North Carolina, wrote an article in *The South Atlantic Quarterly,* a journal that he edited with the intention of creating a forum of intellectual respectability in the South. In "Stirring Up the Fires of Race Antipathy," Bassett admittedly set out to prompt debate on the race issue. "A man whose mind runs away into baseless optimism," he reasoned, "is apt to point to Booker T. Washington as a product of the negro race. Now Washington is a great and good man, a Christian statesman, and taken all in all the greatest man, save General Lee, born in the South in a hundred years; but he is not a typical negro." Bassett argued that blacks would eventually progress and ask for equal rights.

Just as Sledd had his hostile Rebecca Felton, Bassett had Josephus Daniels, editor of the Raleigh *News and Observer*. On November 1, Daniels reprinted the article from *The South Atlantic Quarterly*, but he adorned it with bold print and editorial intrusions. PROF. BASSETT SAYS NEGRO WILL WIN EQUALITY and SOUTHERN LEADERS SLANDERED caught readers' attention and stirred interest. According to Daniels, Bassett was "the first white man in the South" to advocate the ultimate attainment of equal rights for blacks. Daniels, of course, knew that by attacking Bassett at Trinity he was also attacking the school's president, John C. Kilgo, the college, and its benefactors, the Republican Duke family which had established the American Tobacco Company.

Bassett's cause, unlike Sledd's, immediately came to epitomize the issue of academic freedom, and in mid-November he tendered a letter of resignation to the chairman of the board of trustees. In the weeks before the trustees were to meet on December 1, not only other academics throughout the country but the students and faculty of Trinity rallied around Bassett. The trustees voted to support Bassett's right of free expression. "Liberty may sometimes lead to folly," they argued, "yet it is better that some should be tolerated than that all should think and speak under the deadening influence of repression."

While most of the press celebrated the trustees' decision, Daniels argued in the *News and Observer* that freedom of speech "is important and must be preserved, but there is one thing dearer to the Southern people, to wit: the preservation of its civilization, and the purity of the white blood, the supremacy of Anglo-Saxon ideals and white government." It seemed a large gun to shoot at Bassett. Three years later Bassett accepted a position at Smith College, where he pursued his scholarly career, and ultimately Trinity College became Duke University and continued its educational mission. These two episodes showed how differently two Methodist institutions could react to similar crises. A generation later, Baptist schools would have a comparable opportunity. The cases also showed that even moderate challenges to the color line were barely tolerated in the South. A door closed on free discussion of the race issue. No leader emerged to question the assumptions of racism, and if the Sledd and Bassett cases were any indication, politicians, newspaper editors, and the white population at large would not have listened. Even Bassett's defenders stressed that they supported the professor's right to air his views—not his arguments. The South would wander in the wilderness of segregation and oppression for more than the allotted forty years before prophets would successfully challenge the color line.

Xenophobia

Despite its diversity and its manifold traditions, Southern culture when boiled down had a residue of simplicity. Whites were primarily of Anglo-Saxon ancestry and Protestant; blacks also subscribed to similar tenets of salvation. Twentieth-century immigrants to the South, and carpetbaggers earlier, found it difficult to be accepted. Since neither Catholics nor Jews shared the Fundamentalism of the dominant community, they were marked, different. In many cases, however, they were integrated into society anyway, for Southerners often accepted (or forgave) almost any eccentricity so long as it posed no threat to the established order. Indeed, a sizable Jewish population had long lived in the South, and there were large Catholic enclaves in New Orleans and in southwest Louisiana, and elsewhere.

At times, however, waves of xenophobia swept through areas with an almost pogrom-like intensity. Tom Watson, the Populist leader from Georgia, soured after his defeat in the 1896 election, condemned blacks, Jews, Catholics, and others in his newspaper, *The Jeffersonian*. In 1913, when a young Jewish factory manager, Leo Frank, was accused of murdering thirteen-year-old Mary Phagan, a worker in the pencil factory, Watson heaped abuse upon him and demanded his head.

The Frank case became front-page news in 1913; although the evidence against him was flimsy, he was found guilty of the murder and sentenced to death. Two years later, Georgia Governor John Slaton commuted his sentence to life imprisonment, refusing, he stressed, to be labeled a Pontius Pilate. On August 16, 1915, twenty-five masked men took Frank from jail and lynched him, and six thousand people flocked to see his swinging body. The case continued to trouble people who insisted that Frank was innocent, and an eyewitness who was thirteen years old at the time finally revealed that a black janitor, not Frank, murdered the young woman. An attempt to persuade the Georgia Board of Pardons and Paroles to grant Frank a posthumous pardon failed in December 1983. In this case, the mob's taste for a sacrifice turned on Frank, a Jew, just as it could turn on an innocent black. Many Jews fled from the area, fearing a pogrom.

In 1915, the same year as the Frank lynching, the Ku Klux Klan was reborn with all the energy and dedication of many other New South booster organizations. Dredging up the ghosts of the Lost Cause, Colonel William Joseph Simmons launched a new Klan that soon spread far beyond the confines of the old Confederacy and took on new targets where blacks were scarce, especially Catholics and Jews. The mean spirit that the Klan embodied invaded politics and permeated many layers of society. By 1920, the organization stood ready to capitalize on the hate generated by war propaganda and the hysteria of the Red Summer of 1919 when race riots spread across the nation. Armed with slick publicity and businesslike methods, the Klan mushroomed into a large organization. In some ways it represented the fears of people who saw the world changing, who saw threats from every direction. Paranoid about communism, non-Protestant religions, color, and foreigners, the Klan grew into a secret organization that infiltrated communities and sowed distrust and in some cases terror.

When the Klan organized in a Southern community, it sometimes destroyed whatever friendliness and trust existed. In Greenville, Mississippi, former U.S. Senator LeRoy Percy faced the Klan and attempted to discredit it. At a public meeting in 1922, Percy pointed out that the Klan threatened to drive out black laborers from the Delta and ruin the area's agriculture. The city had a sizable population of Jews and Catholics, and Percy defended them. He saw in the Invisible Empire a force that would destroy the fiber of the quiet river town. William Alexander Percy, his son, observed that during the war the Greenville community had been changed by an influx of people from the hills and from the North, "from all sorts of odd places where they hadn't succeeded or hadn't been wanted." The change was slow but sure. "The newcomers weren't foreigners or Jews," he stated. "They were an alien breed of Anglo-Saxon." Many were from areas where the license of a river town seemed like Sodom or Gomorrah, and even though such people were hardly Puritans, they had a streak of vindictiveness that could be turned against such sins as gambling, dancing, or prostitution. Their concerns about race, their position in society, and other issues could be focused and turned into political action, or Klan membership.

LeRoy Percy helped organize the Greenville community and formed the Protestant Organization Opposed to the Ku Klux Klan. He hoped to gain strength from the exclusiveness of the membership. Because its membership was secret, Klan members infiltrated meetings and knew plans in advance, but when Klan members ran for public office, Percy discovered their identities and exposed them. The community, as Percy feared, split. The climax came in an election for local offices, and Percy's anti-Klan candidate won. The battle had been won; black laborers were safe from the Klan's violence, and the Greenville community emerged from the crisis more or less united. The elements that fueled the Klan did not die. When the Supreme Court in 1954 ruled that segregation was illegal, the Klan was again reborn to deal with the forced changes in race relations as well as to support the many people who had moved from farms into cities, where they had to compete with blacks for jobs. Believers in the Lost Cause persisted; they were caught up in the fantasy of an antebellum world that seemed to represent order.

The Context of Violence _____

But it was not just the Klan that resorted to violence in the South. If one were writing a movie script, perhaps no more ghastly scenario could be imagined than the events which took place in Georgia in 1921. The film would open with a high camera shot of a Model T Ford moving across a bridge, a rooster tail of dust trailing behind it. It comes to a halt in a farmyard. Finding the owner away, the two federal agents quiz the black workers about reports of peonage that had reached Atlanta. The camera records the panic on the faces of the laborers when farm owner John S. Williams arrives. Williams casually admits that he had indeed bailed these workers from jail, kept them under guard, and worked them, but, he insists, he would do better. The agents leave. The lens follows the car until it disappears.

The camera returns to the high angle at the bridge; several weeks have passed. Below, a small boy fishes in the early-morning light; the lens zooms closer. The boy sees a foot protruding from the water, his eyes grow large, and he drops his fishing pole and runs for help. Later, two black bodies are lifted from the water. Clues lead the sheriff back to the Williams farm. The black foreman, Clyde Manning, is arrested, taken to Atlanta, and after being promised that he would be protected, admits that he and John S. Williams killed eleven men, eleven peons, to prevent their testifying to a federal crime.

The camera next records the trial of Williams. In vivid detail (and the script calls for flashbacks), Manning describes how he was forced to kill the men, how Williams hinted that unless Manning cooperated with him, his life would be forfeit. Counting on the prevailing racism of the day, Williams tries to turn the case against his foreman, accusing him of being a harsh man, a black demon. The camera comes in tight to record the reaction of the jury and the spectators. The jury believes Manning, and the judge sentences Williams to life imprisonment. A closeup records the look of surprise, incredulity, and outrage on Williams's face. Due to a faulty charge to the jury, Manning's lawyers win a new trial for their client, who had also been sentenced to life imprisonment.

The camera records Manning's second trial as his lawyers build a case to show how macabre the Williams farm was, how Manning had no choice but to carry out Williams's orders. It becomes apparent that blacks had been killed on the Williams farm earlier, some by Williams and some by his sons. When the agents left after their investigation, Williams told his sons to leave the farm, and then he disposed of the evidence of peonage, a federal crime. Manning never loses his composure but relates the crimes, some dating back several years, with confidence and consistency. The jury again sentences Manning to life imprisonment; he dies several years later. And later still, John Williams earns a trusty position at a Georgia prison farm. During a jailbreak, he steps in front of the getaway car and is killed. The movie ends.

The Williams case was only the most horrible of a series of peonage and murder cases that have characterized Southern rural life during the century. Indeed, during the trial, a Georgia U.S. attorney reported that the Williams case was "more atrocious than others only in this, that I know of no other case where more than one peon has been put to death to prevent his testifying." Rural workers walked an uneasy path between freedom and slavery, intimidation and murder, for they were subject to the power of planters, the corruption of local law-enforcement officials, and the apathy of the Justice Department. There were no safe havens for Southern blacks, for trouble could come suddenly and for no apparent reason.

On March 25, 1931, for example, a fight broke out among hoboes on a Chattanooga-to-Memphis freight train, and the whites were driven off the cars. They protested to the stationmaster at Stevenson, Alabama, who had the train stopped at Paint Rock. Not only did the law officers find nine blacks, but they also discovered two white women dressed in overalls. The women claimed that they had been raped.

Before the series of trials internationally known as the Scottsboro case had run their course, nearly every ingredient of race and sex had been aired, communist-supported defense lawyers confronted Southern white women, and any number of people conducted themselves unethically in court and out. It was miraculous that the black men were not lynched, but, it turned out, there are more ways to destroy lives than with a rope. The history of this case, with its tangled testimony, emotional outbursts, draconian verdicts and sentences, heroic but belated pardons, and ultimate TV serialization and ensuing court cases brought by the two women, has been told by Dan T. Carter in *Scottsboro: A Tragedy of the American South*. The book explores the racial climate that drove white men to believe white women when they accused black men of rape even though evidence demonstrated that there had been no sexual contact. The tragedy was not just that innocent blacks served jail sentences, or that good men failed to act on their convictions, or even that white women found it expedient to fabricate a story of rape, but that the entire system of justice proved impotent. There were many well-meaning people who could and should have stopped events from running their course, but they refused to act. In this case the Scottsboro community, the state of Alabama, and many white Southerners united behind two white women of dubious background and found it easy to oppose communist-backed Jewish lawyers from the North. Outsiders united white Southerners when they interceded to protect blacks.

Nearly every intrusion before the New Deal, save that of the federal agricultural program, worked against the white population and for blacks. The white South insisted on being left alone, left to deal with or ignore thorny racial problems, left to wander in the past and romanticize the Lost Cause. For many blacks the way of life that continually straddled the line of freedom and repression did not change. The grid of violence, at least along racial lines, served to remind blacks of their marginal position in Southern society.

4 / Tolling of a Bell

WITH THE ELECTION OF WOODROW WILSON TO THE PRESIDENCY in 1912, the South began a halting march, one step back down the path of the Lost Cause and two steps toward the dream of a New South. Wilson, a typical Southern Progressive, promoted both segregation and reform. Booker T. Washington, meanwhile, lost his national political leverage and died in 1915, doubting, in the end, that his alliance with the "best" white men had furthered black aspirations. His death, like the tolling of a farm bell, called thousands of black Southerners out of the fields, out of the South. When the United States entered the war, W. E. B. Du Bois urged blacks to close ranks and support the war effort, but Jim Crow followed them to military bases and stowed away on troop ships to haunt them in Europe. After the war they endured the riots of 1919—the Red Summer.

The war, migration, and post-war violence created strains in the South, tremors like the first warnings of an earthquake. While most Southerners attempted to settle back into familiar routines after the war, improved transportation and communications brought ideas and fashions from outside the South. At the same time, medical research attacked some of the South's peculiar diseases such as malaria, hookworm, and pellagra. The dissemination of new ideas, communications, health care, and consumer goods remained uneven, but many Southerners were ambivalent about changes set in motion during the war. By 1920 an observer could see, along with plentiful examples of traditional life, portents of change.

Politics and the Past

Woodrow Wilson's election brought Southerners to power in Washington. Not only was half the cabinet from the South, but the Democrat majority in both houses of Congress elevated long-serving Southern politicians to committee chairmanships. Wilson allied himself with these powerful congressmen, often at the expense of more militant agrarians. As a result, nearly all of Wilson's progressive legislation bore the mark of Southern support and influence. Majority leader Oscar W. Underwood in the House and Furnifold Simmons in the Senate guided a tariff-reduction bill through Congress, and it also included a provision to enact a graduated income tax as approved by the recently passed Sixteenth Amendment. Neither did much for poverty-ridden Southerners.

In 1914, however, the Administration dusted off an old Populist idea that allowed farmers to store crops in warehouses and use them as collateral for loans. More important in the long run, Wilson supported a plan to federalize land banks and allow farmers to use land as security for long-term loans. Ultimately, federal and private lenders took over large tracts of farmland when lenders defaulted, and farmers have continued to lose land to any creditor who accepts it as collateral.

Two of the most important farm bills that passed Congress during the Wilson years supported agricultural education. The Smith–Lever Act of 1914 (it could as accurately be labeled the Boll Weevil Act) formalized the Federal Extension Service that Seaman A. Knapp had begun in 1903 to fight the boll-weevil invasion. With new funding and the stamp of congressional approval, the Extension Service revitalized its crusade to modernize Southern agriculture. Extension was aimed at farmers in the field, but the Smith–Hughes

Act of 1917, through grants-in-aid, instituted agricultural education in secondary schools to teach rural youth how to farm scientifically. Both acts had a far-reaching impact on the rural South. The Extension Service taught farmers how to use machinery, select fertilizer, kill pests, and diversify crops. Much of its research went into money crops. High-school teachers, funded by Smith–Hughes grants, instructed farm children in the latest agricultural methods developed at the land-grant universities. County extension programs, secondary education, and land-grant universities grew into a powerful complex of institutions which customarily bypassed the problems of tenants and sharecroppers and instead championed the idea of large landowners and highly mechanized progressive farmers. In every Southern state blacks were shortchanged. Most states only gave token funds to black schools, just enough to appease those who argued that blacks were being ignored.

The rural South was hardly ready for the modernization gospel, for few farmers could afford machines and modern farming methods. Yet those who did grasp these opportunities would be prepared for the new era that emerged in the 1930s. Ironically, the situation would change so quickly that, by the 1950s, children educated in agriculture had difficulty finding land to farm. Instead, many went into the bureaucracy, the agricultural schools, or into other parts of the system, to produce even more ideas to mechanize farming and further shrink the ranks of farmers.

On the state level, Southern politicians shadowed the Progressivism that Wilson personified. In some states the demagogues who revolutionized Southern politics at the turn of the century yielded by 1912 to more progressive, more presentable, less racist leaders. Such governors as Richard I. Manning of South Carolina, Charles H. Brough of Arkansas, Thomas E. Kilby of Alabama, and Locke Craig of North Carolina continued the progressive program by attracting more Northern industries, stressing education, building highways, aiding charities, advocating prohibition, and revising tax, anti-trust, and child-labor laws. Much of this legislation, to be sure, focused on the South's attempts to industrialize and urbanize.

Ironically, the most progressive of Southern governors came from Mississippi. Theodore G. Bilbo, elected in 1915, was the most unlikely of Progressives. He fought Delta planters, revised the state's tax system, built roads, set up state boards, established sanatoriums and reformatories, supported tick eradication, championed prohibition, and even ended public hangings. He shared with James K. Vardaman, who had moved on to the Senate, the dualism of being universally regarded as a demagogue and ridiculed by the polite elements of the state, but loved by the white masses. If he was unsavory and unethical, his followers reasoned that at least he was not boring. In another sense Bilbo embodied the Southern curse that would advocate imaginative reform and at the same time deny blacks both their rights and their humanity.

Woodrow Wilson's Administration may well have personified the progressive spirit to many Americans, but it posed a distinct threat to the precarious existence of black life. Before 1913, when the Democrats regained national power for the first time since Grover Cleveland's second term in the 1890s, blacks had worked alongside whites in the Washington bureaucracy. When Wilson's cabinet members insisted on segregation in federal offices, black leaders complained.

In November 1914, William Monroe Trotter, a brilliant, radical, and outspoken newspaper editor from Boston, had an audience with President Wilson on the subject of segregation. "For fifty years white and colored clerks have been working together in peace and harmony and friendliness, doing so even through two Democratic administrations," Trotter began. "Soon after your inauguration began, segregation was drastically introduced." For forty-five minutes, the black Puritan from Boston, editor of the Boston *Guardian*, argued with the white Puritan, son of a Presbyterian minister, from the South. "Your manner offends me," Wilson retorted, and no doubt Trotter's unyielding arguments outraged him. Perhaps the interview would have been ignored had not Trotter stopped by the press room and revealed the substance of the talk. The next day the meeting played on the front pages of many newspapers. Wilson admitted that he lost his temper with Trotter. It was probably the first time that a black man had treated Wilson as an equal. During the campaign, blacks had considered Wilson, a former president of Princeton University, as an enlightened man who would listen to reason, and several leaders supported him. They were bitterly disappointed, not only with his support of the segregation of federal employees, but also with his enthusiasm for *Birth of a Nation,* D. W. Griffith's brilliant but racist film.

Griffith's film epitomized the confluence of several streams of intellectual endeavor. The director took his plot from Thomas Dixon's novel *The Clansman.* Dixon, like Griffith, personified the post-Civil War generation that turned to radicalism in the matter of race. As historian Joel Williamson has shown, "Tom Dixon had very deep psychic needs of which he seemed unaware. He needed devils, and he needed gods. Or, rather, in his case, he needed goddesses. He found both of these outside of himself, devils in black people, goddesses in white women." Dixon tried graduate school, acting, and the law before becoming a highly successful preacher who held pastorates in prestigious New York and Boston pulpits. In 1899, in his mid-thirties, he left the ministry, settled in Virginia, and began writing novels.

Griffith, born in 1875 in Kentucky, was obsessed with the Lost Cause and the problem of race. He also was a brilliant and innovative filmmaker. *Birth of a Nation* was set in the South during Reconstruction, and it followed Dixon's *The Clansman* in dwelling on bumptious black politicians and the danger of rape to white women. In one episode the white heroine throws herself off a cliff to save her virginity from a black man, and in the concluding scenes the Klan rides in, much as the cavalry customarily did in Westerns, to save a white family besieged by blacks. When the NAACP protested the excesses of the film, Griffith defended himself by quoting Woodrow Wilson's high praise and pointing to the President's *Division and Reunion* (1889) and to histories by James Ford Rhodes and Walter L. Fleming. Griffith thus popularized a trend in historical scholarship that portrayed the Reconstruction as a time when blacks, allied with Northerners and poor whites, gained control over Southern politics and ruled through graft and greed.

More recent scholarship (and W. E. B. Du Bois as early as 1903) has challenged this interpretation of Reconstruction, but Griffith was correct in noting that most scholars of the day supported his and Dixon's interpretation. "Griffith's epic of the war and its aftermath, then," historian Jack Temple Kirby has written, "amounted to a completion of a great historiographical tour through the media of the day." Indeed, a generation of scholars, influenced by Columbia University professor William A. Dunning, had written of the Reconstruction as a time of black excesses that excused white violence in regaining power. By relating Southern history in this manner, historians, novelist Dixon, and filmmaker Griffith perpetuated the depiction of blacks as beasts and, in a sense, intellectually justified the unfair treatment that continued in American society. Film, radio, and later TV depicted the South as a land of aristocratic whites and subservient, musical, or deranged blacks. The idea that average people lived and worked south of the Potomac River never subverted the mythmaking media.

The Great Migration

Politics in the age of Wilson had as little relevance to the lives of ordinary Southerners as *The Clansman* or *Birth of a Nation*. The migration of blacks from the South, however, became one of the most significant population movements in American history. Historians have listed ample reasons why, around 1915, black Southerners began leaving for the North in droves. Yet many of the conditions cited—segregation, poor education, violence, lynching, floods, the boll weevil, unfair settlement of accounts, and poor cotton prices—had existed since the Civil War. And such problems did provoke migration, notably to Oklahoma and to other Western states (and Bishop Henry M. Turner's dream of a return to Africa), in the last decades of the nineteenth century. In other words, there had always been good reason to leave the South. What was new as war swept through Europe in 1914 was what had changed in the North. The vanguard of blacks who had already migrated observed that the flow of European immigrants had ceased because of the war, that industries needed workers (usually at the lowest level), and that the opportunities for education, employment, housing, and health care were much better in most Northern cities than in the rural South. Relatives and friends who scouted out Northern cities wrote back in glowing terms of the promise of life. To a people who had escaped from slavery and held biblical images in great store, the new opportunity to cross the Jordan River (or, more correctly, the Mason–Dixon line) took on the nature of a religious pilgrimage.

Employment opportunities that had driven blacks to the Delta, to Texas, and to Oklahoma refocused on the North. The Chicago *Defender* played a central role in publicizing reasons for escaping from the South. Edited by Robert Abbott, the *Defender* became a clearinghouse for migrants headed for Chicago. His paper graphically reported on violence in the South and juxtaposed it with stories of opportunities in the North. The circulation of the paper rose from 10,000 in 1916 to 93,000 in 1918. When some Southern towns confiscated the paper (much as the slave South had rounded up abolitionist papers), Abbott relied on Pullman porters to drop off bundles to distributors, and he persuaded black entertainers to hand out free copies at performances. He printed letters from those who had obtained jobs in Chicago and other cities, and he sorted through the thousands of letters sent by prospective migrants.

Sharecroppers left plows in the fields, entire church congregations vanished overnight, families secretly made plans and simply disappeared, and a gang of railroad section hands left their tools and did not pause at the pay window. Labor agents moved through black communities providing information and sometimes tickets; some were frauds who collected money and disappeared. The *Defender* warned against such abuses, but some migrants entrusted friendly agents with their savings and never saw either again. It also provided a primer on manners, advising migrants to dress properly, bathe regularly, behave on the streets and in public transportation, and stop using such expressions as "sir," "captain," and "major" to whites.

Once in the cities of the North, migrants sometimes were victimized by agents who collected money to place them in jobs, but the Urban League and other agencies helped Southern blacks make the transition. The pay for factory jobs was good, compared to fieldwork in the South. In Pittsburgh laborers earned from $3 to $3.60 a day, and a Newark dye plant paid $2.75 a day, furnished a free room, and paid the fare from the South. In the South farm laborers earned about $15 a month, or at most $1 a day. Of course, expenses were higher in the North.

Exactly how many blacks left the South remains unknown, for federal census data do not track migrants. Even the Department of Labor could only estimate that from 200,000 to 700,000 blacks left the South in 1916 and 1917. The migration during World War I began a trend that ebbed and flowed until the 1970s. No doubt, improved communications played a great part in the migration. Migrants remained in contact with relatives and friends by mail or telephone. The isolation that had characterized the rural South for so long was breaking down. Dreams of a better life in the North could no longer be hidden in the myth that blacks died of the cold in Northern cities.

The poorly documented black migration is better understood than the white exodus. Many of the same factors that drove blacks from the South—poor schools and health care, low wages, increasing sharecropping, and the promise of better jobs in the North— also drove out whites. According to one estimate, more than 2.3 million whites left the South in the first twenty years of the century, and in the next decade another million joined the migration.

Battle Lines

While many black and white Americans migrated from the South, others joined the army to fight in the war, and the war changed perspectives. Few migrants to the North or soldiers from the South had ever been far from home. Plucked out of Southern byways, uniformed, shipped to Europe and war, many discovered that battle was the most important event of their lives.

William Alexander Percy first joined the Belgian relief effort, became dissatisfied with his noncombatant position, and then joined the army. He sat behind a desk in Paris, yearning for front-line action, and volunteered for line officers' training school. Instead of getting a combat assignment, he became an instructor and was assigned to the 92nd, an all-black division. Eventually he reached the front. He wrote to his father, LeRoy Percy: "I have been through hell and returned without a scar." His letter evaded reality, or rather the unreality of life at the front. "But it was all unreal," he wrote later in his autobiography, "like a slow-motion nightmare, and unreal incidents kept happening." The death beside him and the dogfights above left him thinking that civilian life could never rival combat. When the war ended there was ambivalence—happiness and despair. He saw the war as "great" and "heroic," and he dreaded the return to civilian life in Mississippi.

While William A. Percy found a place in the war, fellow Mississippian William Faulkner failed to find glory. He unsuccessfully tried to enlist in the U.S. Army, wandered to Connecticut and worked as a clerk, and in 1918 went to Canada to train in the Royal Air Force. He later returned to his home in Oxford, Mississippi, in R.A.F. uniform, hobbling about with a cane, and hinted that his plane had been shot down in action. It would be more than ten years before he admitted in a brief note to an editor what he really did in Canada. To get into the Canadian Air Force, he had forged documents purporting English citizenship. He never left Canada but did crash several times. This episode, like so many in his life, was bent and twisted in the retelling and was never corrected by Faulkner. He harbored his privacy and often gave out false or misleading biographical information. But, like many other Southerners, he thirsted for battle.

For blacks the military experience proved bittersweet. Colonel Charles Young, a West Pointer who had served in the Spanish–American War, in Liberia, and in Mexican border skirmishes, asked for a promotion and command of a division. When declared physically unfit to serve, he rode a horse from Ohio to Washington, D.C., to prove his fitness—to no avail. With great difficulty, blacks obtained an officers' training school in Des Moines, Iowa, and the War Department enlisted Emmett J. Scott, who had been Booker T. Washington's secretary, to monitor the problems of black soldiers. Most black troops unloaded ships or performed other support duties. When manpower became crucial, they were rushed into battle with little training but fought well. At every turn they were confronted with racism. U.S. troops spread rumors that blacks had tails, that they were rapists, and that they could not speak English. One white officer even wrote an order warning the French not to fraternize with blacks.

Ultimately, the rumors of rape led the government to appoint Robert R. Moton, the president of Tuskegee Institute, to investigate the charges. After conducting numerous interviews and studying the records, Moton concluded that only three blacks had even been charged with rape, and only one had been found guilty. Moton also spoke to black troops, advising them to behave in Europe and be prepared for segregated life in the United States upon return. His unctuous speeches outraged some black soldiers, but conditions in the United States in 1919 defied any preparation. After fighting to make the world safe for democracy, blacks returned to find it unsafe for themselves.

On another level the war helped to heal sectional wounds. Descendants of those who fought in the Civil War, as historians William B. Hesseltine and David L. Smiley wrote, "mingled their blood with that of descendants of Union veterans at far-away places whose names they could not pronounce: Château-Thierry, Saint-Mihiel, and villages in the Argonne forest." Southern states, benefiting from the mild climate, attracted military bases, named for the great soldiers on both sides of the Civil War—Meade, Lee, Jackson, Wheeler, Sheridan, Beauregard.

While most Southern congressmen voted for war, James K. Vardaman vehemently opposed it, as did North Carolina congressman Claude Kitchin. To pay for the war, Kitchin engineered an excess-profits tax that outraged businessmen. Kitchin observed that businessmen were "willing to fight this war out if somebody else will do the fighting. They are willing to pay for the war if somebody else will do the paying." Still, most Southerners supported the war and shared in the phobia of all things German that swept the country. Indeed, the propaganda generated by George Creel and his committee created a spirit of intolerance that did not grow less violent until after the war ended. The changes in American life— in urbanization, transportation, and fashion—also upset many Americans and set the stage for the unrest that exploded in 1919.

James Weldon Johnson, who had held minor diplomatic posts in Latin America and written newspaper editorials after forsaking a songwriting career, in 1919 was an executive of the National Association for the Advancement of Colored People. He called the central months of that year the Red Summer. The name had a certain irony, for many Americans expected the "reds" in Russia, who had overthrown the czar, to press for a worldwide revolution. Johnson, however, referred to the red blood that was spilled, much of it from black bodies. There were perhaps twenty-five race riots during the year, including four major outbreaks in the South—at Charleston, South Carolina; Longview, Texas; Knoxville, Tennessee; and Elaine, Arkansas.

Blacks who had moved from the South discovered that prejudice followed them. Riots in Chicago and Washington, D.C., took a large toll. In some ways, these riots reflected increasing white tension over black competition for jobs, recreation, housing, and public transportation. Racial violence grew beyond the bounds of the old Confederacy and increasingly came to typify race relations throughout the country. The Red Summer made it clear that white Americans feared blacks on many levels and that the war, with its migration, black involvement in the military, and Northern job market, made the problem of the color line a national concern. It also opened the eyes of young black and white Southerners who did tours of duty in Europe to the debilitating life in the rural South. Many Southerners paused in the North when discharged from the army, and some never returned home. Part of the migratory stream consisted of the brightest people, who sought more freedom for their creativity. The South as a land of opportunity had fallen on hard times. Those who stayed behind, however, discovered that the war and its aftermath had set a new agenda.

The Strains of Rural Life

Despite the disruption of war, most Southerners continued to work on farms and use mules and simple implements. Most farmers, no matter what their status, tinkered with machinery. Farm wagons, plows, houses, and barns all demanded constant upkeep. Given the lack of financial resources, this often required ingenuity. Some farmers had more complicated machinery—cotton gins, hay balers, threshers, tractors, and trucks. During the first quarter of the century, Southerners saw their first automobiles, airplanes, gasoline tractors, and became acquainted with many new implements.

While some interpreters of Southern life viewed mules as a symbol of backwardness, farmers treated them as pets, as favored members of the farm family. Indeed, many farmers spent more time with their mules than they did with their wives and children. Mules are hybrid animals, the offspring of jackass studs and mare horses. They are born male and female but are sterile and cannot reproduce (there have been rare cases of mules having offspring). By 1925, before tractors had made much impact on the South, the mule population stood at some four and a half million. There was, as historian Jack Temple Kirby has written, a direct correlation between mules and the cotton and tobacco cultures; farmers on the fringes of that area preferred horses and oxen. Most farmers bought mules that were bred in Missouri, Tennessee, and Kentucky. Mules were more expensive than workhorses, so Southerners offered justifications for choosing these draft animals over horses and oxen. Some argued that mules had a thicker skin than horses and could better bear beatings. More practical farmers argued that mules were more surefooted (they had smaller hoofs), had better resistance to disease, worked better in the hot climate, and were smarter and stronger than horses. There is justification for all these arguments except for the last. All farmers agreed that mules had a different and more complex personality than other work stock.

In Southern storytelling, mules have earned a place of distinction. When posing for portraits, families often placed mules (and usually dogs) in a prominent place. Some farmers made pets out of their mules, while others carried on a constant war with the animals. Nate Shaw in his autobiography gave one of the best accounts of the importance of mules in the life of Southern farmers. He remembered the name and disposition of every mule he ever owned, and he not only petted his mules but in at least one instance interceded when a white man was beating his animals.

Mules responded to simple commands—"gee" for turning right, "haw" for turning left, "whoa" for stopping, and "come up" for getting started. Yet mules had their own minds about these commands. In tobacco fields, mules pulled sleds alongside the primers, but they sometimes refused to "whoa." They also understood that lunch was served when the farm bell rang; they plowed faster going toward the barn, and, according to most accounts, were individualists. A North Carolina tobacco farmer often gave his mule a chew of tobacco and shared soft drinks with it.

Nate Shaw worked with mules into the 1950s, when most farmers were buying tractors. "I knowed as much about mule farmin as ary man in this country," he boasted. "But when they brought in tractors, that lost me." According to mule trader Joshua A. Lee, owning mules and watching them work was much more than a matter of simple utility; it was an emotionally rewarding way of life.

Southerners not only grew tobacco; they also used it in extraordinary amounts in pipes, cigars, snuff, chewing tobacco, and cigarettes. Few establishments risked not providing cuspidors until the century was half over. Southerners, moreover, deemed it a God-given right to spit on public sidewalks and out of car windows. Tobacco users insisted that it had a soothing effect, and it also stunted the appetite, relieved toothaches, and was an important ingredient in many folk remedies. Women gradually gave up pipe smoking during the century, but many continued to chew and dip as well as smoke cigarettes.

One indication of Southern nicotine dependence emerged during the 1927 Mississippi River flood when a relief administrator in Mississippi pointed out that "we have been faced in this disaster with a situation wherein we find that tobacco and snuff is just as much a portion of the rations given to negro tenants on these plantations as is molasses and bread." Tobacco was one of the few luxuries that rural people, black and white, could afford.

No amount of tobacco, however, could substitute for a balanced diet and medical care. Because of the furnishing system (landlords provided only a set amount of food) and the prevailing poverty, most rural people ate large portions of corn and pork—white food. Many landlords discouraged their tenants from planting gardens, which, they argued, drained effort from cash crops. By the turn of the century, nutritionists realized that some of the stereotyped Southern laziness came from pellagra, caused by a niacin deficiency. As late as the 1927 Mississippi River flood, nutritionists understood that supplements of yeast cured pellagra, but they did not fully comprehend the nature of the disease. Malaria also sapped energy, and in an area that bred mosquitoes, many Southerners contracted the disease. Hookworm, an intestinal parasite that attacked people who went about barefoot and picked up larvae from feces, was widespread. For lack of privies, shoes, and greens, then, many Southerners were drained of their energy. By the 1920s, some of these maladies were under control, but poor people were the last to benefit from medical advances.

No matter what the conditions among the population at large, women bore an uncommon share of misery. Women married young in the South, and girls at a young age took on household chores. They were prepared early for the responsibility of being wives and mothers. The women of the house usually rose first, cooked breakfast, sometimes milked the cow, and often worked in the fields. They also cooked dinner and supper, washed dishes, and cared for the children. Since many farm families depended on their children for additional labor, large families were the norm. Even those who knew about family planning seldom had the finances to buy the necessary preventives. Some women thrived in this environment, and those who did bragged of their prowess in the fields and in the home.

Southerners had an ambivalence about explicit discussions of sex. Some young women were not informed about menstruation and were ashamed and frightened by it. Parents perhaps reasoned that children were supposed to learn about sex from barnyard animals that surrounded them. Barnyard humor suggests that Southern men were often more frank about the reproductive capacities of bulls and roosters than about wives or children. It was as if people were more willing to joke about sex than to confront human problems that arose from sexual relations.

Birthing practices during the World War I years were making the transition from home to hospital, from midwives to doctors. When a woman became pregnant, she usually had the support of her family and that of the community. In towns and cities, a doctor could easily be summoned to help in the delivery—if there was money to pay the doctor. Many physicians tended the poor, knowing that they would never receive any pay. Improved roads and the use of automobiles enabled doctors to cover more territory as well as permitting rural people to travel to town. Midwives, often called granny women, delivered many rural children. Few had any education or formal training, but most were savvy in special ways about delivery. They apprenticed themselves to other midwives, and their methods were traditional. As modern medicine introduced professionalism, granny women became rare. In some cases, midwives also prescribed potions that would induce abortion, but most women chose to bear their children. Although midwives had high status among the poor people of a community, many of the wealthy, including doctors, regarded them as nuisances. Once, a midwife, realizing that the delivery had become complicated, arrived at a small-town doctor's house after midnight to ask for help. She knocked for a quarter of an hour, and the doctor finally opened the door, cursed her, dallied about, and arrived after the infant had been born. Even in the 1950s, midwives served poor blacks and whites who could not afford doctors.

Given the work load, large families, and lack of medical care, the lives of many rural women were demanding and hard. Pride in large families was tempered by the strain of pregnancy and childbirth, and love of fieldwork was balanced against the demanding chores of the household. Some women, perhaps many, simply endured the numbing routine of constant pregnancies, cooking, washing, ironing, fieldwork, and child care. Added to these burdens for sharecropper wives was the constant round of moves from one shabby house to another. In this context, the companionship of other women and the support of the community became especially important.

Life was easier for women if they had a caring husband, but testimony from oral histories and other sources indicate that married couples often argued and fought. Men drank, prowled, and sometimes beat their wives and children. In this culture, divorce was practically unknown; further, society placed strong sanctions on divorced women. So couples stayed together in an uneasy truce. A North Carolina tenant wife observed that her husband was more considerate of the mules and dogs than of her and the children.

The drama of life for rural people was acted out on farms that had rudimentary buildings and conveniences. The system of small farms tilled by tenants emerged after the Civil War, and at first slave cabins were moved from the slave quarters to isolated tracts. As cabins deteriorated, landlords constructed simple one-story dwellings that can more aptly be described as shelters. The more attractive houses had front porches and a long hallway that provided ventilation. Kitchens were often set off from the main structure to minimize the danger of fire. Frame houses constructed in the twentieth century were often simply boards nailed against framing, with no ceilings, interior walls, or insulation. Many farmers joked that they could see the stars at night and watch the dogs and chickens run underneath the house through cracks in the floor. Glass windows were a luxury, and most cabins had shutters. In many areas of the South, homes were heated by cookstoves and fireplaces. Large families huddled in such housing, and often as many as three children shared a bed. Such homes lacked electricity, telephones, indoor plumbing, and running water.

Just as the more affluent farm owners could afford better implements, they could also afford better housing. Modern conveniences, however, were often unavailable. Until electric lines spread through rural areas under the New Deal's Rural Electrification Administration, fewer than ten percent of the country's rural families had electricity, unless they bought a Delco generating plant or could rig a windmill to provide current. In some cases, more affluent farm families moved to towns in order to enjoy the comforts of life.

Rural Southerners would continue to watch the incremental changes that altered their lives, but the larger transformation awaited the thirties. In other areas of life, however, forces that had bypassed the South arrived to challenge traditional institutions. Although still a colony in many respects, the South moved closer to the nation at large. It could no longer ignore every new idea that swept the country.

5 / The Coat of Many Colors

In many ways, the South after World War I continued to be a backwater of rural peasants eking out a living cultivating cotton, tobacco, sugar, rice, and other crops in the slowly revolving seasons that ruled their lives. In political life the racist campaigns of the early years of the century gave way to more conservative candidates. The calm façade that masked the thoughts and actions of Southerners hid a new spirit of introspection. A fault line appeared, one that cut across the South and divided society. Questions seldom asked about the structure of Southern society, especially class relations, increasingly provoked controversy and protest. Many Southerners realized that the war had generated strong forces that would challenge tradition.

Blacks who supported the war hoped to reap economic and social gains, while most whites battled to maintain the racial status quo. A surprising series of incidents exploded on black campuses, where students rebelled against standards of conduct and curriculums better suited to the nineteenth century. Tuskegee Institute's president, Robert R. Moton, supported providing a veterans' hospital for blacks with an all-black staff. While blacks sought entry into the twentieth century, white students faced the nineteenth-century-inspired evolution debate. Southern writers struggled, mostly unsuccessfully, to break out of the Victorian literary mold and write realistically about the South. During the decade, country music spread across the land, popularized by the recording industry and the radio. Southern millworkers launched a series of strikes. The South had many threads in its coat of many colors, but the final design remained elusive. The old and the new continually battled for supremacy.

Black Pride

When the Treasury Department decided in 1921 to build a veterans' hospital for blacks near the Tuskegee Institute campus, Robert R. Moton, president of the school, secured the word of Veterans Bureau officials that blacks would staff it. When the hospital neared completion two years later, the bureau reneged on its promise, and Moton appealed successfully to President Warren G. Harding for support. Yet Veterans Bureau administrators in Washington continued to hire whites, and Moton discovered that his complaints offended the Tuskegee white population. He curtailed his public role but secretly helped orchestrate the protest that followed. The availability of hundreds of highly trained black doctors and nurses challenged the stereotype that blacks were capable only of menial labor. That well-paying federal positions would go to professional blacks embittered whites who wanted the jobs. As the hospital geared up for full operation, Alabama whites and their Veterans Bureau allies attempted to intimidate blacks and control the hospital.

The crisis came on July 3, 1923, when John H. Calhoun, Jr., arrived at the hospital to take a clerk's position formerly held by a white woman. A threatening letter signed by the Ku Klux Klan awaited him, and the Klan planned a march through campus that night. Calhoun, denied a room at the hospital's staff quarters, complained to the head of the Veterans Bureau. The commandant of the Tuskegee Cadet Corps organized alumni volunteers, who poured onto campus, armed, to protect the school. In the dark shrubs and on top of buildings, black men, some of them veterans, sighted down rifles, waiting for trouble. The Klan marched that night, but it was peaceful, and the next day the Alabama press claimed that whites would control the hospital. Within a year, however, the hospital staff became all black. The NAACP, an organization that usually opposed segregation, strongly supported the plan to seg-regate the staff, while the segregationist Klan wanted to integrate the hospital staff and even hire white nurses. White Alabamans not only lost the battle but were ridiculed by fellow whites across the South. A Jackson, Mississippi, newspaper argued that a "hospital operated exclusively for negro patients is no place for a white woman."

An Alabama state senator put into a nutshell the irrational fears of local whites when he observed that the crisis "demonstrates clearly and conclusively how rapidly a negro grows in presumption, courage and the attempted assertion of power, when he is dealt with on the basis of a white man, and treated with consideration and courtesy." Southern whites also learned that the NAACP and the all-black National Medical Association could generate wide-spread support, not only in the black community but in the Re-publican Administration in Washington. Once again, when faced with federal intrusion, white Southerners were forced to yield. Fed-eral aid to blacks in the Tuskegee case was a portent of what would happen in the 1960s.

The militance that led the Tuskegee blacks to arm and that rallied Moton, the NAACP, and the National Medical Association set the tone for other demonstrations on black campuses. Whether it was part of the spirit of black pride generated by black nationalist Mar-cus Garvey, the militance born of war and frustration, the creative drive of the Harlem Renaissance to redefine black intellectual life, or a frontal attack on an outdated Victorian morality and racial stereotypes, black students eagerly sought a more equal place in academic life. Demonstrations at Fisk University and at Hampton Institute epitomized the strains.

Fisk University in Nashville, Tennessee, had been founded after the Civil War, and by the 1920s it reflected the ambivalent status of black college students. A white president, Fayette McKenzie, headed the institution, placating what seemed universal white apprehension of blacks being in control of schools, hospitals, or army units. Students were rigidly controlled by chaperones, rules of conduct, dress codes, the mandatory singing of spirituals for visiting whites, and other guidelines that were designed to please the white community's idea of how blacks should behave. When W. E. B. Du Bois attended his daughter's graduation there in 1924, he criticized the administration and its petty rules, arguing that they stunted the search for excellence. Later he toured the country, calling for McKenzie's resignation.

When the trustees met in November 1924, they were greeted with a delegation of student leaders and a student demonstration calling for the president's ouster. A demonstration on February 4, 1925, provoked McKenzie to call in the Nashville police, but by the time they arrived, the students had already gone to bed. McKenzie hounded the seven student leaders by having them arrested for inciting a riot and giving them the option of denouncing the riot or leaving school. Alumni were outraged at McKenzie's calling in the police, while, predictably, Nashville whites supported him. McKenzie pretended that he was a white scapegoat, but students argued that McKenzie's color was not the point. After five weeks of protest, at least three hundred students still refused to attend classes. McKenzie resigned on April 16, 1925, and Thomas Elsa Jones, a white Quaker, took over. His color never interfered with his plan to make Fisk a university that would serve the needs of black students, and he introduced courses in black history and eased the Victorian restrictions. Jones remained at Fisk for twenty-one years, a time of growth and harmony at the institution.

Hampton Institute, founded in 1868, epitomized the tensions in Southern black education and the imperative to please the neighboring white community with platitudes about training blacks for non-professional careers and stressing their secondary place in Southern society while quietly moving from a high school to a college curriculum. Booker T. Washington, the school's most famous alumnus, founded Tuskegee Institute in 1881, and both schools trained black students in education and in trades. Administrators tried to straddle their precarious place in Southern communities by, on the one hand, ruling the students with an iron hand and parading them about as marionettes and, on the other, appealing to Northern philanthropists to aid in uplifting the children of former slaves. By 1920, Hampton Institute was moving away from its distinctive role as a vocational high school and becoming a college. Yet the search for academic excellence was often sublimated to the archaic rules that governed student behavior. Life revolved around the school bell and the thick book of rules that organized every waking moment of a student's life. Curfews, daily chapel, rules against sex, alcohol, and tobacco, and strict observance of the Sabbath cut down on fun and enthusiasm.

Hampton's growing pains coincided with a movement within the state to cement segregation even more solidly. Because Hampton often was host to speakers and concerts that appealed to the white population in the Hampton–Norfolk–Newport News area, whites attended campus events and took whatever seats were available. Guests, in other words, had to treat blacks as equals. When a dance company performed at the school's auditorium in 1925, the young wife of Newport News *Daily Press* editor Colonel W. S. Copeland was seated beside some blacks, and the colonel's reaction provoked a crisis as he wrote that Hampton advocated social equality.

Hampton president James E. Gregg's patient reply did not calm Copeland, who continued his assault on Hampton, dredging up specters of racial amalgamation, social equality, and the decline of the Anglo-Saxon heritage. The latter topic obsessed some whites, who imagined threats from blacks and immigrants. Virginian John Powell, who championed Anglo-Saxon clubs and later sought in mountain music the glorification of the Anglo-Saxon past, sponsored legislation to enforce segregation on the Hampton campus. In addition, some white teachers openly opposed hiring black teachers, and some half dozen of them had marched with the Ku Klux Klan when it demonstrated in support of the segregation law. For students, who were shifting from industrial and agricultural subjects into academic pursuits, such behavior challenged their view of education.

It was fitting that the crisis at Hampton came not over events of great magnitude but from the administration's decision to leave the lights on in the back of the auditorium during the Saturday night movie, a not very subtle slap at student behavior. The next evening, students refused to sing spirituals, despite pleading from the administration and the presence of an important white guest. A boycott of classes started on Monday, and on Tuesday night a student committee met Gregg to present seventeen complaints, primarily arguments for a relaxation of social rules and a tightening of academic standards. When the boycott continued, Gregg shut down the university on Friday, October 14. To reenter school, students would have to sign an oath to obey the rules. Quickly, Gregg dismissed four men, suspended nineteen more, and refused admission to thirty-eight others. Ultimately, he suspended sixty-nine students and placed hundreds on probation. Hampton had purged its best students. The strike collapsed, and on October 25 the school reopened.

The returning students were defeated, but they were not compliant. Gradually the school began to change as trustees acquiesced to changes in the archaic codes of behavior. Some teachers also protested the high-school atmosphere and the hypocrisy of posing as a vocational school while aspiring to be a college. The tension increased, and in May 1929 Gregg resigned. Hampton continued to struggle with its identity for another generation, but student resentment did not flare up as it had during the 1920s.

Evolution and Fundamentalism

While black students attempted to fight their way out of the nineteenth century, white students were experiencing the trials of twentieth-century worldliness. Many Southerners saw in World War I a catalyst that unleashed evil forces upon the world. They were appalled that children no longer stayed at home but rode in automobiles, attended movies, listened to jazz, danced outrageously, and discussed sex frankly, and that young women wore short skirts, voted, and argued for equality in all aspects of life. Industrialism and urbanization further challenged traditional ways. Southerners sought solace in the past, and for many, religious Fundamentalism became more important than ever as a safe retreat from current questions. Others looked to the agrarian heritage for security, if not escape. As the Bible fell under the scrutiny of higher criticism and the theory of evolution found its way into religious discussions and textbooks, Southern religion grappled with the forces of modernism.

Evolution became the symbol of change, and in the 1920s twenty state legislatures debated bills that would prohibit teaching such theories in the classroom. In 1925, the Scopes trial in Dayton, Tennessee, attracted national attention. John T. Scopes, a high-school biology teacher who taught the theory of evolution, became the focus of a celebrated trial. William Jennings Bryan, three times a candidate for the presidency and Woodrow Wilson's Secretary of State, represented fundamentalism, while Clarence Darrow, an atheist and the personification of new ideas, represented liberalism and free speech. H. L. Mencken, editor of *The American Mercury*, found in the trial, in the revivals, and in the commercialism ample ammunition to further ridicule the South.

The presiding judge found Scopes guilty and fined him a hundred dollars and the state supreme court upheld the law forbidding the teaching of evolution, but Scopes's conviction was overturned on a technicality. The carnival at Dayton, however, was actually a sideshow that demeaned Fundamentalists as freaks rather than as people under siege from new, and to them, ungodly ideas. The teaching of evolution, in their minds, had to be defeated, and they took a stand against it. To most Fundamentalists, evolution threatened their basic beliefs and their faith. Mencken and Darrow could not understand how Bryan could articulate a defense of Fundamentalist beliefs that relied on faith rather than fact. Nevertheless, the trial became a symbol of the South's inability to face the modern world. Bryan died days after the trial, no doubt still puzzled by some of Darrow's probing questions.

The troubles of fundamentalists were not all displayed at Dayton. Fundamental religion distilled the Old and New Testaments into a core of beliefs that included original sin, the divine inspiration of the Scriptures, the virgin birth of Jesus, atonement, resurrection, the Trinity, the second coming of Jesus, and a final judgment. The theory of evolution challenged the creation story in the book of Genesis; it certainly relegated the story of Adam and Eve to myth and symbol. If they accepted evolution, many Fundamentalists feared, the remainder of the fundamentals would fall.

While some religious people feared evolution, William Louis Poteat, the president of Wake Forest College in North Carolina, accepted the theory, taught it in his biology classes, and wondered why some people still thought it controversial. By 1920 several vehement fundamentalists attacked him. A man of exemplary character who was educated in Europe, Poteat presented a formidable target. Even while president of the school, Poteat continued to teach freshman biology, and he instructed the mostly rural students in the theory of evolution.

For Poteat, as for many educated Christian laymen, evolution did not contradict the biblical story of creation. By 1920, however, Thomas Theodore Martin, author of *Hell and the High Schools* (a treatise against teaching evolution), began a series of attacks on Poteat. Replying to these and other attacks with "May a Christian Be an Evolutionist?" in *The Biblical Recorder*, Poteat attempted to reconcile evolution and Christianity. A controversy erupted, and by 1922 the pages of *The Biblical Recorder*, the forum of North Carolina Baptists, were filled with opinions on evolution. Students and alumni strongly supported Poteat, as did most Tarheel editors. When the Baptist State Convention met in December 1922, many representatives debated evolution, its dangers, and the problem of having Poteat on the loose at Wake Forest College, a Baptist-sponsored institution. To silence the discontent, Poteat spoke for an hour, defining Christian education, observing that science presented no threat to religion. His talk left his enemies defenseless, and the next day the convention formally commended Wake Forest and its president.

Poteat saw his faith not as a barrier to new ideas but rather as a context in which to make them comprehensible. No doubt, many of his students saw in his open-minded approach a model for facing disturbing questions of science and social change. Others, however, saw evolution as a symbol of modernism, a threat to the old order of Fundamentalism. Three years later the evolution fight shifted from the Baptist State Convention to the North Carolina state legislature when in February 1925 D. Scott Poole of Raeford introduced a bill that would prohibit teaching evolution in the state's schools. The House of Representatives defeated it sixty-seven to forty-six.

Poteat's travail did not end with the defeat of the Poole bill but increased as local Baptist leaders capitalized on the issue, no doubt caught up in the frenzy of the Scopes trial in the summer of 1925. When the convention met in Charlotte later in the year, Wake Forest alumni from all over the state converged on the auditorium. The Fundamentalists watered down their demands to the point that even Poteat voted for them. Perhaps the convention might be compared to a football game when the alumni turn up to support their team and coach. Many of them did not understand the fine points of the game, but they cheered the home team against all enemies. "He merely stood his ground and whistled," Wake Forest alumni and writer Gerald W. Johnson observed, "and instantly around him sprang up a thousand alumni, grim alumni, with red eyes and no scruples about flying at a Fundamentalist throat."

William Louis Poteat personified the synthesis of fundamental Christianity and modern ideas of science and higher criticism. He never doubted that his religion was stronger and more flexible than the series of fashions, theories, and innovations that invaded society. He was a quiet leader, a man who stood by his convictions, and set a model of deportment and intellectual integrity. In an age of change, Poteat found an inner security that radiated hope for both Christians and heathens.

The Literary Undertow

Just as Southern churchgoers confronted change, Southern writers emerging from the Civil War and Reconstruction swam against several undertows, primarily the strong current of the Lost Cause cult and the more universal tide of Victorianism. Dealing with defeat while avoiding its consequences chained Southern writers to apology, while the Victorian emphasis on the superficials of life inhibited the exploration of such themes as sex and race. Great literature did not spring from the travail of Reconstruction any more than it did from the leisure secured with the work of slave labor. Southerners boasted that the upper class was genteel, well read, and creative; sparse evidence supported these claims. Southern writers looked north, not only for publishers but also for critical approval. No Southern city contained a publishing center, and in this sense the South was as dependent upon Northern publishers as it was upon Northern credit; it was a penniless cultural colony, lacking financial and literary capital.

Post-Civil War literature vacillated between simple Lost Cause romance and more creative romanticism. Joel Chandler Harris wrote his Uncle Remus stories about plantation life and glorified black slaves rather than planters. He faithfully captured the dialect of Georgia blacks as he related the body of folklore he had soaked up. The themes in *Uncle Remus: His Songs and His Sayings* and Harris's other volumes eventually became a Walt Disney movie, *The Song of the South*, a cartoon in every sense. If Harris's work was plundered for happy, sensational, or innocuous themes, so were other works, such as *Uncle Tom's Cabin*, which had a half dozen or more screen incarnations. The South, if one learned of it from film, had but two classes—rich whites and happy blacks. Movies avoided the lives of average Southerners and any footage of class divisions. They were all happy down there.

Thomas Nelson Page defended his class, the Virginia aristocracy, with short stories and novels such as "Marse Chan" and *In Ole Virginia*. In none of these works could the reader find material about sharecropping or the lives of white yeomen or hard-working blacks. While many people worshipped Harris and read Page's stories with interest, George Washington Cable explored the color line in his novels, and race relations in non-fiction. He left in 1885 to live in Massachusetts, because he was depressed by the South's harsh criticism of his work.

One of the more remarkable turn-of-the-century writers, Kate O'Flaherty Chopin, grew up in St. Louis, married Oscar Chopin, moved to New Orleans in 1870, and by 1879 had six children. When Oscar's business failed in 1880, they moved to a small town in Natchitoches Parish, and there Kate Chopin learned about Cajun culture, which contrasted so sharply with the Creole culture of New Orleans. When Oscar died in 1882, Kate returned to St. Louis, taking with her the rich store of material about Louisiana that would inform her literature. During the 1890s, she wrote short stories and novels and in 1899 published *The Awakening*, a disturbing book that undermined the myth of happiness in upper-class New Orleans. Contemporary readers and critics ignored her work, but she has since become recognized as an important and innovative novelist.

As much as any Southern writer of her day, Ellen Glasgow personified the effects of breaking with convention. Born in 1873 into an upper-class Richmond family, she rebelled against her unfeeling father and conventional religion. Her mother buckled under the cares of rearing eleven children and became an invalid. Ellen suffered from neurosis and depression and sought through psychiatric treatment to maintain a balance. Poor health prevented her attending public schools, so she studied at home. Later the University of Virginia denied her admission because of her sex.

In *Barren Ground*, she explored the world of a yeoman family and especially of Dorinda Oakley, who as a young girl thought "the one thing immutable and everlasting was the poverty of the soil." As yeomen lost their carelessly tilled land, they rented other farms and ran them down. Her mother had become an addict to work, and "the habit had degenerated into a disease, and thrift had become a tyrant instead of a slave in her life." Her father, likewise, "had known nothing but toil; he had no language but the language of toil." After making love with a local young man whose parents then insist he marry a respectable woman, Dorinda grows to hate him and runs away to New York. Her pregnancy is ended when a cab strikes her; the experience leaves her cold and stoic. She returns home to bring life to the barren land, to nurse her former lover, whom she despised as cowardly, and finally to marry a man she does not love. Glasgow wrote that Dorinda "exists wherever a human being has learned to live without joy, wherever the spirit of fortitude has triumphed over the sense of futility." Glasgow moved through the world with ambivalence, searching for a break with the past, but constantly drawn back to her father's Calvinism.

Southern writers as late as the 1920s had not reconciled the Lost Cause and Victorianism with the new currents of the post-war era.

Groups of literary-minded people gathered in New Orleans, Nashville, Chapel Hill, and Charleston. In New Orleans, *The Double Dealer* provided space for Sherwood Anderson and the fledgling William Faulkner, among others. At Vanderbilt University in Nashville, *The Fugitive* provided an outlet for Edwin Mims, John Crowe Ransom, Allen Tate, Donald Davidson, and Robert Penn Warren. In Charleston, DuBose Heyward wrote *Porgy* (1925) and romanticized primitive blacks, much as white critics in New York treated the Harlem Renaissance.

These attempts to escape the undertow of the past were promising, but in fact Southern literature had not found the material or the spirit that would make it nationally important. Most writers lacked the complexity or the willingness to experiment that modern fiction demanded. In many ways, the upper-class South never lived up to the promise so often articulated about a creative leisure class. Southern creativity in the first two decades of the century came not from the upper class but from the lower. It came not from poems and novels but from music.

Country Music

Country music, like blues, is preterite music; it speaks of lost loves, missed opportunities, and hardship experienced by working people. It is the music of the damned—not the elect. It incorporated influences sacred and profane, black and white, mountain and plain. No matter how isolated, rural Southerners sang, fiddled, played pianos, banjos, harmonicas, and guitars. Some tunes came from England, while others evolved from unique American experiences and influences.

By the turn of the twentieth century, fiddling contests, minstrels, tent shows, and community sings had long been a staple of Southern life, and musicians continually explored new instruments and arrangements. Rural music was never static but continually changed as musicians borrowed and improvised. Alexander ("Eck") Campbell Robertson, credited with the first country record, won fame in fiddling contests at Confederate veterans' reunions. In 1922, he and Henry C. Gilliland left the veterans' convention in Richmond and traveled to New York unannounced to make a record for Victor. Their session, especially Robertson's "Sallie Goodin," produced classic old-time fiddling, and Victor released the record in April 1923. Recorded country music was thus born. In the same year that Victor released Robertson's record, Virginian Henry Whitter recorded "The Wreck on the Southern Old 97" for Okeh Records, the first of Whitter's fifty-five solo numbers.

John Carson, no doubt, wielded the greatest influence on early recorded country music. Born in Georgia near the Tennessee border in 1868, he was the perpetual star at the Atlanta fiddling contests, which he won seven times. In 1922, Polk C. Brockman, Atlanta's Okeh record distributor, saw Fiddlin' John Carson on a newsreel and tipped off Ralph S. Peer, Okeh's field man. Peer went to Atlanta to record Carson, just as he had recorded black musicians in the field for Okeh's race record market earlier. After a slow start due to Okeh's doubt that the records would sell, Carson became a recording pioneer in country music. Some of his songs were of English vintage, but others came from the minstrel heritage and reflected the diverse roots of Southern music. Although Robertson and Whitter recorded first, it was Fiddlin' John Carson who found the vast market for country music.

The spinning 78 rpm records captured Southern music that had been generating for centuries—ballads from England, love songs, country ballads, church songs, blues, songs that had gained favor among rural people. Suddenly, one could hear such music in one's house, and with the growing distribution of radios in the 1920s, music became more important than ever in many homes. Since many rural people were illiterate, singing or listening to music became a chief form of recreation. They preferred music that dealt with themes close to home—average people and their work, loves and heartbreak, music about dogs, mothers, train wrecks, and death. Polite society scorned country music, which had an energy born of working people and a tradition that would endure, expand, and ultimately become tamed and further commercialized. But that was after Jimmie Rodgers.

Jimmie Rodgers had a profound impact on a whole generation of country singers. He came from a broken home; it was broken by his mother's death when he was six years old. While his father worked on the railroad, young James, as he was then called, lived with a succession of relatives in Mississippi and Alabama. Much of his young life he spent in Meridian, Mississippi, frequenting soda shops, carnivals, tent shows, circuses, and minstrels, and he watched street life with its hustlers and pitchmen. Too mobile and restless to attend school regularly, Rodgers got his education on the streets and later on the railroad and in hobo jungles. At an early age, Rodgers decided he wanted to be an entertainer; he joined a medicine show when he was thirteen. A year later, he was working on the railroad as a section hand. At twenty, he married Stella Kelly, but his poverty and roaming broke up the marriage. Unknown to Jimmie Rodgers, his wife was pregnant, and it would be years before he saw his daughter or even knew she existed. In 1920 he married Carrie Williamson, and that marriage endured despite his hard luck and migratory life. Around 1923 he learned that he had tuberculosis.

By the mid-twenties, Rodgers had friends across the country, for he remembered names, loved the gathering places of working people, and had a charming but unassuming personality. In 1927 he moved to Asheville and sang over the new radio station WWNC. In August 1927 Rodgers learned that Ralph Peer was recording country musicians in Bristol, Tennessee. From another direction the Carter family arrived at the session. "These two famous acts represented distinctly different stylistic approaches to country music," historian Bill Malone has written, "and they embodied strongly opposing impulses—the deification of home, and the glorification of the wanderer—which have ever since endured among country musicians." In the six years still allotted to him, Rodgers's music struck like an earthquake across the country, and he became the first authentic star of country music. While he liked new cars with every option a salesman could attach, he always mixed with his working-class friends and played the small towns that he knew so well from his travels. Like most blues singers, Rogers could not read music, so his recording sessions required hard work to make the pieces come together.

People who heard the Blue Yodeler sometimes could not fathom whether he was white or black. His songs incorporated so many influences and his backup bands were so diverse that nearly all influences, black and white, were represented. He recorded with the Carter family, Louis Armstrong, Joe Kiapo (an itinerant Hawaiian steel-guitar player), and in Louisville he teamed up with Clifford Hayes's Dixieland Jug Blowers, a black band. He accepted a hundred dollars for his first session, which produced "The Soldier's Sweetheart" and "Sleep, Baby, Sleep." Later his Blue Yodel, "T for Texas," became one of the most popular and enduring tunes. "Jimmie's Texas Blues" contained the line "The blues ain't nothing but a good man feeling bad."

By the fall of 1932, Rodgers became ever weaker from tuberculosis. A year earlier, he had recorded "T.B. Blues," taking the suffering themes in country music to a new level as he seemingly detached himself from his own reality. Increasingly, his public performances were short as he gasped for breath, drank prescription liquor to ease the pain, and sucked lemons to steady his voice. In May of 1933, in the midst of the hectic first Hundred Days of Franklin D. Roosevelt's Presidency, he went to New York to record. He endured coughing and fatigue, had to be propped up with pillows for some sessions, but bravely made his last stand. He died the day after the session, during the night of May 24. The train that carried him back to Meridian gave a long whistle when it arrived, and on May 29, 1933, the thirty-five-year-old yodeler, the singing brakeman, was buried in Meridian.

His work not only inspired a generation of country musicians but was representative of the changes that spanned the 1920s. Motion pictures, especially the talkies after 1927, ended the old tentshow tradition in the South. At the same time, Victrolas and radios provided music for the multitudes. To people buffeted by depression and drought, by government policies and mechanization, Jimmie Rodgers's music about drifting and the blues became part of their heritage. As he sang in "Mean Momma Blues": "I've been from several places, and I'm going to be from here." The line reflected his life and that of thousands of fellow Southerners who drifted upriver, uptown, and the farther they removed themselves from the country, the more alluring country music became.

What the phenomenon of Jimmie Rodgers revealed was not so much the coming alive of country music but rather its striking resemblance to music sung by black Americans. His rise to stardom was in effect the intersection of black and white music. Just as black blues singers made the listener feel that the hardship was personal, so did Jimmie Rodgers. His music, like that of black musicians, was the music of the lower class, unfiltered and unbridled by middle-class and upper-class tastes. Many were offended; others ignored his music. Nonetheless, lower-class Southern musicians of both races fueled a significant creative force, one that quickly spread to Europe. It was American music, some of it derived from Africa, some from England, but much of it simply generated by the oppression that was the lot of working-class Americans. Unlike musicians in the classical tradition, most of these musicians could not read notations; this was felt music.

Mill Towns

Before World War I, Southern textile workers resisted routinization by moving from mill to mill, by being skeptical of company-sponsored social programs, and by maintaining a sense of community. Mill-owners failed to restructure communities and work habits. After the war the textile industry entered a depression, and to survive in the new environment, millowners launched a new attack on workers. The assault on the mill workrooms came from college-educated managers, professionals recruited from outside the factories. Indoctrinated with management's point of view, these supervisors had little sympathy for workers; promotion from within the factory to managerial ranks became more difficult. Workers no longer had direct contact with owners; orders and complaints flowed through a chain of command. In addition, mills became more routinized and housed new and more efficient equipment that spread out and speeded up work. With the stretch-out, workers tended more machines, and catching up and taking a break became impossible. The new organization required fewer workers. Counters installed on machines called for workers to reach a production goal and not work at their own pace. At the same time, electric motors on each machine not only drove the machines faster but also prevented an entire line of machines being idled.

When the United Textile Union of America began organization work in the South in the 1920s, it found workers interested in joining unions. Millworkers had always been clannish and proud, so uniting to protest work conditions was a logical step. In most cases workers faced immense odds. Factory owners were prepared to lock out workers, bring in scabs, and use the police power of the state and local authorities to break strikes. In a larger sense, managers created an ideology that made union membership synonymous with second-class citizenship and equated union members with blacks and foreigners. Managers also hinted that they could hire blacks to replace strikers.

Given their culture, many mill families opposed laws that prohibited child labor, yet progressive forces continued their crusade. The coalition that opposed child-labor legislation included the National Association of Manufacturers and the American Farm Bureau Federation. These organizations argued that such laws derived from foreign influences, threatened the sanctity of the family, and even threatened Christianity. Obviously, such organizations had no shame when it came to protecting their source of cheap laborers.

Lint in textile mills inflicted respiratory ailments, and workers rarely saw the sun; they marched into the factories before light and left after dark. Ten or eleven hours a day, plus half a day on Saturday, added up to fifty-five or sixty hours of work per week. A worker could earn about $670 a year in 1927, which was better than the $519 average for farm workers. The benefits of workman's compensation, minimum wages, and safety did not reach most of the textile areas until much later.

Even as the cotton culture spread west, the textile industry moved from New England to the South as it consolidated in the face of decreasing sales. By 1929 the South had a majority of the country's spindles and accounted for nearly seventy percent of the spindle hours of production. In order to continue profitable operations, millowners resorted to wage cuts and heavier work loads.

The conditions in textile villages were shared by coal miners, steelworkers, and lumbermen. Each industry had its own work routines, which varied as much as commodity cultures in agriculture, but whether one looked to farms, mill villages, the log woods, or the shanties surrounding the steel mills, the housing and sanitation were primitive. Some workers did band together in unions. Railroad brotherhoods were notably successful, and typographers and builders also founded unions to promote their welfare. Such unions rarely proved radical; rather, these skilled and stable workers were conservative and hoped to preserve their jobs from competition from the mass of unskilled workers.

During the labor unrest in 1919, several Southern strikes yielded mixed results. The post-war decline in business, however, destroyed unions and led to lower wages. When experts entered the cotton mills, stopwatches in hand, and reorganized the work routine, workers understood the implications. In 1927, in Henderson, North Carolina, several hundred workers struck for higher wages. The strike failed but left a residue of union members. The American Federation of Labor moved haltingly into the South to instruct workers on their rights and on the possibilities of opposing millowners. By 1929 textile-mill workers began to organize and resist changes in factory organization.

Workers testily endured mill authority, which extended into their churches, and welfare workers, who actually checked on absenteeism. When the Loray Mill in Gastonia, North Carolina, in 1927 and 1928 instituted the stretch-out system, workers were irate. The Loray management acted quickly and ruthlessly, installing new machinery, sometimes doubling the number of machines tended by a worker, and within fifteen months reducing the labor force from 3,500 to 2,200. Lowered wages and demotions accompanied the stretch-out. When workers complained about the arbitrary way that management changed the work routine, the superintendent imported workers from South Carolina who worked for lower wages. Church membership dwindled. The stability of the mill village fragmented. In March of 1928, weaving-room workers struck, but they had no effect. "It used to be you could git five, ten minutes rest now and then, so's you could bear the mill," one worker complained. "But now you got to keep a-runnin' all the time. Never a minute to get your breath all the long day." He had tended six drawing frames previously, but with the stretch-out he tended ten.

The National Textile Workers Union (NTWU) was organized in September 1928; it was a communist union. In March 1929, Fred E. Beal started to organize in Gastonia among the Loray employees; it was a ripe field despite some concessions by management. Beal did not stress his communist affiliation, and his demands were those of a trade union—minimum wages, reduced hours, an end to the stretch-out, better sanitary conditions, rent reduction, and recognition of the union. NTWU organizers ridiculed the less militant United Textile Workers and the American Federation of Labor. The Loray management discovered the communist link, but the unabashed organizers openly boasted of the benefits of the communist system. Organizers flocked to Gastonia, advocating an overthrow of the capitalist system, which bred the problems. Some two dozen communist workers were in the city during the strike, representing, among others, the International Labor Defense, *The Daily Worker*, the Young Communist League, and the Young Pioneers. The attempt to enlist black union members in what was an almost totally white work force largely failed. Organizers also soft-pedaled their antagonism to the church, because of the obvious religious bent of the workers.

After some violence along picket lines and some scuffles with police, the governor called out the National Guard. The union tried to win over the soldiers, but there were arrests. The strike began on April 1, and two weeks later, in most respects, it was broken. Management recruited outside workers, and strikers drifted back. The union became isolated, and evicted workers huddled in a tent colony at the edge of the village. On June 7, a group of union members marched toward the mill but were turned back by police, who followed them back to the tents. A scuffle broke out and several people were wounded; the chief of police died from wounds the next day. This put the union on the defensive. Most important, management stressed that outside agitators dominated the union, that communists and atheists had no place in the community. Quickly, almost the entire community united against the strikers. The Rhode Island owners somehow avoided the outsider label; at least, it was not an issue.

The leaders of the strike stood trial for conspiracy, but on September 9 a mistrial resulted when one of the jury members went insane. That night a caravan of cars rode through the country, terrorizing union members. Union leaders planned a meeting in South Gastonia for Saturday afternoon, September 14. A truck headed for the rally was turned back near its goal; shots were fired. Ella May Wiggins, who had composed ballads and had been active in the strike, was killed. Violence continued for another week. Some union members were taken from the state and beaten, while five men indicted in the murder of Wiggins escaped conviction. At Wiggins's funeral, two Methodist ministers announced that her five children would be taken in by an orphanage. The union leaders, meanwhile, were convicted of conspiracy and then fled to Russia, forfeiting bail. Later Fred Beal returned and served out his prison term.

Even when factory managers could not portray strikers as outsiders, they had power to break strikes. In 1929, in Elizabethton, 550 women inspectors walked out of the American Glantzstoff rayon plant, protesting a fellow worker's demotion for asking for a raise. Quickly, organizers appeared, but the local government as well as the Tennessee governor helped break the strike, and some thousand workers lost their positions.

Even as the Gastonia and Elizabethton unrest continued, workers in Marion, North Carolina, struck against the stretch-out system and the degrading conditions in the village. Compromise failed. When workers in one mill walked out on October 2, the sheriff fired tear gas into the ranks of the strikers, and deputies opened fire on them as they retreated. Six workers died and another twenty-five were seriously wounded, shot in the back. Local preachers refused to conduct funeral services, but a mountain preacher from the area prayed, "I trust, O God, that these friends will go to a better place than this mill village or any other place in Carolina." R. W. Baldwin, the head of the milling interests in Marion, summed up the attitude of his class. "I read that the death of each soldier in the World War consumed more than five tons of lead. Here we have less than five pounds and these casualties. A good average I call it." There are few lines in literature that so succinctly summarize the conflict between workers and owners.

Although workers lost these battles, strikes swept across the

Southern textile area, and in many cases local workers spontaneously walked out. Indeed, when national union leaders offered help, many workers spurned them. Like Southern farmers, mill-workers sprang from independent roots that had no tradition of premeditated protest. Even the reorganization of mills could not completely break down that heritage. In a decade usually seen as one of labor complacency, Southern workers set a tone of militance. Southern blacks and whites, musicians and writers, sinners and saved, were struggling for dignity.

6 / The Conservative Revolution

In the South, the Great Depression slowly eroded what was already poor economic soil. Farmers had watched their fortunes decline during the 1920s, and as depression struck, many more went broke and became sharecroppers or left the land to huddle in small towns or cities or fled north or west in search of opportunity. Factories closed, and unemployed workers, with no government program to help, roamed the land looking for work. The lumber industry of the South declined, for much of the good timber land had been cut over. Overproduction in other businesses, such as oil, idled drilling rigs, and bank failures wiped out the savings of many. State governments, with a reduced tax base, could not provide services and were practically helpless to inaugurate work projects. Urban people, in some cases, headed for the country to live with relatives or attempted to subsist on small farm plots. Farmers replaced them in cities, for they saw opportunity far from the land and the landlords who abused them.

When disaster struck, such as in the 1927 Mississippi River flood, the Red Cross, with logistical and matériel support from the federal government, aided refugees. In that flood some million people were displaced, many of them sharecroppers from the Delta lowlands who fled to Red Cross refugee camps. Planters feared that balanced meals, health care, and recreation would raise sharecroppers' expectations and undermine their power, or that labor agents would persuade refugees to move north.

In the spring and summer of 1930, a drought spread across large areas of the South. This disaster came slowly, and relief agencies were not sure when officially to declare a disaster. The Red Cross sent investigators to the parched areas, and though most reported that people were suffering from lack of food, the gears of Red Cross relief did not turn. Part of the reason derived from the local Red Cross chapters, which were largely controlled by community leaders hesitant to start relief programs before the fall harvest. Cotton planters, for example, feared that workers would refuse to pick cotton if they were supplied with relief food.

Throughout the fall and winter of 1930–31, the Red Cross studied the situation, and Congress debated bills to offer relief to the victims. President Herbert Hoover's philosophy called for local people to aid each other; failing that, the Red Cross would offer relief. The drought was so widespread, so destructive, that farmers needed both food and credit to survive. The Red Cross could only keep people alive; it could not put a credit plan into action. Ultimately, the Red Cross did bring relief, but many people suffered from starvation before it arrived.

The impact of drought and hunger proved devastating. The United States, in the minds of most people, provided opportunity, and to fail at making a living reflected not the collapse of the system or even drought; rather, it meant that they had failed as Americans. Most people did not want relief if it could be avoided, but conditions became so stark that they guiltily took it. This set of contradictions bred shame in people and broke their spirit.

Both the flood in 1927 and the drought three years later gave a taste of Red Cross relief to millions of Southerners and suggested that when local resources failed there would be relief from outside the community. As the depression deepened and communities tightened their belts, it became obvious that a disaster had once again visited the South, but in this case it was economic disaster. At that point the South, and the nation, faced the question of assigning the responsibility and drafting a program to care for people plagued by poverty, unemployment, and despair. In another sense, Southerners saw a biblical warning in the flood, the drought, and economic disaster. Surely such terrible events came as warnings. Whatever the causes of hardship, Protestant religion offered hope of salvation, and in the dark days of the early 1930s, people looked for signs of a savior.

The conditions in Mississippi were typical of other Southern states. In 1932, the state was bankrupt, and when Governor Theodore Bilbo left office in 1932 it owed $14 million and had barely a thousand dollars in the treasury. Since depression struck in 1929, the number of jobs in manufacturing fell from 52,000 to 28,000, and unemployment in the state's larger cities rose above ten percent. Per-capita income fell from $239 a year in 1929 to $117 by 1933. The shrinking tax base throughout the South resulted in cutbacks in state services, and as schools closed, road construction ended, and government offices closed, more workers were laid off. Low commodity prices and farm failures made a shambles of the South's economy. Figures on unemployment during the depression are unreliable, but probably from ten to thirty percent of Southerners had no steady job.

As the depression continued, waves of people roamed the country in search of work. Men left home, hoping to land jobs and then send for their wives and children. In other cases entire families packed up their automobiles and headed west or north. Large tracts of land fell under the hammer of foreclosure, and banks, mortgage companies, life-insurance companies, and other lenders took over the land. Hoover carts, made from automobile axles and tires and pulled by horses or mules, carried people about, for they were too poor to buy gasoline or license tags. Herbert Hoover, who had first earned international attention for organizing relief abroad and then ran the relief effort during the 1927 Mississippi River flood, watched helplessly as the economy unwound. Ultimately, the Reconstruction Finance Corporation loaned funds to corporations, but for the poor, Hoover had no imaginative program, no lifeline. Dispossessed, broken-spirited, and searching for jobs, many people hoped for economic recovery or for a leader who could offer a bold program. Until this time, in the minds of most people, government aid seemed alien, even socialistic, but as hard times continued, they saw no other hope. Federal intrusion, so long feared, offered their only salvation.

The Kingfish

There is something haunting in the newlywed photographs of Huey and Rose Long taken in 1913 and of Jimmie and Carrie Rodgers taken ten years later. Two smiling young couples faced the camera and the future. Within a few years, both of the men would become legendary figures; both would die young. Since the Civil War generation passed away, there had been few role models for Southern youth, but Long and Rodgers lighted hopes and dreams; they furnished heroic images to emulate. Jimmie Rodgers moved across the country (he holds his suitcase in the photograph) and became the friend of drifters and those who searched for the frontier of opportunity; he sang of the common people. Huey Long, who championed the poor, evoked reverence among his followers. Before making a speech, Long customarily waited until the last moment; then he would walk through the crowd to mount the podium. His biographer, T. Harry Williams, observed that while Long was a hero to many people, he was "not like them or of them." People "would touch his sleeve, lightly, almost religiously. Some people would follow him from meeting to meeting, hearing the same speech over and over, just to touch him again, as though they derived some special kind of grace from this laying on of hands." Although Jimmie Rodgers was more accessible, his fans also worshipped him. There would be no such giants to walk the South again for a generation.

Huey Long emerged as the political leader of Louisiana in the mid-1920s, the same time that Franklin D. Roosevelt reentered politics and became governor of New York. These two men were to have a tremendous effect on Southern history, on the hopes and dreams of a section of the country that lagged far behind in nearly every index of well-being. Roosevelt was an aristocrat who was struck down by polio and who, to the minds of many, had been humbled by this experience. Long came from Winnfield, Louisiana, and was born in a log house—a rather large log house. Winn Parish had a maverick political heritage—Unionist in the Civil War, Republican during Reconstruction, Populist in the 1890s, and Socialist in 1912. By the standards of the comparatively poor parish, the Longs were well-off landowning yeoman farmers. Born in 1893, Huey Long was too young to remember much about the Populist movement. Roosevelt was eleven years older than Long, and he spent his youth in idyllic and bucolic Hyde Park, in the best schools, and with the best, or at least the most aristocratic, people. Mostly self-taught, Long worked as a traveling salesman, studied law at Tulane University, and realized that he was destined for a political career. As different as the two men were in background, both had charisma, both could move crowds, and both wanted power. They had radically different dreams of the country's future, and they differed on how government should be used to restore prosperity. Even today, both names kindle love and hate, for few people in the 1930s or since could talk about either man without passion.

Until 1969, with the publication of T. Harry Williams's *Huey Long*, historians had been content to treat Long as a sideshow, a comic but dangerous man who at his worst was a Southern-bred fascist and at his best was an inept and ill-mannered politician who surrounded himself with lackeys, crooks, and bodyguards. Whatever the merits of that interpretation, more recent scholarship has explored his significance, and as the books accumulate, Long's career has become central to understanding the choices that were present in the depression South. At the center of his program, Long advocated a redistribution of wealth. First as Public Service Commissioner, when he enforced laws regulating large corporations, and then as governor, when he took on the Standard Oil Company, Long did not flinch from fighting corporate wealth. When he became governor of Louisiana in 1928, his opponents believed they could coopt him, drive him into their arms or into foolish mistakes. When he persisted in carrying out his program of building roads, furnishing free textbooks to schoolchildren, updating health care, promoting university education, and pressing for tax reform, his opponents tried to impeach him. They failed.

In the next few years, Long consolidated his power by building a political machine that had one purpose—to promote Huey Long. His opponents could not counter this brilliant drive for power, and ultimately the only way they could retain any power was to approach Long, hat in hand, and accept what he might offer. Having packed the state house with loyal allies, Long ran for the U.S. Senate in 1930 and won, but he remained governor until 1932, both to prevent the lieutenant governor from taking over and to push through other segments of his program. He supported Franklin D. Roosevelt at the 1932 Democratic Convention and expected Roosevelt to defer to him. Instead, Roosevelt bowed to the Southern power structure, realizing, as had Woodrow Wilson before him, that he needed it to put his program through Congress.

Long, the only Southern politician in the 1930s who unabashedly argued for a redistribution of wealth, criticized Roosevelt for not restructuring tax laws. The same people, mostly the poor and the dispossessed, supported both Long and Roosevelt. In New Deal programs Southerners enjoyed government aid for the first time— agricultural programs that raised prices, work programs such as the Civil Works Administration (CWA) which gave them jobs, and even the Civilian Conservation Corps (CCC), which sent young men to camp to earn money helping to conserve natural resources. To the poor of the land, even the few federal dollars they pocketed each month meant better food and housing. To Long this was not enough; it would have no enduring positive effect. Indeed, Long quickly realized that the bounty of the New Deal helped the wealthy proportionately more than it helped the poor.

Long's ideas were often unconventional, for he relied not on a brains trust, as did Roosevelt, but upon common sense and ideas picked up from people around him. In 1930, for example, a bumper cotton crop threatened to reduce the price of cotton to six cents a pound, far below the cost of production, and create a mammoth surplus. While the Federal Farm Board and the Hoover Administration urged cooperative efforts to cut production, Long, after listening to some north Louisiana farmers, suggested that no cotton at all should be planted in 1931. The simplicity of the program appealed to many farmers and businessmen. Critics argued that ginners, seed crushers, fertilizer salesmen (and companies), and furnishing agents would all go broke, but Long countered by stressing that if his program was enacted, the price of 1930 cotton would double, and the economy would actually be healthier after a year's vacation from the cotton fields. Most important, the plan would treat all farmers equally, unlike the later New Deal farm program, which penalized small farmers and tenants and rewarded large operators. Though cotton prices remained low, Huey Long's stock rose; he had championed the common man, though he had been defeated by vested interests. It was a familiar theme in Southern history.

Ultimately, Long went to the Senate and, after getting established (and creating a legend for his night life), emerged as a progressive legislator, one who fought Roosevelt and advocated tax reform. By 1934, Long became a national leader, and his radio addresses, which had been so popular when he was governor of Louisiana, reached national audiences. Like Roosevelt, Long was a master of the radio. While Roosevelt spoke with patrician articulation, Long purposefully assumed a down-home manner and mispronounced big words to show he was just an average American. In one address, he had songwriter Harry Link sing a jingle, "Every Man a King." Much as in a commercial, every few minutes Link would tune up on a piano and sing; sometimes Long would join in.

In such addresses Long quoted from philosophers and from the Bible to prove that his plan was not radical. He undermined New Deal programs at every turn. In a 1935 talk, he cited a Federal Trade Commission report showing that in 1930 one percent of the population owned fifty percent of the wealth; in 1935, Long insisted, they owned more. There were more people unemployed in 1935 than in 1933 when Roosevelt took over, he announced. His Senate bill to limit income to $1 million a year and to tax inheritances had only gotten six votes; Roosevelt had opposed the legislation. The New Deal farm program, he observed, was a failure; it drove people off the land. He reintroduced a theme from the drop-a-crop plan of 1930 by suggesting that farmers should grow all they wanted, and when they had accumulated a year's supply, they could take a year off from farming and work on government projects or go to school.

Whatever the merits of Long's programs, he realized that the early New Deal was not benefiting poor people at large. Sharecroppers and small farmers received less of the bounty of federal money than the wealthy did. While federal credit programs aided some farmers, they also propped up lending institutions. Instead of being paid for by additional taxes on the wealthy, the New Deal program operated off deficit borrowing which the average taxpayer would ultimately make up. Long could never accept the existence of large fortunes side by side with the suffering of the masses. Share our wealth, he argued again and again. By 1935 millions of Americans were listening to Long, and thousands were forming Share Our Wealth clubs across the country. Long hoped to cash in on this constituency in 1936 and challenge Roosevelt for the Presidency. His dreams ended in the fall of 1935, when he was assassinated in the Louisiana state house.

His death ended the last attempt by a Southern politician to redress the imbalance of wealth in the country. Long avoided the racial politics that had dominated the South for years. He was simply inept at using the race issue; when he tried, it lacked conviction, probably because he knew it was a false issue. He openly admitted that if poor whites prospered, so would poor blacks, and saw the future shared by all classes of Americans and dominated by none. Sharing wealth meant restructuring the economy from the bottom up. In the end, the New Deal restructured the economy too, but from the top down.

With the exception of Huey Long, Southern politicians in the 1930s varied little from those who had dominated politics since the turn of the century. Some historians have made much of such liberals as Lyndon Johnson of Texas, E. D. Rivers of Georgia, Dave Sholtz of Florida, Olin Johnston and Burnet Maybank of South Carolina, and Lister Hill of Alabama. This handful of liberals (and their liberalism shifted with the political winds) were but a small percentage of the whole, and most simply basked in the glory of Roosevelt and his New Deal programs. More important, Roosevelt's liberal program had significant conservative implications. Upon analysis, New Deal programs could be seen as a mammoth attempt to prop up the toppling system of capitalism. Ironically, those who profited most, the capitalists, hated Roosevelt, while those who ate the crumbs that fell from the table, the poor, worshipped him as a savior.

Alphabet Porridge

The National Recovery Administration (NRA), passed by Congress in 1933, awarded a Blue Eagle to those businesses that codified their operations to fit national guidelines. Much as the Progressive legislation of the first few decades of the century rationalized business, the NRA attempted to update and modernize such guidelines. In western Tennessee and Kentucky, for example, NRA codes threatened to force tobacco growers to sell their crops in warehouses. Many farmers had previously sold their tobacco directly to factories to avoid warehouse charges. Even though such codes opened the way for unions to organize without harassment, such freedom was long overdue and, in the South, hardly a factor in recovery or reform. By the time the Supreme Court struck down the NRA in 1935, it had become widely criticized for centralizing corporate power. Its codes of competition aided large corporations, which could absorb higher wages and government guidelines.

The Tennessee Valley Authority (TVA), established in 1933, ruthlessly moved people from the land, as recent scholarship has demonstrated. The water behind Norris Dam, the first of the system's lakes, covered the land, homes, schools, churches, and graveyards of pioneers and their descendants who were poor but attached to their homesteads. One man committed suicide, refusing to leave the land. Almost a half century later, many who relocated were still bitter or at best ambivalent about the impact of TVA.

True, many Southerners worked for TVA, and the dams did develop electricity and recreational facilities. TVA transformed the Tennessee Valley, but corporations and the federal government profited as much as people from cheap electricity and navigable streams. Alcoa, the aluminum company, for example, depended on TVA to provide power for its electricity-hungry operations, and during World War II, Oak Ridge used TVA power to produce the atomic bomb. Like other New Deal programs, TVA radically changed the relations of people to the land and to each other. It was another evidence of government intrusion, of outside experts deciding how people should live. The agency never asked if people desired such changes; to stand in the way of TVA meant one was backward and benighted. Dam after dam rose to trap the waters and flood the farmland and homes, and long after there was any need for or justification of such works, TVA continued to build them. When it had dammed up every fast-flowing stream in the valley, it constructed coal-fired electrical generating plants that burned strip-mined coal. The plant at the ironically named Paradise, Kentucky, spewed so much ash from its gigantic chimneys that the town had to be abandoned. Finally, TVA turned enthusiastically to nuclear power and lost billions of dollars in the process. The need for bureaucracy to feed on itself seemed more important than conservation or the life of communities.

While TVA earned the reputation of being an intrusive agency, the Rural Electrification Administration (REA) encouraged local people to form cooperatives and chart their own plans. Founded in 1935, REA furnished the expertise and loans to run electric lines far into the country. At that time, only about ten percent of rural homes in the United States had electric power because private power companies had avoided servicing sparsely settled areas. Although many rural people looked with suspicion on power lines and lights, many farm women realized that electricity could ease some of their more burdensome chores. Women rose at daybreak, built a fire in the wood stove, and cooked three meals over the hot stove. They toted water from a spring or well for kitchen use and for washing clothes in cast-iron pots in the yard. They heated heavy sadirons atop the stove for ironing. Either a springhouse or an ice box (the iceman called once a week with blocks of ice) kept milk and other perishables from spoiling.

Rural electricity meant not only that women could regulate the cook stove but that they could have running water (hot or cold), indoor toilets, electric irons, refrigerators, and radios. Farmers lighted their barns so that chores could be done after dark with no danger of kicking over a lantern and starting a fire. Some bought electric motors to power machinery. More important, lights, which is the way most people referred to electricity, meant that rural people were as good as their urban cousins, for once the electricity came on, rural people took on another degree of dignity. They also moved into the consumer society. Co-ops, appliance dealers, and home-demonstration agents stressed the usefulness of electric appliances. It was a quick leap from lanterns to lightbulbs, from privies to indoor bathrooms, and some farmers weighed their purchases carefully, deciding where convenience confronted luxury. The REA was a grass-roots program and relied on local residents to sign up members, secure rights of way, plan distribution, and construct lines. Federal administrators offered managerial suggestions and lent funds to local cooperatives. Among co-op members, there was also a sense of having beaten the private companies at their own game.

Years after the New Deal and TVA's main work, William Faulkner mused on the destruction of the Big Woods and the disappearance of the civilization that it harbored. "The Big Woods, the Big Bottom, the wilderness, vanished now from where he had first known it; the very spot where he and Sam were standing when he heard his first running hounds and cocked the gun and saw the first buck, was now thirty feet below the surface of a government-built flood control reservoir whose bottom was rising gradually and inexorably each year on another layer of beer cans and bottle tops and lost bass plugs . . ." William Faulkner, in addition to understanding the dynamics of Southern history, understood the potential of entropy inherent in government-forced progress.

And if William Faulkner understood such loss, his brother John understood the effect of the Works Progress Administration. In *Men Working*, John Faulkner portrayed the travail of a farm family as it relocated in town and went to work for the W.P. and A. The book presented a dismal view of federal bureaucracy and its impact on poor people. Most of all, it showed that neither Roosevelt nor his brains trust had a concerted plan for rebuilding prosperity and saving the old culture.

Southern politicians made sure that race relations were not upset, but in a larger sense such programs helped clear the land of surplus laborers and paved the way for commercial farming. This is not to suggest that many government programs were unwanted or were not useful. The significance of such programs would only become apparent later, when the structure of the South had changed. From the beginning of the Great Depression to the end of World War II, the South was metamorphosed. The wreckage of the old system was washed away; in another generation much of the caste system would also undergo a revolution. The ledger book on that revolution is still not balanced.

Some federal agencies entered the South with apprehension. In 1934, the Federal Emergency Relief Administration (FERA) conducted a survey to determine if relief pauperized recipients, and it gathered a great deal of information about rural conditions. The profile of Morgan County, Georgia, offered a microcosm of some of the forces that swept through the South. The county had a population in 1930 of 12,488, and fifty-eight percent was black. Only a decade earlier, the population had numbered over 20,000 but boll-weevil destruction and black migration ("The more virile and adventurous types left," the report observed) weakened the economic structure of the county even before the depression hit.

In the summer of 1934, the FERA had sixty-four white and seventy-one black families on relief, or 4.7 percent of the county's residents. Forty-four of the families were headed by women, most widowed. Only thirteen of the heads of household had attended school past the seventh grade, and most had dropped out by the fourth. Morgan was an agricultural county, and the 1930 census reported that eighty percent of farm operators were tenants and half were sharecroppers. Among black farmers, ninety-two percent were tenants and two-thirds were sharecroppers.

The Agricultural Adjustment Administration (AAA) had paid $85,000 to county cotton farmers in 1933, and the Civil Works Administration had paid out over $20,000. The Civilian Conservation Corps had accepted sixty-four whites and six black recruits, a proportion that demonstrated the racial bias of the South. The report concluded that four-fifths of the relief population was "content" to remain in that condition, but it "pointed out in extenuation that the rolls include many who have become habituated to receive aid in times of stress because of the established relationship between landlord and tenant." Indeed, Southern tenant farmers had long been part of a system that resembled relief, but the New Deal substituted a federal landlord for the local counterpart.

What has become apparent is the key role the Agricultural Adjustment Administration (AAA) played in turning the South from sharecropping to agribusiness. From the evidence available in archives and other documents of the time, it appears that most Southern farmers wanted to stay on the land. In the cotton South, the AAA program first reduced acreage (and thus the demand for labor) and then stabilized prices, so that larger farmers could invest in machinery. Landless refugees moved to cities or towns to seek government work, or trekked west or north in search of the new frontier of opportunity. Ultimately, nearly all crops would undergo such changes, as the South became enclosed; the old paternalism inherited from slave days came to an end, and government control took its place. The federal government replaced the old paternalistic system and became the master of Southern agriculture.

The New Deal agricultural program, the AAA, attempted to raise the price of commodities by controlling the supply and paying farmers for cooperating to reduce the surplus. Each commodity had a section of the AAA to look after it, and each section chief had a certain autonomy within the guidelines. When the Cotton Section decided to set up a voluntary program to reduce supply by plowing up part of the growing 1933 crop, it paid for the land taken out of production. In 1934 acreage was reduced across the board for all farmers, and a penalty drove mavericks to cooperate. Quickly, planters saw the advantages of cooperating with the government. For land taken out of production, they collected government payments, and the crops from land kept in production sold for a parity price (a figure that equaled what other workers in the economy would make for similar work). Sharecroppers complained that not only did some planters cheat them out of federal money but in some cases they were turned off the land in violation of AAA guidelines.

The structure of the AAA and the agricultural educational complex of land-grant universities, extension agents, and the Department of Agriculture made it well-nigh impossible for a sharecropper to appeal eviction. In the Arkansas Delta, thousands of sharecroppers banded together into the Southern Tenant Farmers Union (STFU), founded by blacks and whites in the area. H. L. Mitchell, a co-founder of the STFU, fearlessly called strikes in the cotton fields and carried his case to Washington. There, such leaders as Cully Cobb, the head of the AAA Cotton Section, refused to accommodate the union's complaints. Instead, he fired the union's supporters in the AAA. Back in Arkansas, the situation in several counties became tense as planters beat some union members and attempted to intimidate the entire STFU organization.

What is crucial about the fight between the STFU and the AAA is that the former was the conservative element, battling to preserve and reform the old system of sharecropping. The AAA, while denying that its purpose was to force social change, supported planters in their fight against sharecroppers. They, and to some extent USDA employees, saw that by reducing the number of sharecroppers and reverting to wage labor, owners could streamline their operations, change the status of their workers, and take in more government money. During the first years of the AAA, large cotton planters did just that. By the mid-1930s, planters invested their government money in machinery such as tractors. This enabled them to reduce their labor force even further. These elements—the AAA, large planters, and the agricultural educational complex—saw the possibility of making a revolution in the rural South. They, not the STFU, were the radicals in the 1930s. Whatever non-commercial aspects of agriculture had persisted since the Civil War disappeared into government programs. Even as many planters complained of federal intrusion, they greedily took government money, invested it in machinery, rationalized their farm operations in a more businesslike way, and looked to the end of the rainbow, at the pot of federal money, at a host of farm machines, and at chemicals.

The process of aiding larger farmers involved not just government payments to farmers but also the tilting of payment and credit to larger growers. A Senate investigation, not surprisingly, revealed that much of the money went not to poor farmers but to banks, mortgage companies, and life-insurance companies, which controlled vast amounts of Southern farmland. In most commodity programs, landowners received most of the benefit payments, so federal money propped up larger farmers at the expense of those displaced from the land.

The temporary programs that gave work and relief to needy and unemployed became permanent—and so did the AAA. Looked at in a long perspective, the AAA created a social revolution in the cotton culture during the 1930s, and in later decades it would also reconfigure other commodity cultures. In the 1950s rice farmers dwindled as acreage reduction cut into their number, and in the1970s tobacco farmers left the land to make way for machines and new government programs. No matter what the verdict on TVA, WPA, CWA, CCC, REA, and other programs, the AAA created a revolution in the rural South. The old cultures were swallowed up in the belly of government or cut down by machines. Only migrant workers, still toiling in primitive conditions and often held involuntarily, served as a reminder of the old labor-intensive culture. Yet who could mourn the passing of such an exploitative culture as sharecropping?

What one could mourn was the passing of the underpinnings of the old culture—the families that were broken and dispersed to the cities, the communities that wilted, the small rural churches that had bonded such communities, and the neighborliness that allowed such deprived people to endure even the vicissitudes of sharecropping. In 1936, James Agee and Walker Evans, a talented writer and a notable photographer, studied three families in Hale County, Alabama, and produced the classic book *Let Us Now Praise Famous Men*. Agee not only reflected the ambivalence of his feelings about the tenant system but also the love-hate relationship these tenants had for the cotton culture. Evans's photographs have become classic images of the last generation of sharecroppers. Much that was miserly and exploitative passed away, but things of value also disappeared as people left the land.

Such people had no say in their fate. Many would have preferred to remain on the land; they left, driven away by government and machines. The war sucked up many such wanderers, giving them jobs in defense plants or pushing them into battle. The war, not the New Deal, saved them from unemployment, and a permanent war economy would keep them working. Thus, the government ultimately became the planter, the master, not only of those who stayed on the land and worked under government programs but also of those who fled to work in the cities.

In the end Huey Long proved to be a prophet. Had even a token of his Share Our Wealth program been adopted, the fate of the dispossessed would have been far different. His program called for no control over farmers but allowed them to work at federal jobs if they overproduced. Instead of paying people to keep their land idle, he would have rewarded them with jobs and educational opportunities. Instead of enriching corporate owners and large planters, his program would have democratically benefited all farmers. Some farmers suggested that acreage be reduced on a sliding scale, as in the income tax, but this common-sense idea never received the serious attention of legislators or the AAA. Thus, the opportunities to stem the tide of government intrusion evaporated. The federal government and machines reconfigured the rural South. Only a seer could decide whether the things lost offset the increased productivity and more businesslike operations that would characterize the rural South.

Legitimizing Unions

Despite the strikes of 1928 in Marion, Elizabethton, and Gastonia, unions made little headway in the South before the New Deal. During the 1930s, however, union organization increased. The primary catalyst of change was provision 7(a) of the National Industrial Recovery Act, which stated that workers had the right to organize and receive protection from unfair labor practices. Yet, in a region that only selectively obeyed laws, the protection was often more on paper than in reality. The NRA guidelines, while stating that unfair labor practices were illegal, did not specify what was unfair. The National Labor Board, established in 1933, proved inept in policing the provisions of the act. Established a year later, the National Labor Relations Board improved enforcement only incrementally. In 1935, Congress passed the National Labor Relations Act, or the Wagner Act, and spelled out unfair practices. Roosevelt reluctantly and belatedly backed the bill. In 1936, Congress set wage and hour guidelines for firms with government contracts, and two years later minimum-wage guidelines covered all industries engaged in interstate commerce.

More important than the laws, however, was the split in the American Federation of Labor (AFL) when John L. Lewis of the United Mine Workers in 1938 founded the Congress of Industrial Organizations (CIO), which concentrated more on industrial workers than on skilled laborers. Labor unions flourished under the New Deal in most areas, but in the South the benefits were uneven. By 1940, the South had about half as many union members proportionately as did the country at large, 10.7 percent to 21.5 percent.

Still, the CIO boosted Southern labor. It organized steelworkers, and, of course, the United Mine Workers was central to its success. Predictably, the cotton mills remained almost entirely free of unions despite a wave of strikes in 1934. The Carolinas and Georgia, where most of the textile mills were located, had few unions, but in Kentucky, Alabama, and Tennessee, the seat of manufacturing and mining, unions increased. In a larger sense, the NIRA sanction of unions, the President's murmured support, and the Wagner Act eroded the idea that unions were un-American.

Perhaps the best example of unionization during the New Deal came from the coal industry. During World War I, union membership rose dramatically, but by 1930 it had dropped off drastically. In Harlan County, Kentucky, the UMW dwindled, and its organizing efforts at the end of the 1920s faded. In May 1931, a battle in Evarts, Kentucky, led to deaths on both sides. From this dismal situation, John L. Lewis seized on section 7(a) of the NIRA in 1933, and in two years had enrolled over a half million workers. In the mining area of West Virginia, union membership rose from 7 in June 1933 to over 85,000 in two years. Even though the government sanctioned unions, much of the increase came from the dogged organizing tactics of the CIO and the UMW. Some mineowners simply ignored the labor guarantees written into statutes. To satisfy their demands, unions struck, and in some cases strikers benefited from government food distribution. Even in Harlan County, the UMW in 1938 won a contract for over 13,000 miners.

With his gains in the coal industry, Lewis moved into the steel areas of Birmingham and won representation quickly. His success came from several factors, including the Northern ownership of some of the firms. Perhaps as important, the steel industry realized that with the support of the President, who in 1936 had won another term, with the ruling on constitutionality by the Supreme Court, and with profits pouring in, the better part of wisdom was to avoid a strike. Even industries that held out during the 1930s yielded in the war years, for the government awarded contracts to firms that had good labor relations.

Despite CIO gains in mining and manufacturing, the textile trade remained the stronghold of non-union sentiment. By 1940, the South had seventy-four percent of the nation's spindles. Although textile workers first greeted NIRA's section 7(a) with joy, by 1934 they saw that strikes would be their only redress. In July, some 20,000 workers struck in Alabama. By September, there were 400,000 workers on strike as the movement spread across the industry, and several people were killed. When Congress passed the Wagner Act, John L. Lewis moved in to win the United Textile Workers, which had split from the AFL. Still, to a large extent the textile industry resisted organization.

The CIO also stressed that blacks were equal partners in labor, although in practice discrimination continued. Whereas the AFL allowed locals to decide the issue of race, the CIO insisted that blacks be included. In the mining industry, Lewis argued that omitting blacks would spell the end of the union effort. To placate whites and give token leadership roles to blacks, the CIO hit upon a formula that included a white president, a black vice president, a white secretary-treasurer, and some black minor officials. There was little integration in the social activities of workers, but blacks belonged to the union and benefited from its successes.

Southern businessmen and politicians vehemently fought the Wagner Act and any attempt to strike down the right to pay lower wages. When the Fair Labor Standards Bill was introduced in 1937, Southern politicians denounced it, claiming that it was intended to enslave the South. Lumbermen insisted that increased wages would ruin them. Naturally, such assertions did not convince working people that the bill was a threat to them. Southern political campaigns in late 1937 and 1938 indicated that the bill had strong support among voters, and in June the bill passed, legislating a forty-hour work week, and a minimum wage of forty cents an hour, which would be achieved by gradual steps. The bill exempted agricultural workers and several other categories.

The New Deal atmosphere that encouraged unions did not have a magical effect, but it did move the South one more step toward realizing that to achieve parity in wages it had to unionize and dissolve the lines that separated the races. Though the gains were in some ways spectacular, the South remained a stronghold of anti-union sentiment. During the 1930s, however, several Southern politicians accepted union backing and repaid it with support of labor legislation. By World War II, a host of politicians sought union votes.

Ironically, union members credited Franklin D. Roosevelt with their successes, just as farmers attributed higher prices to him. In the case of agriculture, the New Deal restructured the South by aiding the more able farmers and driving off sharecroppers, but even ex-farmers, the dispossessed, worshipped Roosevelt. His New Deal seemed to offer hope even to those it ignored. Although Roosevelt had been lukewarm toward labor and actively detested John L. Lewis, union members saw in Roosevelt their savior. And in a sense the federal government did act as a savior, for it intruded into the relations of capital and labor. The South would from time to time become the battleground of labor struggles, and it would cherish right-to-work laws as no other region. The spirit that moved settlers from the coast to the mountains, and failed and sent them back to the mills, and stressed independence over collective action, died hard.

A Southern Literature

Most accounts of the poverty of Southern literature before 1930 quote H. L. Mencken's "The Sahara of the Bozart." Lillian Smith made much the same point. But she was a Southern writer. "In nearly two hundred years of white southern culture there was not one artist or critic or poet or dramatist or musician or writer (if we except Poe) produced here who was comparable to his contemporaries in Europe," she wrote in *Killers of the Dream* (1949). "This conspiracy of blindness, this collaboration with authority, entered into voluntarily but later made obligatory by custom, closed a heavy door on the mind and the senses." Indeed, many white Southerners ignored the unpleasant or the embarrassing. "Perhaps the wasting away of our people's talents and skills," she concluded, "has been the South's greatest loss." By the end of the 1920s, the trance had worn off, minds cleared, and the door opened.

In October 1929 William Faulkner's *The Sound and the Fury* was published—a book that taps into the stream of consciousness of the narrators, including the idiot, Benjy Compson. A short time later, Faulkner took a job working the graveyard shift at the University of Mississippi power plant and wrote *Sanctuary*. A year later, as the country sank into depression, he purchased an old plantation in Oxford and named it "Rowan Oak." As many Southerners struggled against changes set in motion first by depression and then by New Deal policies, Faulkner went about establishing himself as a writer and recluse. Although he did not have formal schooling in Southern history, he read widely and listened to the stories passed down through his family and neighbors. His creative life became a search for meaning—in the contradictions of slavery and the class divisions that troubled white society, in the tangled bloodlines created by miscegenation, in the obsession with the Civil War, in the violence and paranoia of the Reconstruction years, in the rise of a new type of Southern businessman, in the decline of the old aristocracy, and finally in the civil-rights movement. Most of these themes were developed in the 2,400 square miles of Yoknapatawpha County, populated by 6,298 whites and 9,313 blacks. Faulkner was the sole owner and proprietor of the county; it existed only in his mind and in his fiction.

In many ways Faulkner's fiction transcends location and dwells on the South as a universal theme. He was born in 1897 in New Albany, Mississippi. As he drifted about the United States and Europe in the mid-1920s, he had failed to discover a vehicle for his ideas. "You're a country boy," author Sherwood Anderson told him in New Orleans, and "all you know is that little patch up there in Mississippi where you got started from." In 1927, while writing *Flags in the Dust*, Faulkner discovered the wealth of material in his "little patch." As literary critic David Minter explained, "he found everything he had heard, seen, felt, and thought suddenly available: the sense of a shadowy past, at once cursed and glorious; of self-preoccupied individuals and families; of several entangled and doomed ancestors and descendants; of two entangled and doomed races, and two entangled and doomed sexes."

Throughout the thirties, he worked away, producing, in addition to short stories and movie scripts, seven novels: *As I Lay Dying* (1930), *Sanctuary* (1931), *Light in August* (1932), *Absalom, Absalom!* (1936), *The Unvanquished* (1938), *The Wild Palms* (1939), and *The Hamlet* (1940). Despite this incredible output, Faulkner failed to gain wide recognition until 1946 when Malcolm Cowley put together *The Portable Faulkner*, calling attention to the body of his work. New York City and the expected round of publishing parties rarely attracted Faulkner, and on some New York visits he simply got drunk and failed to keep his appointments. He usually remained in Oxford, sailed, puttered around his plantation, and wandered into town to visit with friends. If his neighbors thought he was a bit peculiar and wrote incomprehensible books, they extended him the right to be eccentric. On Christmas Day 1932, he wrote to Bennett Cerf, his publisher: "Rotten weather here, as usual. However, I have a keg of good moonshine and four pounds of English tobacco, so what the hell, as the poet says."

Ultimately, Faulkner's shadow became so long that it became oppressive to other Southern writers, yet modern writers as diverse as García Márquez and Salman Rushdie find in Faulkner inspiration for their work. He attempted to write his way through the myths that paralyzed his land, and in the end he spun a vast and intricate web that in 1950 earned him the Nobel Prize for Literature. Needless to say, many Southerners neglected Faulkner—out of ignorance, out of disgust at his grotesque treatment of Southerners, or because they understood all too well that by pushing open the literary door and raising questions, he had invaded the sanctuary of Southern life.

Richard Wright, like William Faulkner, did not flinch from dealing with the unsavory reality of Southern life. Born near Natchez, Mississippi, in 1908, Wright grew up in poverty and hunger. His autobiographies, *Black Boy* and *American Hunger*, depict the search for escape from the South. His life, as he recounts it, was a series of horror stories. "Hunger stole upon me so slowly that at first I was not aware of what hunger really meant." In school he learned about books, how to count, how to ask questions, and like other youth, black and white, he learned about segregation. When his father abandoned the family, he and his brother spent some time in an orphanage.

His mother moved the family to Elaine, Arkansas. There his imagination was fired by a teacher who boarded with the family; she read to him and answered his questions. His grandmother, a devoutly religious woman, forbade the teacher to go on reading to him, so he did not learn how the book *Bluebeard and His Seven Wives* ended, but it stirred something in him. It was, he remembered, "the first experience in my life that had elicited from me a total emotional response." He hungered for knowledge.

His life became more unbearable, a round of constant slappings, beatings, and hunger. His Uncle Hoskins owned a saloon and was, by the standards of rural Arkansas, a prosperous man. He often took Richard for rides on his wagon. A white man murdered his uncle out of envy of his thriving liquor business. "There was no funeral. There was no music. There was no period of mourning. There were no flowers." The family fled to West Helena, fearing retaliation from whites, who threatened to kill all his uncle's relatives. The family could not claim his uncle's assets, and when Richard asked why they had not fought back, he was slapped.

His mother suffered a stroke and became paralyzed, and the children were parceled out to relatives for a time. He soon joined his mother at his grandmother's house in Jackson. For a while he refused to join the Church, but finally relented and was baptized. He felt nothing, and, he discovered, neither did his friends. He saw the North, not Christianity, as the means of salvation. "I dreamed of going north and writing books, novels. The North symbolized to me all that I had not felt and seen; it had no relation whatever to what actually existed." He had to escape; he was fifteen.

Wright took a job at a sawmill, then at a clothing store and at a drugstore. He became a bellboy and saw naked white prostitutes. "It was presumed that we black boys took their nakedness for

granted, that it startled us no more than a blue vase or a red rug."
Then he became a ticket taker at the local movie house. He would
hold out tickets so that they could be resold, and four of the con-
spirators would pocket the money. Then he broke into a college
storehouse and stole fruit. With his earnings from petty theft, he
left Jackson and in 1925 arrived back in Memphis. He worked for
an optical company and saved his money, and he read profusely.
He finally fled the South. "I was not leaving the South to forget
the South, but so that someday I might understand it, might come
to know what its rigors had done to me, to its children." His
reputation rests on his autobiographies and the novels *Native Son*
(1940), the story of Bigger Thomas, and *The Outsider* (1953).

The South obsessed him. A quarter century after his father abandoned the family, Wright traced him to a remote plantation in
Mississippi. He found him "standing alone upon the red clay of a
Mississippi plantation, a sharecropper, clad in ragged overalls, holding a muddy hoe in his gnarled, veined hands—a quarter of a century
during which my mind and consciousness had become so greatly
and violently altered that when I tried to talk to him I realized that,
though ties of blood made us kin, though I could see a shadow of
my face in his face, though there was an echo of my voice in his
voice, we were forever strangers, speaking a different language,
living on a vastly distant plane of reality."

Like Faulkner and Wright, Erskine Caldwell spanned the years
of unsettling change in the twentieth-century South. Born in White
Oak, Georgia, in 1903, Caldwell came from a respectable middle-
class family; his father was a Presbyterian minister. His fourth book,
Tobacco Road (1932), portrays poor white Georgia cotton farmers.
He treated these poor farmers in a humorous manner, in the tradition of Southwest humor. Through it all runs sharecropper Jeeter
Lester's lamentation that he wants credit to finance one more crop.
"When the smell of that new earth turning over behind the plows
strikes me, I get all weak and shaky," Lester says. "It's in my
blood—burning broom-sedge and plowing in the ground this time
of year. I did it for near about fifty years, and my Pa and his Pa
before him was the same kind of men." In *God's Little Acre* (1933),
Caldwell again stressed the conflict between farming and factory

work. Caldwell's books, with what was then considered risqué sexual encounters and lowlife humor, appealed to a wide audience. He also understood the tension created by a dying sharecropping system and an emerging factory system. His books remained popular, and as a play, *Tobacco Road* set Broadway box-office records.

Faulkner, Wright, and Caldwell saw the Southern world changing, and they wrote with ambivalence about it. They knew that as the South moved slowly into the mainstream of American life, it would lose some of its distinctiveness. This concern attracted other writers, and none wrote a more thoughtful series of essays than twelve Southern writers headquartered at Vanderbilt University in Nashville. What makes *I'll Take My Stand* (1930) significant, though it does not deal with race and tends to mythologize the past, is the head-on confrontation with the notion of progress and the sanctity of industrialism.

Industrialism, the twelve writers agreed, had "little regard for individual wants." They saw it as collectivist and driven by science; by 1930 it had "enslaved our human energies to a degree now clearly felt to be burdensome." Working people had lost their sense of vocation. John Crowe Ransom charged that industrialism led to "the strange idea that the human destiny is not to secure an honorable peace with nature but to wage an unrelenting war on nature."

Andrew Nelson Lytle raised questions about the preachings of the land-grant colleges, the Extension Service, and the USDA. "One common answer is heard on every hand: Industrialize the farm; be progressive; drop old-fashioned ways and adopt scientific methods." This, farmers were told, would lead to wealth. "A farm," Lytle reasoned, "is not a place to grow wealthy; it is a place to grow corn." In a larger sense, the essays discussed a stage in world history, a time when a backward part of a technologically advanced country was threatened with absorption.

Author Lillian Smith later faulted the twelve authors for ignoring the dark side of Southern history. "The basic weakness of the Fugitives' stand, as I see it, lay in their failure to recognize the massive dehumanization which had resulted from slavery and its progeny, sharecropping and segregation, and the values that permitted these brutalities of spirit," she wrote. "They did not see that the dehumanization they feared the machine and science would bring was a *fait accompli* in their own agrarian region." The agrarians, like most Southern whites, only counted the problems that white people faced, and in their myopia blinked at larger realities. There were, as Faulkner so well knew, two doomed races, and the spirit of progress would threaten both. Despite its shortcomings, *I'll Take My Stand* remains a testament against acquiescence to industrialism and the blind acceptance of the notion of progress.

Thomas Wolfe, born in Asheville, North Carolina, in 1900, concentrated on small-town life. When ranking his contemporaries, Faulkner attributed first place to Wolfe, not because of what he produced but because of his ambition, his attempt. In his autobiographical novel, *Look Homeward, Angel* (1929), set in Altamont (actually Asheville), Wolfe explores the dynamics of the Gant family. He extends his explorations in *Of Time and the River* (1935). Although Wolfe spent most of his short adult life (he died in 1938) in New York, he looked homeward for the subject of his fiction. He wrote prolifically and left mounds of unedited manuscripts. Two posthumously published novels, *The Web and the Rock* (1939) and *You Can't Go Home Again* (1940), added to his reputation.

Carson McCullers, born in Columbus, Georgia, also explored small-town life, in *The Heart Is a Lonely Hunter* (1940). The dreams of young Mick Kelly and the haunted Mr. Singer captured the sense of desperation in the small-town South. McCullers was but one of a host of Southern women who emerged in the thirties as important novelists. Margaret Mitchell's *Gone with the Wind* (1936) is, of course, the best-known work on the South, selling more than a million copies the year it appeared. In 1939, David O. Selznick transformed the book into a film, and in some respects the movie version of *Gone with the Wind* was an updating of *Birth of a Nation*. The flirting and devious Scarlett O'Hara, robust Rhett Butler, serious and troubled Melanie, domineering Mammy, and brave but tragic Ashley Wilkes are stereotypes, as are black field hands. In 1935, W. E. B. Du Bois's *Black Reconstruction in America, 1860–1880* challenged earlier interpretations of the Reconstruction era, but its message was largely ignored. *Gone with the Wind* shows Southern whites losing a glorious war, suffering under blacks, carpetbaggers, and scalawags, and winning back their power through violence. Mitchell's novel and Selznick's film have continued to represent to the public the Civil War and Reconstruction eras, and although historians have reinterpreted these struggles, the myth lives on.

Mitchell won the Pulitzer Prize for Literature in 1937, and four years later Ellen Glasgow won it for *In This Our Life*. The list of Southern women writers lengthened—Carolyn Gordon, Rebecca Yancey Williams, Josephine Pinckney, Marjorie Kinnan Rawlings, and Frances Parkinson Keyes, to mention a few. "No other section," historians William Hesseltine and David Smiley wrote, "could boast so extensive a roster of important women writers."

A host of writers, artists, and photographers spread across the South during the 1930s, interviewing people, cataloguing historical documents, and stopping action in photographs. The depression years, ironically, gave opportunity to young artists. Eudora Welty found her first job with the Works Progress Administration as a junior publicity agent, and she crossed Mississippi, camera at the ready, writing and taking photographs, combining the skills of Agee and Evans. Her book *One Writer's Beginnings* tells how she grew up in Jackson, Mississippi, obsessed with reading and then with writing. Her account of Southern values in Jackson is precise and compelling. Richard Wright and Eudora Welty lived in Jackson at the same time—two powerful writers, so different in background and in temperament, with never a chance of communicating.

James Agee may not have realized it, but the three sharecropper families described in *Let Us Now Praise Famous Men* were the last generation of sharecroppers the South would produce. Beneath the poverty lay human feelings, dreams, aspirations—and desperation. In this book and in the work of other Southerners, there is a sense that the old ways are in jeopardy. The thirties continue to have a hold on the country's imagination because the documentary record so vividly portrays, at least in the case of the South, a traditional culture under attack. It was not just the forces of depression but also the revolutionary intrusion of the federal government that confused people. In these years one could hear the death rattle of the old culture. It would not long endure the invasion by the federal government, technology, and the effects of the approaching war.

7 / The Two-Front War

As the threat of war grew, Southerners had no difficulty in marshaling their own vehement brand of patriotism. In many ways, Southerners had always seen the world as sharply divided between good and evil, us and them, black and white. Southern politicians responded positively to impending war and Presidential entreaties to support an increasing United States role in international affairs. When some politicians insisted on neutrality or isolationism, Southerners, whose very isolation made easier the insistence on intervention, became impatient as war spread in Asia and in Europe. Many white Southerners, true to their heritage, were spoiling for a fight.

While Southern politicians backed Roosevelt on matters of war and peace, they increasingly disagreed with him on the thrust of the New Deal. On the assumption that the President would not seek a third term, they backed his Vice President, Texan John Nance Garner, for the Democratic nomination. Garner, like many other Southerners, disagreed with the President over his support of labor, his attempt to purge several conservative Southern politicians, and the amount of government intrusion he advocated. But Garner was quite old (at least by the standards of 1940) at seventy, and the Democrats had no other man with stature enough to challenge the President. Southerners rebelled against Vice Presidential choice Henry A. Wallace, however, and gave congressman William B. Bankhead 193 of the 248 Southern convention votes.

Factories and Farms

Of course, Roosevelt and Wallace won the election, and the emphasis on the New Deal quickly turned to almost total concentration on the approaching war. The South provided not only mild weather, which attracted training camps, but also a climate of support that favored military installations in the form of shipyards and defense plants. In 1941, the South attracted relatively little of the defense expenditures; only 24 of 302 defense plants were designated for the South. Slowly, the proportion increased. New shipyards sprang up and old ones were refurbished. The Newport News Shipbuilding and Dry Dock Company geared up for production of aircraft carriers and battleships, as did navy yards in Norfolk and Charleston. The list of private yards grew as almost any port with enough water to float a rowboat began producing warships—Houston, Tampa, Mobile, Pascagoula, Beaumont, Wilmington, Brunswick, and others.

The war led to unprecedented urbanization throughout the South. Workers invaded the new defense centers, making demands on housing, food, sanitation, public transportation, and segregation. Wartime wages brought wide-eyed amazement to workers who had for years shared a crop or wandered from job to job. At last, these people had a purpose, a job, and while some worked, others joined the armed forces. Thus, people went from the crisis of unemployment and hopelessness to the crisis of war, and for many the war became their New Deal.

In addition to employment in ship construction, Southerners labored to manufacture aircraft, chemicals, ammunition, petroleum, synthetic rubber, aluminum, and other products. Southern war plants attracted about $4.5 billion during the war, a disproportionate part of it going to the Gulf Coast. Such immense expenditures and construction for war production, of course, raised the question of what would become of such plants once the war ended. One estimate is that the South gained forty percent in industrial capacity as a result of the war.

Southern cities were unprepared for the flood of people. Workers quickly filled available housing and then turned to house trailers, tents, hotels, conversions of all manner of structures into apartments, and the "hot bed" solution of people working and using the bed on shifts. City services collapsed under the strain—reservoirs dried up, sanitation services and trash collection failed, public transportation groaned under the weight of numbers, and schools ran double shifts. Some young people, freed from farm chores and discipline, formed gangs and became hoodlums. During the war, Mobile almost doubled its 1940 population of 114,000, and other places simply grew from towns to cities, with little attention to urban planning or zoning. Women, who a few years earlier had hoed cotton or strung tobacco, worked in defense plants, and even middle-class women joined the work force. Some women flocked to military installations, became camp followers, and, while lifting the morale of troops, also caused concern because of the spread of venereal diseases. It seemed as if Southerners thrust aside their Puritanism during the war, as men and women escaped from confining communities and crossroads settlements in the hinterland and virtually re-created Sodom and Gomorrah. Old traditions died out, for the war broke down traditional ways of life and threatened family structure. While many refugees from the land settled in Southern towns and cities, over 1.6 million others moved north and west between 1940 and 1945.

Southerners who remained girded for war by buying war bonds, conserving fuel and food, and working for the war effort. The shortage of rubber kept many automobiles up on blocks, and gasoline rationing limited pleasure rides. People tightened their belts and used less sugar and luxuries. Desperate days of depression yielded to the flush times of war; jobs were plentiful. Because of the patriotic spirit, Southerners deemed unions more radical and alien than ever. The infusion of money into the South, the frenzy of wartime, and urbanization revolutionized its way of life.

The changes in Southern agriculture during the war continued the revolutionary structural shift encouraged by the New Deal. Regions differed remarkably in how they reacted to war, mechanization, and government programs. The cotton culture, for example, continued to move westward, and for the first time since the invention of the cotton gin, Southern farmers voluntarily turned to growing other commodities and in some cases actually underplanted their cotton allotments. Farm owners, desperate for workers, insisted on using prisoners of war and laborers from Jamaica and the Bahamas. Farmers feared that their labor supply would vanish and were alarmed at wage increases. The county agricultural agent from Chickasaw County, Mississippi, complained to his congressman in February 1943 that government policies confused local farmers. Establishing goals for farmers and then penalizing them if they did not achieve ninety percent of the goal seemed unreasonable. "If we could receive a few more tractors, combines and etc. we could meet and exceed every war goal set up for Chickasaw County," wrote H. J. Vickery. Local farmers did not care for subsidies or incentive payments. "They only want a fair price for their products." Many farmers, of course, feared that their workers would be drafted.

Rice growers in the prairies of the Gulf Coast and Arkansas solved the labor problem by turning to combines. While this saved labor, it created the necessity of building driers for the moisture-laden rice. Thus, the work culture and the processing of rice changed radically. Residents who left the area when binders still cut the rice, workers shocked it by hand, and several weeks later a crew hauled it to a thresher, returned after the war to find combines handling the entire process in one step. The seasonal jobs that the old culture offered had disappeared, and because of more expensive machinery, the cost of engaging in the culture of rice escalated. Rice farmers, alarmed at federal distribution of their crop to foreign nations, feared that when the war ended, the usual unreliable domestic demand for rice would evaporate.

In the flue-cured-tobacco-growing area, small farmers prospered. The tobacco culture avoided mechanization and farms remained small; some tenant farmers even bought farms. The price of tobacco rose dramatically, and though tobacco was neither food nor fiber, it seemed necessary for the war effort. Indeed, cigarettes became a form of currency, and movie stars who were seen smoking, as well as the President with his stylish cigarette holder, made smoking appeal to millions. The federal tobacco program continued to work well, for after the 1939 vote against the AAA plan, growers cooperated with federal programs. In at least one case, a German prisoner of war replaced a farmer who was drafted into the army. Some prisoners of war became virtually a part of tobacco-growing families until they returned to Europe after the war. Despite the labor shortage, some tobacco farmers continued to make the annual pilgrimage to Canada to help cure the Canadian crop there.

As late as April 1946, Louisiana U.S. Senator Allen J. Ellender insisted that prisoners of war be kept in Louisiana to provide farm labor, and some 1,500 remained there that spring. Southern farm owners, looking at wage increases for farm workers, longed for free labor from POWs and cheap labor from foreigners. Most farmers who lived through the disastrous 1920 collapse of prices feared that they would face a similar crisis when the war ended.

While nearly all farmers, whether engaged in growing peanuts, sugar, rice, tobacco, or cotton, prospered, significant structural changes forever altered Southern agriculture. In many areas livestock replaced cotton, and machines replaced laborers. The mechanical cotton picker was in its infancy during the war, and after the war it rapidly became a major economic force. It was first used in the flatlands of California and Texas and then entered the Mississippi Delta. Upland areas and the Black Belt, besieged by the boll weevil and characterized by smaller units of production, were weaned away from cotton. Then the size of farm units increased and the mix of crops changed. Farming became more of a business, subsidized by government programs and represented by the Farm Bureau in the halls of Congress.

Southern politics continued to be conservative. The congressional elections in 1942 showed this trend, for Republicans picked up nine Senate and forty-six House seats. Southerners attacked New Deal programs and used their positions of leadership to undermine the WPA, NYA, CCC, and FSA. Yet, for most Southerners, Roosevelt remained a hero, so political leaders were, in this sense, out of touch with their constituencies. When the Democratic Convention met in 1944, Henry A. Wallace lost to Harry S. Truman as Vice Presidential nominee, in part because of Wallace's stand on civil rights and unions. Roosevelt in the winter of 1945 appointed Wallace Secretary of Commerce, again arousing a storm of protest from Southern politicians. In many ways, the New Deal was over before Roosevelt died in April 1945.

Perhaps the fate of the Farm Security Administration (FSA) illustrates the reactionary trend in politics as well as any other agency. The FSA remained outside the federal-state agricultural establishment and was a threat to the ideology of the Farm Bureau–USDA–land-grant college complex. FSA programs such as cooperative farms, aid to small landowners, and concern for tenants and sharecroppers were but stopgap attempts to preserve some semblance of the old order. The FSA never had the funding to mount anything like a massive assault on rural problems generated by depression and could not counter the restructuring dynamics of the Agricultural Adjustment Administration.

The attack on the FSA, which escalated during the war, provides a case study of how the established agricultural network isolated, impugned, and then destroyed a rival agency. The massive collection of photographs generated by Roy Stryker's historical branch of the FSA, in part to publicize the need for the agency, showed an aspect of rural America that offended those dedicated to progress and, in their estimation, to a more wholesome view of rural America. The images of migrants, sharecroppers, down-and-out drifters, sagging houses, and even proud and defiant farmers shocked Americans, who customarily ignored rural realities. The USDA and its satellites realized that the AAA, the war, and increasing mechanization offered an opportunity to further restructure Southern agriculture. The FSA's defense of sharecropper rights seemed a backward step to agricultural planners who longed for the day when farm machinery would replace human labor. It was the agricultural establishment that proved radical, for it sought to remold rural life. The FSA was the conservative agency, attempting to preserve and reform the old structure.

During the war, however, the Farm Bureau and its allies portrayed the FSA as radical. The Southern mood had changed from the days when Roosevelt's innovative programs were welcome. For larger and more prosperous farmers, the New Deal programs offered stability, and they believed that the destabilizing effects visited on the tenant class should be ignored. Ultimately, charges of communism were leveled at the FSA. Author John Dos Passos picked up on this theme when he asked an Alabama farmer how a program that favored the family farm could be communistic. "Well, around here communism's anything we don't like," the farmer replied. "Isn't it that way everywhere else?" If it wasn't then, it soon would be. The FSA lost its battle, and in 1946 its remnants were incorporated into the Farmers Home Administration.

The rising cost of farm labor and higher commodity prices turned many farm owners against the New Deal. Such farmers took government subsidies and damned the government for supporting tenants. "We are letting creep in with the labor policy of the government a lot of communism and state socialism," the head of the Mississippi Farm Bureau told a meeting. On the other hand, those who criticized the drift toward larger farms, the power of the Farm Bureau, and the USDA's favoring of larger farms were deemed radical. It was a clever ploy, one that continues to cloud rural issues.

Fascism at Home

In the midst of changes, bizarre rumors circulated throughout the rural South. Fearing black militance, whites in 1942 spread rumors about Eleanor Clubs (named for Eleanor Roosevelt), associations of black women which were planning to boycott white women's kitchens. Rumors persisted that blacks were buying and stockpiling ice picks for use on a day of revolt, that as soon as white men were off in the army, black men would fall upon the remaining men and then seize white women and mongrelize the white race, and that black women had formed a conspiracy to try on clothes in department stores. Obviously, there was no basis for these fantasies, but they showed that Southern whites felt the world was closing in on them and Eleanor Roosevelt's encouragement of civil rights was partly to blame.

Race relations were further strained by the war atmosphere. Since the late 1930s, lynching had changed from a spectacle in which an entire community joined as witnesses, to what became known as "streamlined" lynching, where a small group of white men would quietly do the killing. As more black Americans put on uniforms, white fears grew. Near many military bases across the South, the communities where soldiers went on liberty became ripe for trouble. At several forts small incidents reflected racial unrest, warning of trouble to come. Blacks, especially those in uniform, often refused to buckle under the Jim Crow system as readily as before the war, and whites were more alarmed that the structure of white supremacy was breaking down. Lynching increased during the early years of the war; three lynchings within a week in Mississippi outraged many citizens, including Governor Paul B. Johnson. Still, grand juries failed to return true bills. A federal effort by the Justice Department resulted in January 1943 in indictments against five whites, but in April a jury failed to find them guilty.

Just as World War II speeded up the reconfiguration of Southern rural life, it also undermined segregation. During World War I, many blacks closed ranks, as W. E. B. Du Bois recommended, hoping that the war to make the world safe for democracy would mean improved conditions for black Americans. Little changed, and the recalcitrance of white Southerners in 1940 still proved absolute. The Red Cross, for example, kept its blood banks segregated. The state of Mississippi kept its textbooks segregated, and it required that all references to voting, elections, and democracy be deleted from textbooks used by blacks. The hypocrisy in fighting for democracy and against fascism did not escape black Americans. The rhetoric that had persuaded blacks to close ranks in the First World War proved less successful in 1941. One revealing story told of a Southern sharecropper who commiserated with his boss: "By the way, Captain, I hear the Japs done declared war on you white folks."

German and Japanese propaganda had an unexpected effect. When enemy broadcasts and leaflets accused the United States of tolerating lynching, the Justice Department, at the request of the President, moved against lynching and other civil-rights abuses and publicized its actions. As an assistant attorney general wrote to a U.S. attorney in Texas after a peonage case had been dropped: "Enemy propagandists have used similar episodes in international broadcasts to the colored race, saying that the democracies are insincere and that the enemy is their friend." During the war, the Justice Department brought two successful peonage cases to the Supreme Court. The black press constantly stressed the similarity between Nazi Germany and the white South.

As the war effort began in earnest in 1941, A. Philip Randolph, the leading organizer of the Brotherhood of Sleeping Car Porters and a nationally recognized union organizer, proposed a march on Washington to protest the lack of defense jobs for blacks. His proposal epitomized a new spirit of protest. Upset at this militance, Roosevelt attempted to stall the march, but Randolph would not budge. At last, Roosevelt capitulated and signed an executive order a week before the proposed march; it outlawed discrimination in defense industries and established the Committee on Fair Employment Practices (FEPC). The FEPC conducted hearings and gave some publicity to discrimination in defense jobs, but it lacked the teeth to punish those who disregarded its directives. In many minds non-discrimination meant in effect integration, and few Southerners in the war years crossed the color line. When Roosevelt in 1943 established a second FEPC after the first one proved impotent, white Southerners deemed it communistic.

Even before the 1940 election, Roosevelt had made concessions to blacks. In September the White House announced that 36,000 of the first 400,000 draftees would be black and that the Air Force would organize black air units. Yet many blacks believed that such "fortunate" draftees would be placed in non-combat positions; certainly, they would be segregated. Ultimately, some 920,000 blacks saw duty in the war. Most of these troops received basic training in the South.

Black troops continued to alarm white Southerners. In August 1941, for example, the 94th Engineer Battalion, a black unit from Michigan, went on maneuvers in Arkansas. At every stop they confronted hostile whites, and at Gurdon, where they went on passes, the whites insisted that the blacks leave town. A few days later, while marching along the highway, the troops were confronted by more state police, who began pushing them off the highway. White MPs stood by as the harassment proceeded. That night about sixty of the men went AWOL; they wanted to get out of the South. Most of them turned themselves in once they had escaped from what they perceived as a threat to their lives. This incident gained national attention, and other such incidents flared across the South. The military moved to counter this trend with black MPs and special officers to deal with racial problems.

Well-paying jobs drew in refugees from the poor land, and they strained city public services. In desperation, Beaumont turned hogs on to the garbage dumps to dispose of rotting food. The strains produced by instant urbanization would have been difficult enough without the added burden of racism. In public transportation, for example, blacks customarily sat in the back of buses, behind a Jim Crow sign, and whites sat in front. Public transportation became more important during the war, as thousands of new workers crowded into buses and trolleys. Such a way of life was a new experience for rural folks, both black and white, and neither quite knew where the conventions of Jim Crow began and ended.

Mobile, Alabama, epitomized the problems generated by war industries and urban growth. "The mouldering old Gulf seaport with its ancient dusty elegance of tall shuttered windows under mansard roofs and iron lace overgrown with vines, and scaling colonnades shaded by great trees," John Dos Passos wrote in March 1943, "looks trampled and battered like a city that's been taken by storm." The storm, created by a near-doubling of the 1940 population in three years, put Mobile on the government's "most critical" list. A government report gave an official view of what happened when country people moved to town. It found that Mobile had taken in "primitive, illiterate backwoods people," who when faced with urban strains became "hostile, defiant, suspicious, and terrified." The "undisciplined hordes," as the report put it, felt the strain of poor housing, rickety transportation, a nine-to-five workday, foremen shouting instructions they were unfamiliar with, and a new relation with blacks. All across the South, racial violence flared up. Riots on and near military bases, shootings in cities, incidents on city buses, and lynchings were frequent. It was as if both blacks and whites knew that one result of war would be to change race relations. Whites tried to maintain the status quo; blacks tried to undermine it.

In Mobile, defense contracts brought in some $400 million from 1940 to 1944, most of it in shipbuilding, and most of that went to the Alabama Dry Dock and Shipbuilding Company (ADDSCO), which by 1943 employed some 30,000 people. Blacks comprised sixteen percent of the work force, but most of them performed menial tasks. Since 1938, the Alabama Dry Dock and Shipbuilding Company had been organized by the CIO, and although the union's announced policy was non-discriminatory, few blacks held skilled positions. In late 1942, after hearings on discrimination in hiring and job placement, the FEPC demanded that ADDSCO train and promote blacks; management responded by hiring more blacks but not promoting them. Talks between ADDSCO management and the War Manpower Commission (WMC) dragged on as one plan after another floundered.

On May 25, 1943, management assigned a dozen black welders to replace whites on one of the ways during the graveyard shift. The effect was electric as word spread across the yard, and at 9:30 in the morning, whites began attacking black workers. To escape from Pinto Island, the location of the shipyard, blacks had to run a gauntlet of whites as they were funneled onto a drawbridge, a tunnel, or a ferryboat landing. White foremen intervened to protect black workers, but many blacks were seriously injured in the melee. By noon, the violence had ended, miraculously with no deaths, but rumors spread that a number of black workers had been thrown into the Mobile River and drowned.

The next day work slacked off as black workers were not on the job, and some thousand asked to be transferred out of the yard. Other blacks were outraged, for they had bought war bonds and paid their taxes, and in return were the victims of violence. At first, some officials suggested that enemy agents had provoked the violence, but it soon became apparent that it was a spontaneous riot.

Two days later, when some blacks reported for work, several hundred whites walked off the job, and only the presence of law officers prevented more violence. Meanwhile, the yard had lost some 160,000 man-hours of work. Negotiations continued to solve the problem and return the men to work. Representatives from ADDSCO, the CIO, the NAACP, the FEPC, and other groups failed to find a way to please all factions. Ultimately, these representatives compromised and decided to offer four segregated ways to blacks. After much recrimination and finger-pointing, the plan went into operation.

During the unrest in Mobile, editor R. B. Chandler of the Mobile *Register* condemned the rioters and rumor-mongers and urged them to stop aiding Hitler. On May 29 he offered a thousand-dollar reward if anyone could prove that there were deaths as a result of the riot. "Rumors and lies, spread by idle tongues and empty heads," he wrote, "continue to whiz over the telephone wires, across the back fences and up and down the streets." No one collected his reward. The city eventually booked three whites on charges of complicity in inciting the riot, and a few people were fined. Despite the fact that four entire ways were never given over to blacks (they got two complete ways and two half-ways), these workers had the last laugh in the end. In May 1944 black workers completed the S.S. *Tule Canyon* in seventy-nine days, breaking the yard record. Some white workers quit their jobs in disgust. The feat of the black workers almost caused another riot.

The summer of 1943 flickered with racial incidents on military bases, in nearby towns, and in cities both north and south. There were some 250 racial outbreaks in the country in 1943 alone, and major riots ripped through Los Angeles, Beaumont, Detroit, and Harlem. Although blacks were usually the victims of this violence, military and civil authorities at first attributed the incidents to radical newspapers or agitators. The army attempted by 1943 to face some of its racial problems. A committee headed by Assistant Secretary of War John J. McCloy suggested that the army take a stand regarding equal opportunity. Chief of Staff George C. Marshall issued a statement in July 1943 that "under no circumstances can there be a command attitude which makes allowances for the improper conduct of either white or negro soldiers." Further, the army began treating the black press with respect, inviting correspondents to report on the accomplishments of soldiers. Black Americans, starved for news of black troops, eagerly read such reports. The army even made a film, called *The Negro Soldier*, and published *Command of Negro Troops*, which reviewed problems and offered constructive suggestions.

During the war, farsighted army leaders realized that a segregated army was not the most efficient. Even if not convinced that segregation was debasing and un-American, the armed forces faced the facts. If they could not end segregation, they at least tried to offer equal opportunities to all servicemen. In July 1944 the army formulated a policy that forbade segregation in post exchanges, in transportation owned by the military, and in theaters; it also set up enforcement machinery.

Southern politicians were quick to see the threat to the old order. A host of politicians condemned the army's policy. It is ironic that, in the midst of a war, Southern congressmen and governors condemned the army for attempting to implement equal rights for blacks in uniform. Instead of seeing equal rights as a fulfillment of democracy, Governor Chauncey Sparks of Alabama charged that it harmed race relations in the South and "grievously handicaps those of us in leadership positions who are trying to bring about a better relationship between the two races." Instead of seeing the order as a reward for blacks for fighting for their country, Congressman A. Leonard Allen of Louisiana charged that the order "is a blow at the Southland and it is a slap at every white man from Dixie wearing the uniform."

As the war ground on, the Pittsburgh *Courier's* double V slogan (victory at home against racism and abroad against the country's enemies) became more significant. An increasing number of Americans, Southerners included, came to realize the danger of racism. Hitler's openly racist pronouncements and increasing rumors about his Jewish policy sent chills through many people. Was the Nazi stance a mirror of the South? Did not the peonage, lynching, and everyday violence and hatred based on race parallel Hitler's racial policies? Blacks were marching off to fight such perverse ideas; how could anyone fail to see that black Americans had endured slavery and violence yet were proving once again that they were patriotic?

The government became more and more sensitive to enemy propaganda that held up America's racism as a symbol of hypocrisy. While the government did not magically convert Americans to accept integration or even equal rights in a segregated society, it did for the first time use its power to promote significant changes in the relations between the races. This was the very intrusion that Southerners feared most, for it brought back the ghosts of abolitionists, of carpetbaggers, of neo-abolitionists, and of other crusaders against racism.

During the war, Southern white liberals and black leaders attempted to assess changes initiated by the war. This uneasy alliance had continued since Booker T. Washington's day, and neither group ventured outside well-meaning ideas on incrementally improving race relations. White liberals realized that segregation, so long ignored, had become a crucial issue. Education, lynching, poverty, and disenfranchisement had been the agenda of the Commission on Interracial Cooperation for years, but in 1943 the organization disbanded. Its demise was a blow to racial liberals. Several meetings of blacks and whites during the war timidly attempted to define goals and aspirations. A meeting of blacks in Durham, North Carolina, in 1942 went on record opposing segregation, but a carefully worded statement reiterated that ending discrimination headed their immediate concerns. A year later a meeting of black and white leaders in Richmond basically agreed with the Durham statement. The Southern Regional Council, founded in October 1943, continued the mission of cooperation between white liberals and black leaders.

Because liberals carefully weighed the potential reaction of radical racists before any announcement, they postponed challenging segregation until, in some far-off time, white public opinion would be prepared for the idea. They overestimated the power of hardcore racists and underestimated the reservoir of goodwill toward blacks that many white Southerners held, for side by side with conventional talk about the importance of segregation existed uneasiness, an understanding that blacks as fellow human beings deserved an outlet for their aspirations and dignity that only first-class citizenship could offer. The war against fascism and especially Hitler's anti-Jewish fanaticism pricked America's conscience.

White and black leaders both were increasingly out of touch with changes in public opinion. No better indication of this comes to mind than the tremendous growth of the NAACP during the war years. As far back as World War I, the NAACP had attracted Southern members, who, sometimes at great personal risk, started local chapters. During World War II, the NAACP grew from 355 branches to over a thousand, and membership increased from just over 50,000 in 1940 to over 450,000 by 1946. White racists in the South no longer had as convenient whipping boys Southern white liberals and black leaders; they instead confronted a well-funded national organization that was spoiling for battle. This change would confound segregationists, who had always been able to head off assaults on their often violent ways by intimidation. At the same time, the South had changed radically during the war, for those millions of Southerners who moved to cities never returned to the farms. The war moved the South into the urban age, and at the same time moved it closer to the nation at large. The problem of race was no longer a Southern rural problem, or even a Southern urban problem; it was a national concern highlighted by revolutionary changes in the international colonial system.

8 / The Movement for Civil Rights

To UNDERSTAND THE SOUTH AFTER WORLD WAR II, IT IS HELPFUL to look beyond the boundaries of the United States to the Third World, to the liberation movements in Africa, South America, and Asia, for in many ways the South resembled a colony. Many Southerners, black and white, pointed to Northern financiers and businessmen as their economic oppressors, and in a general way this view had merit. Over them presided factory managers, foremen, and plantation owners, and over them loomed the merchants of capital, located mostly in the Northern states. Southern politicians preached platitudes, defended the status quo, and, hobbled by their careful attention to segregation and racism, evaded issues that challenged the South's colonial status. Like other colonial people, Southerners were restless, impatient with the oppression of the past, and uneasy about the direction of the future. National political leaders realized that the racial system of the South presented a diplomatic problem, for to attract countries emerging from colonialism, the U.S. could not afford the embarrassment of segregation and disenfranchisement.

The war left the South more prosperous than ever, but it also stirred issues that had lain dormant for years. Some Southerners, upset at urbanization and at challenges to the color line, looked to the past for tradition. Others, realizing that a return to labor-intensive agriculture and a continuation of segregation and disenfranchisement was futile, dreamed of a future that would move the South closer to the nation at large. The South was no longer the backwater of industrialism and poverty, nor was it magically transformed into a prosperous land. Rather, it was undergoing continuous change. The generation that suffered depression and then war wanted jobs and homes and an end to strife. To younger Southerners, who did not remember the depression or much of the war, such goals seemed tame and stultifying. The South was again standing at a crossroads.

Although Southerners had entered the consumer society, their wants differed remarkably from those of Northerners. In a discussion of the Point Four Program in 1949 (President Harry S. Truman's plan for support of the United Nations and post-war recovery in Europe), for example, one man observed that he knew of a Chicago businessman who dealt with a backward part of the world, "and that was some certain part of the Southern states." This man's Chicago firm, a mail-order house, found goods "that had completely gone out of style for the Northern market." In the South, on the other hand, "either there were no styles or a style five or ten years old that had just about reached them. And they were gathering what was junk in the Northern market and it was just as good for the Southern market as the new styles of stuff." His firm dumped out-of-style goods in the South as if it were a colony.

The South of the immediate post-war era, in retrospect, was another country. The heritage of Populism lingered; it was tinged with a colonial-like bitterness toward the power of capital that dictated the destinies of Southern people. Blacks, segregated and exploited, lived in a colony within a colony. Their emancipation from slavery after the Civil War was only partially completed, for they remained isolated from the centers of power. The post-World War II South moved slowly into the traditions of the country at large. In one sense the changes were a liberation movement; in another sense, they brought the South closer to the North and sacrificed unique elements of Southern culture to national conformity.

Pioneers

The post-war South was witness to ironic incidents, juxtapositions, contradictions, conversions, and confrontations. Jackie Robinson personified many of the themes that emerged during the era. Robinson's mother moved her family of five, recently deserted by her sharecropper husband, from Georgia to Pasadena, California, in 1920, a year after Jackie's birth. Even as war fervor grew in the early 1940s, Robinson set records at U.C.L.A., earning letters in four sports—football ("He is probably the greatest ball carrier on the gridiron today," one sportswriter wrote), basketball (he led the Pacific Coast Conference in scoring for two years), track (1940 champion in the broad jump), and baseball. He also managed to win the Pacific Coast golf championship, swam in championship meets at U.C.L.A., and played competitive tennis. "It is probable," historian Jules Tygiel wrote, "that no other athlete, including Jim Thorpe, has ever competed as effectively in as broad a range of sports."

In 1942, after dropping out of college in his senior year to help support his mother, Robinson was drafted into the army. His career was a series of confrontations along the color line. The army baseball team was segregated, and the coach refused to allow him to play; the football coach then tried to entice him, and still bristling from the baseball coach's slight, he refused to play even when a colonel insisted. Stationed at Fort Hood, Texas, Robinson in July 1944 refused a bus driver's command to sit in the back of the bus and created an incident that ended in a court-martial; he was acquitted.

In August of 1945, after a season with the Kansas City Monarchs (a black team), he was signed up by Brooklyn Dodgers owner Branch Rickey, at first to play in the International League with the Montreal Royals. The reaction was mixed; some sportswriters wrote that it was an overdue move, while others, especially Southerners, criticized the threat to segregation. Significantly, the first institutions to challenge the color line were the military and major-league base-ball, and Jackie Robinson had been part of both. Rickey warned Robinson that his road would be rough, that not only spectators but also rival players (and even teammates, it turned out) would give him a hard time.

In February 1946, Robinson married his fiancée of five years, Rachel Isum, and two weeks later they left California for spring training camp in Florida. Arriving in New Orleans by plane, they were bumped off their connecting flight and discovered that the restaurant was segregated; they refused to eat. The hotel accommodations for blacks "almost nauseated" Rachel Robinson. At Pensacola they were "bumped" for two white passengers, and the room they could rent for the night was in a crowded house. They decided to take a bus to Jacksonville, and for sixteen hours they endured the Jim Crow section, where the seats, unlike those in the white section, did not recline. At Jacksonville, they were relegated to a Jim Crow waiting room, and again they refused to eat. At last a sportswriter and a photographer drove up from Daytona Beach and took them back to training camp. They arrived three days late. Their trip through the South was typical of what blacks endured in the days of Jim Crow. The web of restrictions was meant to demean, to constantly remind blacks of their assigned lower place in society.

Jackie Robinson ventured south of the Potomac and challenged not only the segregated hotels and restaurants but also baseball. There, in the competitive environment that whites had created, Robinson and other blacks would confront the myth of white superiority. When Southern cities refused to allow the integrated Montreal team to play, Rickey scheduled the games at Daytona Beach, where the city fathers welcomed them. Robinson attracted national press attention, but Southern newspapers played down his role.

Robinson became a hero to black Americans. In those first days in Florida in the spring of 1946, blacks crowded into the Jim Crow bleachers to see him perform; white attendance increased also. Black sportswriter Sam Lacy summed up his feelings: "I felt a lump in my throat each time a ball was hit in his direction." An opposing pitcher tested Robinson by throwing at his head on the first pitch.

The next curve started for his head but broke over the plate; Robinson hit a single. The next time at bat, Robinson was decked by a dust-off pitch; the second pitch he hit for a triple. The Southern-born pitcher told the Montreal manager, Southerner Clay Hopper: "Your colored boy is going to do all right." He had passed the test. Such testing became part of Robinson's initiation into the major leagues. Whatever he may have been thinking in terms of retribution, Robinson usually responded by playing harder. Montreal won the International League championship that year by nineteen and a half games and defeated Louisville in the minor-league Little World Series. Jackie Robinson broke the color barrier, and the next season Rickey signed Roy Campanella and Don Newcombe.

In 1947, Jackie Robinson put on the uniform of a Brooklyn Dodger, and baseball was never the same again. As other blacks followed in his footsteps and team after team capitulated to pressure to sign black ballplayers, the game became a truly American sport. In the South spectators, lacking a major-league team of their own, anxiously watched on the new medium of television. They carefully checked for black faces, seeing in every black ballplayer a threat to the color line. If blacks could play in the majors, another myth was undermined, just as Joe Louis and Jack Johnson earlier had broken through the myth of white supremacy in the boxing ring and Jesse Owens's Gold Medals had embarrassed the Nazis in the Berlin Olympics.

The courts as well as athletic arenas challenged segregation. In 1938 the Supreme Court ruled in *Gaines* v. *Canada* that Missouri, lacking a black law school, should admit Lloyd Gaines to the white school. The Court later extended the ruling in a series of cases involving Oklahoma and Texas. Yet admission to law or graduate schools did not mean that segregation ended. G. W. McLaurin spent his days as a graduate student in education in Oklahoma in a separate classroom, door ajar, where he could hear lectures but not associate with white students. He ate his meals at a Jim Crow table and studied at a separate desk in the library. There was something ironic about an education department teaching how to teach while at the same time degrading a future teacher. In *McLaurin* v. *Board of Regents*, the Supreme Court forbade such treatment, ruling that it denied McLaurin intellectual contact with other students. The National Association for the Advancement of Colored People backed many of these cases.

The NAACP had grown from its inception in 1909 into a major civil-rights organization by World War II. It pressed for equal rights in many areas, its strategy in the courts being first to challenge segregation in border states and then push into the Deep South. By 1950 it had made significant inroads into law and graduate schools along the border. During the war, the white primary, the device by which many Southern states denied blacks the vote, fell before the Supreme Court in *Smith* v. *Allwright* (1944). At that time, only five percent of potential black voters in the South were registered; by 1960, the percentage had risen only to twenty-eight percent.

The Neo-Bourbons

By 1948 the South seemed besieged by change. Not only was the old sharecropping system disintegrating and blacks and whites moving from the countryside and from the South, but blacks were in graduate schools with whites and playing the national pastime in the major leagues. President Harry Truman in 1946 took a strong stand on equal rights, in the wake of lynchings, riots, and post-war reaction to black aspirations, and appointed a Committee on Civil Rights. After every war the South reacted with violence to crush the aspirations of blacks. After the Civil War, a wave of terror had swept the South that killed and intimidated black leaders and led to a conservative, or Bourbon, restoration of the white ruling class. After World War I, a wave of riots, lynchings, and racial violence characterized the Red Summer of 1919. After World War II, President Truman acted in a timely way to prevent violence and advocate civil rights.

In the South, the Democratic Party seemed to be united, but a thoughtful observer could see fissures that threatened to break it apart. There were moderates who stressed business and progress, conservatives who placed race above all else, and liberals who championed racial justice, unionization, and other social causes.

As the issue of race became increasingly important, first in the army, then in baseball, then in Supreme Court cases, and finally in politics, conservatives gained strength. Historian Numan V. Bartley has labeled these men "neobourbons," a throwback to post-Civil War politicians. "Their social, economic, and political outlook was in the tradition of nineteenth century bourbonism," Bartley observed, "and, as an earlier generation of bourbons sought to end the First Reconstruction, neobourbons strove to crush the Second Reconstruction." These men reached out for voters primarily on one issue—race—but they also questioned higher education, Northerners, communism, unions, integration, and the federal government. Their ideology tapped into Southern paranoia about intrusion and the myth of the Lost Cause. No one should doubt either God or General Lee, or any politician who invoked their names in defense of the Southern system of segregation.

Opposed to neo-Bourbons was the rising class of business conservatives, spawned in the growing towns and cities of the South. These voters wanted stability, honest government, and a favorable business climate. In a South that was changing from labor-intensive agriculture to machine-intensive agribusiness, businesses increasingly became crucial in putting unemployed rural people to work. There was little social conscience among such employers, but they did not want such ugly issues as racism to hurt business.

The Southern liberal tradition, such as it was, had never seriously threatened the two other political factions. Since at least the time of George Washington Cable's late-nineteenth-century writings on the sordid aspects of the South, liberals had lived an uneasy but peaceful coexistence with their neighbors. They attempted to aid black education, emerged as conciliators, wrote occasional pieces about racial harmony, and met from time to time with blacks to discuss progress. They were vulnerable to charges of being too friendly with blacks, charges that constantly limited their hopes of reform.

There was, in addition to liberalism, a pent-up realization of injustice and guilt that dated to the days of slavery. Many Southerners suspected that in the matter of race, as Thomas Jefferson had speculated, there would come a day of retribution. The generation that grew up during the Depression and the war saw more clearly the contradictions inherent in practicing racism. There were too many overtones of Hitler's genocide in the lynchings, white-cappings, segregation, and discrimination that shadowed the South. Even as some Southerners looked to their history for clues to attack segregation, national leaders, watching Third World countries emerge with non-white majorities, realized that the South was a great embarrassment and could lose them the Cold War. Forces were building for collision.

In October 1947, President Truman's committee released its report, *To Secure These Rights*. More important, the Democratic Party in 1948 adopted a civil-rights plank, and Hubert Humphrey strode down the convention aisle and called for an end to segregation and discrimination. A large bloc of Southern delegates bolted, formed the Dixiecrat Party, and nominated J. Strom Thurmond of South Carolina as their Presidential candidate. Dixiecrats had the perfect Southern issue—intrusion. The Civil War mentality had been resurrected, and many Southerners united to fight the federal government and its neo-abolitionist allies.

The issues revolved around states' rights, and under this umbrella, Dixiecrat politicians could oppose integration. After Truman's victory in 1948, the Dixiecrat movement lagged but did not die. In 1950 Dixiecrat politicians failed to unseat such stalwart Democrats as South Carolina's Olin Johnston, and the victories of Earl K. Long in Louisiana and Kerr Scott in North Carolina showed that traditional Democrats still controlled the party. Scott appointed the liberal Frank Porter Graham, president of the University of North Carolina, to a vacant U.S. Senate seat.

After 1950, however, the Dixiecrat movement revived. After the *Sweatt*, *Henderson*, and *McLaurin* Supreme Court cases struck at segregation, Southern politicians girded for total war. Already a series of Supreme Court cases that would challenge public-school segregation were building across the South. On the national level, Senator Joseph McCarthy launched his hysterical attack on communists, charging that the State Department was riddled with agents of Moscow. An ugly mood darkened the nation, from California, where Richard Nixon ran against Helen Gahagan Douglas, to Florida, where Claude Pepper took on George Smathers. In North Carolina the issue was liberals soft on communism and segregation vs. diehard neo-Bourbons. In every case, the liberal candidate lost.

In North Carolina, Frank Porter Graham personified the forces of enlightenment. As president of the University of North Carolina, he had defended free speech and championed labor's right to organize. He even supported the state's long tradition of allowing evolution to be taught in the schools. A man of sterling character, Graham discovered, in his Senate campaign against Willis Smith, the power of the media, which portrayed him as a threat to his state and to the South. This election still rankles some Tarheels, and many attribute the acrimony stirred up against Graham to Willis Smith. Handbills circulated across the state urging white people to wake up to the dangers of integration. "Do you want Negroes riding beside you, your wife and your daughters in buses, cabs and trains? Negroes going to white schools and white children going to Negro schools? Negroes to occupy the same hospital room with you and your wife and daughters?" Radio broadcasts reiterated this message, and a doctored photograph depicted Graham's wife dancing with a black man. There was a stream of abuse that in no way reflected Graham's record. Although he denied he had any part in this propaganda, it was not the last time that Jesse Helms, one of Smith's publicity agents, would be linked with such a campaign.

As the threat of integration increased, Southern politicians turned to improving black schools. Old buildings, inadequate supplies, and low teachers' pay had characterized black education since the Civil War. Popular wisdom held that blacks were not able to learn, that education would spoil a good field hand, and that education made blacks dangerous. The pending segregation cases frightened Southerners, for even the *Plessy* v. *Ferguson* decision mandated separate but equal education and implied that schools for both races should be the same. Duplicate schools were expensive, however. Further, the white schools were also inadequate, for in many cases Southern education for whites touched the bottom of the national rankings. By 1952 Governors Herman Talmadge of Georgia and James F. Byrnes of South Carolina led the forces of reaction, and they openly opposed the Democratic Party on the national level.

In 1952 the Democratic Party platform had a civil-rights plank, but it was toned down from that of four years before. Many Democrats in the South openly bolted the party and supported Dwight D. Eisenhower. This signaled the beginning of a regional shift that would culminate both in party-switching by Democrats and in the rebirth of a strong Republican Party in the South. The issue of race proved crucial. Republicans had always had strong support in the hills and among businessmen, but urbanization and a new middle class grew a fresh crop of Republicans. They were joined by whites from the predominantly black-populated areas of the South who feared the Democratic challenge to the status quo in race relations. As the national Democratic Party became more engaged in the civil-rights movement and black voters flocked to its banner, it became a haven for disaffected liberals, union members, blacks, and Southerners who saw the future in terms not of racial strife or strikes but of harmonious race relations, good working conditions, adequate pay, and equal opportunity.

In 1952, Dwight D. Eisenhower won four Southern states—Virginia, Tennessee, Texas, and Florida—and ran well in North Carolina and Arkansas. Whites in areas where a large number of blacks resided feared that the demands for integration would bring the storm they dreaded. In the closet of Southern horrors, the fear of social equality ranked as the most dreadful. Among a people who were ill-educated, poorer than Americans in other areas, prone to see the world in the Apocalyptic terms taught in their churches, and ambivalent about federal intrusion, segregation seemed a rock in a world that was steadily shifting. Although they anchored their beliefs in Jesus and segregation, their Bibles offered few words of justification for the system of discrimination. They took up offerings to send missionaries to Africa and the Orient, but they did not see their non-white neighbors and fellow workers as equals in Christ. Christ had instructed them to preach the Gospel to all people, to accept all people into the church as fellow Christians. Yet politicians preached that blacks were monsters, that they lusted after white women, that they first wanted social equality and then domination. Theories collided. If blacks were inferior, how could they take over? There was something deep inside the Southern psyche that ached to face the race problem, to admit guilt, and to turn at last and admit that there were deep injustices. Southerners were moved more by such contradictory religious feelings than by intellectual attacks on racism.

While some whites struggled with their consciences, others continued to believe that an attack on segregation was an attack not only on the South but on the state, on the family, and, as was so often voiced, on wives, daughters, and sisters. It was this group of Southerners that the approaching storm would move to action. It was not that they ignored the latest sociology, refuted Christianity, or resented Jackie Robinson; they simply did not think about the issue in those terms. Segregation was God-inspired. These were the fire-eaters, the descendants of the South Carolina hotheads and their allies who provoked the Civil War, and in the South of the early 1950s there were politicians willing to lead them. If one supported integration, one must be either mad, a communist, a "nigger" lover, or a liberal. There was no place for moderate opinion. Good people sat by and watched in increasing horror as the South was pilloried on the TV, condemned among nations, and ultimately saved by a black preacher.

Education

The South of the 1940s and early 1950s had strict segregation laws, and such laws were more effective in keeping the races separate in cities than in rural areas, in white-collar more than in working-class jobs. In some instances, several racial codes operated simultaneously. All citizens, black and white, kept the letter of the law, yet friendships grew across racial boundaries. Such affection was sometimes just another manifestation of paternalism; sometimes it was genuine. Frequently, segregation was something practiced in public while in private another relationship could exist. When a logging crew sat down to a lunch of sardines, soda crackers, and soft drinks, it mattered little if the seating on stumps was segregated.

What mattered far more was the lack of opportunity that segregated education dictated. The physical facilities for black education in the South were terrible, but the spiritual deprivation went even deeper. Both W. E. B. Du Bois (in the 1880s) and James Weldon Johnson (in the 1890s) taught in Southern rural schools, and their autobiographical accounts relate the heartbreak of watching gifted children lapse into poverty and despair.

The attempt to integrate schools in the 1950s and 1960s had a precedent, for after the Civil War some Southern areas flirted with integration. New Orleans schools were integrated for several years during Reconstruction, until whites rebelled against the experiment. Gradually, all attempts to have mixed classrooms failed, and schools not only became separated by race, but black schools received only a fraction of public financial support. By the turn of the century, black schools were far behind white schools, and white schools lagged behind those in other sections of the country. As Louis R. Harlan observed in *Separate and Unequal: Public School Campaigns and Racism in the Southern Seaboard States, 1901–1915*, black school terms were shorter, states expended less money per pupil, facilities were deplorable, classrooms were crowded, library books were scarce, and salaries were extremely low. Black schools were poorer in every respect.

The ideology behind inadequate schools proved complex, for whites, in many cases, did not care to have their children well educated. Farmers saw little advantage in having children finish high school, for most were expected to work in the fields for the rest of their lives. Some blacks shared this thinking, although being denied education whetted their appetites for learning. Farm owners, at least those who employed tenant help, insisted on marginal education. They did not care to have sharecroppers or tenants who could calculate their annual settlements and challenge the figures.

In the fight for equal schools, the Supreme Court's *Brown* v. *Board of Education of Topeka* decision in 1954 was the culmination of an appeal process that had started years earlier in Kansas, Virginia, Delaware, and South Carolina. In Clarendon County, South Carolina, where one of the cases originated, the school system for blacks was atrocious. There were sixty-one inadequate one- or two-teacher schools that served 6,531 black pupils and had a budget of $194,575. A dozen schools served 2,375 white pupils and ran on a budget of $673,850. The white superintendent of schools, L. B. McCord, was a Presbyterian pastor in Manning; he was also an ardent segregationist. The county provided thirty school buses for whites and none for blacks. In 1947, J. A. DeLaine, a black minister and schoolteacher, asked for a bus for the black children; McCord refused the request, pointing out that blacks did not pay enough taxes to warrant the bus. Blacks dug into their pockets and bought an old bus that continually broke down and used a lot of gas; the county would not pay for the gas either. With support from the NAACP, DeLaine persuaded a black farmer, Levi Pearson, who owned a 160-acre farm with his brother, to bring suit against the county on behalf of his three children. In 1948 the suit failed on a technicality.

In 1949 the NAACP tried to get twenty plaintiffs to bring another case, but since most blacks were sharecroppers and could be evicted from their farms, it proved difficult. The principal of one school had already been fired because whites suspected he had been involved in the Pearson case. When a corrupt principal replaced the one fired, the black community rallied and called on DeLaine to lead them. They asked for a hearing, and DeLaine was fired from his teaching job. DeLaine collected affidavits and went to Columbia to continue the suit.

A white superintendent made some concessions and offered DeLaine a teaching job—if he would stop the protesting. He even offered DeLaine's wife, Mattie, the acting principalship of a school. Meanwhile, the committee obtained the necessary twenty plaintiffs. The first name on the list was that of Harry Briggs, a black filling-station worker (the case became *Briggs et al.* v. *Elliott et al.*). At Christmas, after several threats, Briggs's boss gave him a carton of cigarettes and fired him. His wife was fired from her chambermaid job at a motel. Four years later, after trying to farm and having all credit denied them, the Briggses left the county. The people on the list were singled out and many were fired or, if they farmed, were denied credit.

In January 1950, DeLaine wrote a three-page open letter and circulated it around town. "Shall we suffer endless persecution just because we want our children reared in a wholesome atmosphere?"

he asked. "What some of us have suffered is nothing short of Nazi persecution." DeLaine paid a heavy price for the letter—threats from the Klan, intimidation, and a suit against him for $20,000 by the ousted black principal. A white jury awarded the principal $2,700 in damages; DeLaine refused to pay it. His supervisor assigned him to a church thirty-five miles away, one that his father had founded, but he returned home often to lead the fight for better schools.

Shortly before one o'clock on May 17, 1954, Chief Justice Earl Warren began reading the Supreme Court's unanimous decision in the *Brown* case, which included the Briggs appeal. After reviewing the history of segregation, the Chief Justice declared that "education is perhaps the most important function of state and local governments." It was the springboard to success, and "it is doubtful that any child may reasonably be expected to succeed in life if he is denied the opportunity of an education." Warren then concluded that segregation deprived minority students of equal educational opportunities. Earlier cases had only dealt with the lack of equal segregated facilities. He rejected the findings in *Plessy* v. *Ferguson* (1896) that separate facilities did not stamp a badge of inferiority upon blacks. Warren then announced that the Court had unanimously concluded that "in the field of public education the doctrine of 'separate but equal' has no place. Separate educational facilities are inherently unequal."

Warren well understood the significance of this decision and of its impact on the South. He made it clear that the decision did not affect just the four cases included under *Brown*; it was a class action case. He announced that the Court had scheduled further hearings in the autumn and invited all concerned states to participate. No amount of conciliation could hide the fact that this decision reversed a long history of legally approved segregation and, before that, of rulings that blacks were not entitled to the benefits of United States citizenship. In the South the storm broke as whites armed for legal and political battle. Blacks, knowing the history of the first Reconstruction, faced the second Reconstruction with apprehension.

The impact of the *Brown* decision was uneven. Among whites, the ruling was of concern to adults, the generation that had lived with segregation, that had not known the Populist movement or the possibilities of racial harmony before the turn of the century. White youngsters, protected from such adult concerns, seldom talked about the implication of *Brown*, for, like sex, the topic was forbidden. Blacks, young and old, responded to the hopes for equal rights implicit in the Court's decision. A few days after the decision, near Walls, Mississippi, Leslie B. McLemore, his brother Eugene, and their friends chopped cotton and naïvely discussed which white high school they would attend when they entered high school the next fall. At that time De Soto County, Mississippi, had no public high school for blacks. Black public elementary schools were housed in churches, and one teacher taught all grades.

In some areas of the South, whites shrugged and admitted that the decision was just, that segregation had robbed blacks long enough—but these people were leaderless. The forces of reaction, of doom, prepared to resist integration. Southern political leaders reacted bitterly. James O. Eastland charged that the Justices had been "indoctrinated and brainwashed by Left-wing pressure groups." Other politicians, including James F. Byrnes, Harry F. Byrd, and Richard B. Russell, dressed their objections in states'-rights doctrines. Border states of the South attempted to comply with the decision, but states in the Deep South opposed it and vowed to prevent integration, in the words of Governor Marvin Griffin of Georgia, "come hell or high water." Some proposed to do away with public education altogether and set up a private-school system, while others drew up complex school plans that would evade the ruling.

Strom Thurmond took the opportunity to run for the Senate as a write-in candidate and won. In other states moderate candidates such as Kerr Scott of North Carolina and Estes Kefauver of Tennessee won their contests. None of the Deep South states accepted Warren's invitation to submit briefs and argue the implementation of the decision. In Mississippi, Governor Hugh White invited a select group of black leaders to a conference, expecting them to oppose integration. Blacks nearly unanimously supported the Supreme Court and integration.

Novelist William Faulkner urged white Southerners to take the lead in civil rights and not wait for federal intrusion. As Mississippi scrambled in 1955 to build up a black school system that complied with the sixty-year-old *Plessy* decision, Faulkner pointed out the folly. The existing school system, he stressed, was not even adequate for whites. A year later, deeply concerned at the disturbance at the University of Alabama over the admission of Autherine Lucy, a black student, Faulkner wrote: "It is a sad commentary on human nature that it is much easier, simpler, much more fun and excitement, to be *against* something you can see, like a black skin, than to be *for* something you can only believe in as a principle, like justice and fairness and (in the long view) the continuation of individual freedom and liberty."

Reaction and Action

Battle lines quickly formed in the South. Most whites were incredulous that blacks did not bow to their wishes to maintain segregation. They had for years deluded themselves into thinking that blacks actually preferred segregation, disenfranchisement, and discrimination. Despite a resurgence of violence and retribution, again and again they would insist that blacks and whites lived in utopian harmony. In 1955 there were four lynchings in Mississippi; there were no convictions. Blacks petitioned school boards to implement the *Brown* decision, and some of the petitioners lost their jobs. Whites, seeing a conspiracy involving the Supreme Court and its allies such as the NAACP, formed resistance groups. Historian Numan V. Bartley estimated that within a year of the *Brown* decision some fifty such white organizations emerged. The most significant and powerful, the White Citizens Councils, which absorbed many of the lesser groups, had branches in every Southern state.

The White Citizens Council movement started in Indianola, Mississippi, in July 1954, as a Delta plantation manager, Robert B. Patterson, and some friends discussed measures to counter the Supreme Court decision. A circuit judge, Tom P. Brady, made speeches and wrote a pamphlet, *Black Monday*, setting forth his critique of the decision and his ideas on how to organize to circumvent it. The movement quickly grew in Mississippi and spread across the South.

Each state reacted differently. Mississipi, Alabama, Louisiana, South Carolina, and Virginia were the states most involved with the campaign. Although it was difficult to determine membership, historian Bartley concluded that it "was a bourgeois phenomenon" that appealed to the "middle class of the towns and villages." Council speakers found attentive audiences at Lions, Kiwanis, Exchange, and Rotary clubs. Bartley also located support in rural areas, "and state Farm Bureau Federations, presumably reflecting planter sentiment, were very friendly toward the organized resistance." Some whites preferred the Ku Klux Klan as a means of protest; and in some areas, such as northern Alabama, Citizen Councils and the Ku Klux Klan were almost indistinguishable. There the anti-black sentiment spilled over into anti-Semitism, nativism, and anti-Catholicism. In general, neo-Bourbons sprang from the middle class, while the Klan often came from the working class. The Citizens Councils' rhetoric about states' rights and legal niceties was lost on people who preferred direct confrontation with the forces of change.

On the political stage, Harry Flood Byrd came up with the term "massive resistance," which was grounded in the Southern tradition of interposition and states' rights. With the ruling in 1954 and the instructions to proceed in 1955, however, Southern states faced their ultimate challenge. President Eisenhower carefully avoided making a strong stand one way or the other on school integration. It was amid this confusion that Southern politicians began to create Citizens Councils, and sought to interpose the power of the states between the federal government and the white people of the South. The blacks' only ally in the South proved to be the federal government. Thus, the white population looked to their homegrown political leaders for support, while blacks looked to their community leaders and to the federal government.

In Congress, Southerners composed a manifesto of constitutional principles to attack the Supreme Court's decision. Strom Thurmond and Harry Byrd led the movement, and in the end nineteen senators and eighty-two representatives signed it. James O. Eastland attacked the Supreme Court directly, for he saw in integration a communist conspiracy. Taking a clue from Joseph McCarthy, Eastland asked for an investigation of the Court, linking equal rights in education to subversion. Under the banner of free enterprise, he called for a nationwide movement to fight the Court, the CIO, and the NAACP.

Montgomery

Even as white Southerners armed for massive resistance and an ugly mood of racism spread across the South, organized black opposition to the system of segregation began almost accidentally in Montgomery, Alabama. On December 1, 1955, Rosa Parks, a seamstress who said she was too tired to stand in the segregated aisle of a bus and refused to give up her seat to a white man, was arrested. By 1955 the Montgomery black community was poised for action. E. D. Nixon, a Pullman porter; Ralph Abernathy, a twenty-nine-year-old black preacher; Martin Luther King, Jr., pastor of the Dexter Avenue Baptist Church; and others, formed the Montgomery Improvement Association. Rosa Parks was arrested on a Thursday, the improvement association was set up over the weekend, and on Monday morning fewer than a dozen blacks rode the Montgomery buses. At a Monday meeting King was nominated to head the association; that night he addressed nearly four thousand blacks.

Even in his initial address devoted to civil rights, King expressed the impatience that blacks had long internalized. "But there comes a time when people get tired," he said. "We are here this evening to say to those who have mistreated us so long that we are tired— tired of being segregated and humiliated, tired of being kicked about by the brutal feet of oppression." Blacks, he suggested, had sometimes given the impression that they liked the system of segregation and humiliation. "But we come here tonight to be saved from the patience that makes us patient with anything less than freedom and justice." For thirteen years after this, his voice would rise against segregation, discrimination, and finally the Vietnam War, which he believed robbed the movement of its vitality.

In retrospect the demands of the Montgomery Improvement Association were exceedingly modest. It called for courteous treatment by bus drivers, first-come-first-seated arrangements, with blacks filling the rear of the bus and whites the front, instead of whites having the right to ask blacks to stand; and employment of black drivers on predominantly black routes. Until these demands were met, blacks would refuse to ride the Montgomery buses. For over a year, the boycott continued; car pools took black workers to their jobs. The boycott solidified the black community and cut across class lines. The city fathers tried through the press and legal maneuvers to crush the boycott, and militant whites dynamited King's home. King began working out a strategy of non-violent direct action that relied on negotiations, protest, boycotts, non-cooperation, and publicity to confront the segregated system.

As King realized, it was not just the segregation of blacks on city buses that was at issue. Montgomery's fifty thousand blacks earned an average annual wage of $970, some $750 less than whites. Fewer than a third of black homes had flush toilets, compared to nearly ninety-five percent of the white homes, and schools and recreational facilities in the black community were inferior to those of whites. Only two thousand black citizens were registered to vote in the city.

Even as the Montgomery Improvement Association fought the city fathers in Montgomery, the Supreme Court struck down local and state segregation laws on public transportation. On December 21, 1956, King, E. D. Nixon, and a few others took seats on a Montgomery bus and celebrated their success. Yet King tempered black enthusiasm with a stern warning to his followers. "It is becoming clear," he prophesied, "that the Negro is in for a season of suffering." So were white Southerners. They watched segregation break down and also had to deal with the guilt of what it had wrought over the years. It was difficult to face Martin Luther King, Jr., to read about Thurgood Marshall arguing a case before the Supreme Court, and, most of all, to watch on television as many white Southerners ranted irrationally against the end of segregation—and Southern civilization. In the 1950s, a decade that is known for passivity and complacency, the country changed, and a new sense of justice and concern for blacks emerged. Some white Southern leaders shied away from the forces of massive resistance, and many Southern white youth examined their past with a new insight.

For Southern youth the door that had been closed for so many generations opened. National television screens showed the inequality of the system, newspapers reported the crisis, and news magazines editorialized about injustices. While most community leaders hoped that the movement would not succeed, they attempted to answer the questions of young people, questions that were earlier forbidden. No longer was segregation sanctified, no longer could questions be brushed aside. Many white Southerners felt besieged not only by the NAACP and Martin Luther King, Jr., but also by television, by the press, by universities, and by moderate spokesmen throughout the country who urged that the law be obeyed.

Martin Luther King, Jr., became the leader and symbol of the civil-rights movement, and in 1957 he organized the Southern Christian Leadership Conference (SCLC) to coordinate direct action in the South. At first, King seemed a radical; however, events quickly moved King to the middle of the spectrum, and like the NAACP, within a few years King became a symbol of moderation. Perhaps the most telling challenge to King's radical image came in 1958 when the television special *The Hate That Hate Produced* presented Malcolm X and the ideology of the Black Muslims. In the Southern mind, Malcolm X personified every Bigger Thomas in their memory. Here was a man, a movement, that would not compromise. The Black Muslims advocated segregation, but they did so with a contempt for whites that equaled in vehemence anything the White Citizens Councils or the Ku Klux Klan felt.

After the *Brown* decision, Southern white leaders used their ingenuity to plan strategies that would evade the ruling. Southern states drew up intricate plans that would inhibit integration, plans that included closing schools, moving white pupils to private schools, and providing state tuition grants. Despite these desperate moves, border states began token integration. In 1956 black pupils attempted to enter schools in Tennessee, Texas, Kentucky, and Arkansas. In many instances such attempts were met by white violence.

In 1957, when Elizabeth Eckford attempted to enter Central High School in Little Rock, Arkansas, she faced terrible odds. Before she left home, the television reported that a mob was gathering. Once she got off the bus and approached the school, she thought that the National Guard troops would protect her. The other eight black children were escorted to school, but somehow Elizabeth had not heard of that plan. As she walked along the street, whites heckled her and shouted that she ought to be lynched. Her knees started shaking as she walked the block to the school entrance. The National Guardsmen would not allow her to pass, nor would they offer protection. "I tried to see a friendly face somewhere in the mob—someone who maybe would help," she remembered. "I looked into the face of an old woman and it seemed a kind face, but when I looked at her again, she spat on me." Elizabeth finally sat down on a bench at a bus stop, and a white man sat down beside her. "Don't let them see you cry," he said as he put his arm around her. None of the nine pupils gained admission. Governor Orval Faubus had called out the Guard to prevent school integration.

It took several weeks of negotiation before President Eisenhower federalized the National Guard and sent a thousand troops of the 101st Airborne Division to augment it. Inside the school, blacks were not accepted. Rather, whites shoved them, cursed them, kicked and hit them. At the end of the year, one of the black students graduated, and the next year Faubus closed the school. Faubus's excesses rallied the Little Rock white community. In 1959 the school opened, integrated.

In the same autumn that Elizabeth Eckford and her eight friends attempted to integrate the Little Rock school, a similar attempt took place in Birmingham. The Reverend Fred L. Shuttlesworth and his wife escorted two of their daughters and a friend to Phillips High School. When they arrived, Shuttlesworth calculated that there were more Klansmen present than police. As he got out of the car, one of the mob shouted, "This is the son of a bitch; if we kill him, it'll be all over." The mob brutally beat him, while the police stood by. His wife was stabbed in the hip, and they both fled to their automobile. They drove to the emergency room of the hospital. "I remember lying there, like a skinned pig, bruised, most of the skin rubbed off my face," Shuttlesworth recalled. A doctor was amazed that he did not have a skull fracture. "Doctor," he replied, "the Lord knew I lived in a hard town, so He gave me a hard head." Years later, he assigned much of the blame for the violence to the executive branch of the federal government. "You had President Eisenhower, who saw nothing, felt nothing, heard nothing, thought nothing and did nothing."

In Prince Edward County in Southside Virginia, the school board closed all schools in 1959. The public schools stayed closed for five years, and white children attended private schools funded by county tuition grants. Most black pupils went without an education. In 1964 the Supreme Court ordered the county to reopen its schools, but most whites continued to send their children to private schools. Indeed, many white parents all over the South sent their children to segregated private schools as integration began.

Across the region, white leaders experimented with evasions and courts struck them down. While such attempts used interposition and states' rights to justify resistance, the country was moving in the other direction. Martin Luther King, Jr., the Congress of Racial Equality (CORE), and other civil-rights advocates refused to obey state and local segregation laws. Almost a hundred years before, the Reconstruction era had witnessed such a confrontation. As long as the federal government kept its resolve, there had been a chance that blacks would emerge from the Civil War with opportunities to break out of the house of bondage, but as whites gained control of government and as violence marched across the land, Reconstruction faltered and ultimately failed. Quickly, both sides realized that *Brown* v. *Board of Education* was a second attempt at Reconstruction, and the same forces lined up for the struggle.

9 / Domesticated Violence

THE SOUTH IN THE EARLY PART OF THE CENTURY HAD FEW RECREA-
tional facilities, and many people harbored a Puritanical distrust of
frivolous pastimes. During the century, sports, entertainment, and
recreation became central to Southern life, a measure of sectional
pride and accomplishment. There had always been music and dancing, just as there had been contests to match skill with firearms and
brawn, and in the twentieth century such contests became formalized. Football, basketball, and baseball became staples at Southern
high schools, and some colleges made reputations on the skill of
their athletes more than on the intellectual caliber of their faculties.
There was the ritual of fall football games, where students and
alumni dressed up, cheered, drank, and judged life by the fate of
the local team. In the winter, they moved indoors into crowded
gymnasiums to watch high-school boys and girls play basketball or
to cheer university teams. In the spring, baseball was king.

Along with these respectable sporting contests existed the netherworld. Other Southerners attended stock-car races or went even
farther into the hinterland to attend cockfights. These preterite
sports caught up the untamed, the outlaws. At the same time, music

was evolving from waltzes and swing into a more provocative sound that eventually became rock 'n' roll. While one segment of the Southern population moved toward middle-class respectability, another element fought to preserve wilder traditions.

Stock Cars

It is ironic that Southerners, so often thought of as inept at operating machinery, created a race-car culture and, legendary for their rebellion against authority, organized one of the tightest racing clubs in the world, NASCAR (National Association for Stock Car Auto Racing). In the beginning, most of the serious racing occurred off track, either along the Thunder Roads as bootleggers diced with the law or in semi-friendly races among liquor haulers who in their off-hours wanted to test their cars against the best competition. Out of the mountains of North Carolina, Tennessee, and Georgia, cars sped down to Knoxville, Asheville, Atlanta, and other towns and cities, transporting the clear liquor that inhabitants thirsted for. These were no ordinary cars, no ordinary men.

At Daytona Beach, famous for speed records set on the hard sand, promoters in the mid-thirties built a course that went along the beach, cut across the dunes to a parallel road, and then crossed back to the beach. When liquor haulers heard about the Daytona races, they assembled at Red Voght's garage in Atlanta (he modified many of the hauling cars), raced to Daytona, and the survivors took part in the organized race there. The war put an end to racing, but it quickly revived. By 1947, Bill France, a native of Horse Pasture, Virginia, who operated a Pure Oil filling station at Daytona Beach and raced there, realized that both drivers and fans often got cheated. Promoters disappeared with the gate receipts, races were canceled, and disorder prevailed. France, along with Bill Tuthill and Louis Ossinsky, formed NASCAR, promoted a few races in 1948, and a year later suggested racing new cars right out of the showroom. The first such race at Charlotte, North Carolina, drew thirteen thousand people; a Lincoln driven by Jim Roper of Kansas won the race, beating Packards, Studebakers, Henry Js, Nashes, and Hudsons. This was the beginning of Grand National racing.

It was the sport of bootleggers, filling-station hangers-on, and wild young men and women who wanted to drive fast. Long before World War II, automobiles had been important in Southern life. For farmers they broke down isolation; for city people they made living in suburbs possible; and for young people they changed courting rituals. They also gave status. For many they were meant to be driven fast. Young men polished, altered, decorated, modified, customized, washed, waxed, unmuffled, lowered, jacked up, bored, stroked, and stood back to admire their handiwork. There were few "stock" cars seen among young Southern automobile connoisseurs. Despite its relative poverty, the South led all other regions of the country in automobile purchases after World War II. In rural areas, status was sometimes measured by the number of old cars up on blocks in the back yard.

Tom Wolfe, in an article in *Esquire* magazine on the race driver Junior Johnson, observed that racing "was immediately regarded as some kind of manifestation of the animal irresponsibility of the lower orders. It had a truly terrible reputation. It was—well, it looked *rowdy* or something." Automobile racing was not restricted to the mountains or to the South, of course, but in fact Southern race drivers were, according to many accounts, wilder, faster, and meaner than drivers from other areas.

Hauling bootleg liquor trained many of the drivers who dominated stock-car racing, but it was only one aspect of their culture. Making illegal liquor had been an American profession since the early days of settlement; the Whiskey Rebellion exploded when farmers in western Pennsylvania in the early days of the Republic objected to paying a federal tax on their moonshine. From that time on, there has been constant guerrilla war between moonshiners and federal revenue agents. The families who distilled liquor treated it as a business; it was also hard work. The still elements were large and had to be carried into the woods and assembled. The corn, sugar, and other ingredients were hauled in, and finally the corn liquor had to be toted out, loaded into cars, and transported to customers.

The runs down the mountains brought back cash to families to buy the staples that could not be raised on the farm. Some mountain bootleggers sold to the larger cities, which required a "run" down the hills, while others, when they needed more staples, quietly became community suppliers or ran off batches of corn liquor and sold it in mining towns or nearby villages. Moonshining, in other words, was not a one-crop culture but was part of a larger pattern of survival in a world that was modernizing. It furnished an outlaw's way of dealing with change, yet one that was respected by most people, and it kept alive the untamed aspect of mountain culture.

Tom Wolfe recorded Junior Johnson's account of the liquor business in his area of the mountains, Wilkes County, North Carolina. "I'd say nearly everybody in a fifty-mile radius of here was in the whiskey business at one time or another." Junior Johnson was an especially good driver, and a legend grew and spread from Ingle Hollow through Wilkes County and then throughout the country. The revenue agents never caught him on the road, but shortly after he began his racing career, they did catch him tending his father's still. He served time. "Getting caught and pulling time, that was just part of it." In other words, it was a good honest living; it was just against the law.

Of course it was more than business. Tim Flock, one of the most quoted of the old-time drivers (Junior Johnson is a retiring man who has little to say), grew up in what he considered a fairly crazy family. Two of his brothers and a sister raced cars, and another sister liked to jump out of airplanes. The Flock boys all hauled liquor, but his older brothers wanted Tim to go to school. After retiring from the track, Flock could be counted on to relate the adventures of his youth—about sitting in the back of his brother's car holding the cases of moonshine, about bootlegger's turns, about sheriffs who shot out radiators, about drivers who then put the engine in the back, about rolling out of Georgia mountains and driving to Atlanta with a car full of contraband. "It was a challenge at all times, and that was the reason that the people that done it, enjoyed it. It was dangerous. Some people I think likes to live dangerous."

When such men arrived at Grand National racing, they brought with them the elements of their culture. They fought on and off the track, played practical jokes, wrecked rental cars, attracted beautiful women, and created legends. When stock-car racing came into its own in the 1950s, the list of legends grew—Curtis Turner from the Virginia mountains; Joe Weatherly from Norfolk; Tim, Bob, Fonty, and Ethel Flock from Georgia; Junior Johnson from Wilkes County; Lee, Richard (and then Kyle) Petty from Level Cross, North Carolina; Fireball Roberts from Apopka, Florida; Freddy Lorenzen from Elmhurst, Illinois; Tiny Lund from Harlan, Iowa; David Pearson from Spartanburg, South Carolina; Cale Yarborough from Timmonsville, South Carolina; and a large supporting cast. Racing pulled in like a magnet drivers who were tough, hard, wild, and fearless, many of whom saw racing around tracks as more attractive than outrunning the law and risking prison terms. Their mechanics knew how to set up cars to go fast and incrementally "cheat" on the rules to get more speed. They emerged from the necessary seclusion of liquor running or from the byways of the South and the country at large and created another culture, a legend that needed no embellishment in the retelling.

When asked about Curtis Turner, for example, old-timers even now get a faraway look in their eyes, and they will swear that everything ever told about Turner actually happened, only double that. Six foot two, two hundred and twenty pounds, Hollywood-handsome, wild, and charming, Turner was a natural race driver and a fierce competitor. He was, nearly all of his contemporaries agree, the best dirt-track racer among them. Turner seldom fought; he disarmed those who felt wronged on track with his eternal rejoinder: "Another party's starting in about fifteen minutes." Before the Daytona races, Turner and Little Joe Weatherly would rent a house and party for a week. They served drinks from fire extinguishers and used flower vases for glasses, all the better to limit pit stops, they joked. Tim Flock partied with them and recalled that Turner had a string of "baby dolls." Women knocked on Turner's door at all hours, Flock remembered. They still chased racers, he admitted, but drivers were more serious and trained for races. "We used to use girls to train with. Now they usin' ropes and chinnin'."

Women took part in stock-car racing in the early days, but as it became more organized, they were excluded. Ethel Flock Smith learned to drive from her brother, Bob. She once raced at Daytona, qualifying eleventh and finishing fourth; her brothers all fell out of the race with mechanical problems. Louise Smith grew up in Greenville, South Carolina, and she was wild. "I was always outrunnin' the policemen, the state highwaymen, and everybody else." She made a reputation on the tracks and off. "Louise Smith held her own with the men, not only driving, but the other arts that they were accomplished in as well: drinking, cussing, and fighting," Jerry Bledsoe wrote. Women were later banned from major events, but "powder-puff" derbies became a gimmick, to attract crowds.

The role of women has been largely forgotten, but Jerry Bledsoe's interviews recovered that neglected history. He also recounted the unique saga of Wendell Scott, a black driver who started racing in 1949. Just as women were accepted in the racing fraternity, Scott was accepted also—at first as a gimmick. The Danville police pointed out Scott as the best black driver in the area, and they should have known: Scott hauled liquor. "I never made it. I just transpo'ted it," he explained. He first drove in local races and took abuse from fans and drivers. Some drivers, Bledsoe recounted, "were openly hostile, making derogatory remarks and calling him 'nigger' within his hearing. Some laughed at him. A few would deliberately try to run him into the wall on the track." Unlike white drivers, Scott chose not to fight after such incidents; it would probably have been suicidal. "I've never really got involved in too many fights," he admitted. "But I *have* been involved in some right stiff arguments." Some drivers encouraged him and made him welcome. Eventually, he began to win modified races, and in the early sixties he entered Grand National racing. He was the only black man ever to race in that league, but he lacked sponsorship and seldom had competitive equipment. For all this effort, Scott scored one victory, at Jacksonville, Florida, in 1964. No Detroit factory ever offered to support Scott, nor did any black or white businesses sponsor him. He raced because, like the white drivers, he loved it.

By 1973, Grand National racing had become too expensive and too technically sophisticated for Scott to continue alone and unsponsored. The amazing aspect of Scott's career is that he raced at all. His legend, less known than that of Turner or Weatherly, is magnificent all the same. Given the temper of the times and the constituency of Grand National racing, NASCAR to its credit never drew a color line against Scott. Indeed, in opening competition to women and to Wendell Scott, it was far ahead of the times. By the mid-fifties, however, many tracks excluded women from the garage and pit areas; but those exclusions are now gone.

Stock-car racing quickly became big business and dirt tracks gave way to superspeedways. Bill France created a tight organization which remains the envy of many racing clubs. Auto makers in Detroit realized that stock-car racing was great promotion for passenger cars. After all, if a Ford, Chevy, or Chrysler won, it meant that the car was dependable, fast, and glamorous. By the mid-fifties, several factories backed entries and introduced powerful engines and improved suspensions, and tire manufacturers furnished special racing tires. France presided over these innovations, always trying to keep the competition even—he gave and he took away, but he seldom allowed one brand to dominate NASCAR. When Curtis Turner tried to organize the drivers, France cracked down and threatened to pull his sponsorship off of any track where organized drivers showed up. Drivers wilted away, except for Turner and Tim Flock. France banned the duo but later relented and reinstated them. Even an effort by Richard Petty, the King of Grand National racing, who won two hundred races, failed to organize drivers. France was tough, but he was fair. He watched Detroit run hot and cold on racing, drivers organize and then disorganize, and through it all he maintained the respect of a group of drivers who would make most wild men look tame. Most of all, he encouraged safety. Grand National race cars are full racing machines that may resemble showroom cars on the outside but underneath they are pure racers.

Ultimately, the first generation of wild drivers was killed off or retired, and Grand National racing became more organized and characterized by rich sponsors who pasted decals on the cars, making them 200-miles-an-hour billboards. Cigarette companies, banned from television advertising, sponsored races—the Winston Cup series. Beer manufacturers found such billboards attractive, as did fast-food chains, soft-drink companies, convenience stores, airlines, auto-parts suppliers, filling stations, and the like. The truest indication of change was Junior Johnson's when he shrugged and said, "It's been tamed now."

Still, a day at the races, Southern-style, epitomized much of what has made the South distinctive. Since races are customarily held on Sunday afternoon, a church service precedes the race. Spectators reverently bow in prayer even as they pour another drink. They come to the track with coolers of beer, bottles of liquor, and no doubt other distractions. The wilder spectators fill the infield with campers, pickups, rental trucks, often build scaffolds for better viewing, and in many instances fly Confederate flags (the skull and crossbones of would-be outlaws and rebels). They have their favorites—cars and drivers. Drivers earn nicknames—"King" Richard Petty, the "Silver Fox" David Pearson, "Big Man" Buddy Baker. Fans like the noise and they like the "trouble" or "incidents," otherwise called spins and crashes, but they like to see their heroes walk away and wave to the crowd. Stock-car racing combines Southerners' love of automobiles, daring, violence, heroes, and hell-raising. It began as the sport of preterites, and although tamed and commercialized to a large extent, it continues to renew the outlaw spirit.

Rock 'n' Roll

The South survived the First World War with most of its institutions challenged but intact, but after World War II fallen idols littered the landscape. Family life, threatened by the Depression, unraveled further during the war; sharecropping, undermined by government intrusion and mechanization, withered away; cities, absorbing rural refugees and sprouting suburbs, boomed; race relations, static in most aspects, became a central issue; and popular music, keyed to big bands, hit parades, and great white stars, exploded into rock 'n' roll.

Author Nick Tosches in *Unsung Heroes of Rock 'n' Roll* (1984) traced rock 'n' roll to the 1920s. Whether it began in 1922 when Trixie Smith recorded "My Daddy Rocks Me (With One Steady Roll)," in 1931 when Duke Ellington sang "Rockin' in Rhythm," or in 1934 when the Boswell Sisters recorded "Rock and Roll" (Tosches pointed out that Gladys Presley was pregnant with Elvis at the time), the naughty words and the nervous sound had a large audience by the mid-1940s. *Billboard* magazine, trying to keep pace with the evolving music and good taste, changed its "Harlem Hit Parade" list to "race" records in 1948 and a year later settled on "rhythm and blues."

In 1947, as Jackie Robinson was leading the Brooklyn Dodgers to the World Series, Wynonie Harris recorded "Good Rockin' Tonight." In May 1948, Brownie McGhee cut "Robbie-Dobie Boogie," a tribute to Jackie Robinson and Larry Doby. That year, Doby (the first black player in the American League) and the Cleveland Indians went to the World Series. Wynonie Harris personified the neglected early rock 'n' roll singers. Born in 1915 in Omaha, Nebraska, he gave up his pre-medical studies after two years and started singing, moving from Omaha's night spots to Kansas City, Los Angeles, and New York. Harris learned that vulgar lyrics, pills, liquor, wiggling hips, and Cadillacs, among other things, attracted women. He boasted that his music dealt in sex, and his exploits rivaled those of Curtis Turner and Joe Weatherly and their doll babies in the stock-car racing culture. Harris, as had blues singers earlier, admitted that he dealt with the Devil's music. "I don't mix the Lord with the Devil. They are the two I'm most afraid of. As long as I'm with the Devil, I'm going to shake him down for everything, every dime I can get." During his career, he earned a lot of dimes, and he spent most of them on Cadillacs, women, and liquor, investments duly recorded in his most popular songs—"Drinkin' Wine, Spo-Dee-O-Dee," "Bloodshot Eyes," and "I Like My Baby's Pudding."

Rock 'n' roll was the music of release, similar but in its way opposite to revival church music. Church music gave hope for life after death; it nourished tradition ("Rock of Ages"). Rock 'n' roll gave spirit to the present; it was dance music, music that stirred the passions, that celebrated life. It released people from the memories of depression and war, dissolved the last vestiges of the Victorian past, and appealed to both blacks and whites.

The various forces that were building in the late 1940s were leading to an integration of music. Peter Guralnick, in his book *Lost Highway: Journeys and Arrivals of American Musicians* (1979), describes Memphis during that era. The river city had a white hillbilly tradition that had not been commercialized like Nashville's and a blues heritage that dated to the twenties. Two radio stations featured black entertainers, including Howlin' Wolf and B. B. King, and Beale Street still attracted blues singers. King, of course, exerted a profound influence on the development of the blues, as did Howlin' Wolf and Muddy Waters.

The two traditions, two cultures, that had coexisted for centuries began to merge. Significantly, the move was initiated not by blacks attempting to enter white bars and clubs but by white youngsters "picking up on black styles—of music, dance, speech, and dress," Guralnick writes. Until after the war, whites could not enter black clubs, but then black owners allowed whites to stand in a segregated corner as spectators. By the early 1950s, black managers stretched rope across dance floors to abide by segregation laws; soon the ropes came down and everyone was dancing together. A new cult emerged, and Elvis Presley, Jerry Lee Lewis, and Carl Perkins were among those who frequented black bars, doing their graduate work in music.

In 1950, Sam Phillips, a twenty-seven-year-old disc jockey, converted a radiator shop into a sound studio. He had grown up on a farm near Florence, Alabama. When his father died, Phillips left the farm, became a disc jockey, moved to Muscle Shoals, then to Decatur, on to Nashville, and finally to Memphis. All around him in Memphis, a new and largely unappreciated sound was emerging. So Sam Phillips set up his sound studio and brought in black performers such as Jackie Brenston, who recorded "Rocket 88." It was appropriate that one of the first great rock 'n' roll sounds had to do with a fast car. Many of the black men Phillips recorded were the pioneers of rock 'n' roll but are now largely forgotten.

In 1954 he turned his attention from black artists and concentrated on the restless white youth who were eager to sing rock 'n' roll. Elvis Presley gave Sun Records its first big hit. In July 1954, Elvis cut "That's All Right," a blues song written by Arthur "Big Boy" Crudup, and, on the flip side, "Blue Moon of Kentucky," one of Bill Monroe's songs. Memphis disc jockey Dewey Phillips (no relation to Sam) could not play the song enough to satisfy the eager people who called in. He sent for Elvis, and when Elvis admitted he didn't know anything about interviews, Dewey Phillips warned him: "Just don't say nothing dirty."

Presley was ambitious, too ambitious to remain with Sam Phillips and Sun, so after five singles, Phillips released him to RCA for $40,000 and $5,000 in back royalties. Elvis Presley personified, or at the least suggested, the shady side of Southern life. Marshall Frady's description of Elvis, written for *TV Guide* on Elvis's fiftieth birthday in January 1985, echoed the words of Tom Wolfe about Southern stock-car racing. The parallel is worth pondering. "Even before he was on television, he simply sounded, in that pasteurized time, *dirty*—outlaw, wild." With promotion by his protective manager Colonel Tom Parker, his signing with RCA, his army tour, Hollywood B movies, and Las Vegas stands, Presley disintegrated. John Lennon concluded, "Elvis died the day he went into the Army"; that verdict may have been generous. Frady hit the nail squarely when he described Elvis as "a kind of poor ole boy's Liberace, eventually producing himself on Vegas stages as a spangled mummy of his memory in capes and scarves and high-winged Dracula collars, inflated, epicene and hung in heavy shoals of jewelry appropriate to some Aztec corn deity."

But in many ways Elvis never forsook his roots. Graceland, his Memphis residence-museum, remains a shrine—completely tasteless, inordinately suggestive, banal. Millions of people file through to pay their respects; they know that Elvis never left them, either in his tastes or in his spirit. Elvis lives.

If Elvis was the King of Rock 'n' Roll, he was the white king. His music dissolved racial barriers both among performers and among listeners. In the mid-1950s, most rock 'n' roll concerts featured a dozen or more entertainers, representing a spectrum of top songs. Southern fans did not care what color the performers were, and though local ordinances often segregated concert halls, the audiences shouted and danced with equal enthusiasm. The new music generation listened to radios, bought the newly marketed 45 rpm records, danced the bop and shag, turned their collars up, and saw James Dean in *Rebel without a Cause*. Hundreds, thousands, of fledgling performers worked at singing careers, some making tours and signing recording contracts, while others waited in vain for discovery.

In 1953 a young and relatively unknown black singer finished his performance at the Club Matinee in Houston. "This is Little

Richard, King of the Blues," he screamed. "And the Queen, too!" Little Richard was more outrageous and more complex than many of his contemporaries. Born in Macon, Georgia, in 1932, Richard Penniman was different from his siblings and friends, not just because he walked with a limp (one leg was shorter than the other) or was mischievous or got frequent spankings; he was effeminate, and at an early age he got his introduction to sex—with boys and girls. When he was fourteen he started singing on stage, first locally and then with traveling road shows. In 1951, when he was eighteen, he made his first record, but it took him four more years to produce his first hit, "Tutti Frutti." He had been singing the song for years— "Awop-bop-a-Loo-Mop a-good Goddam-Tutti-Frutti, good booty"— but these lyrics had to be laundered for commercial release. When the first frantic notes exploded over the radio in 1955, listeners knew that a new force had arrived on the music scene.

It seemed to matter no more that he was black than that he was gay. His frantic music and unorthodox appearance and wardrobe set him apart from other groups. "His hair was processed a foot high over his head," his manager Bumps Blackwell remembered. "His shirt was so loud it looked as though he had drunk raspberry juice, cherryade, malt, and greens and then thrown up all over himself." In 1956, he recorded "Long Tall Sally" and "Rip It Up," and his concerts became wilder than ever. At the height of his popularity, he withdrew from entertainment and entered divinity school.

For five years Little Richard preached and sang gospel music. Like many performers, he felt ambivalent about religion and secular music. In 1962, he agreed to make a tour of England and perform gospel music, but he yielded to his fans' demands and started singing rock 'n' roll. During this tour, the Beatles performed the opening act at his concerts; the next year, it was the Rolling Stones. Later, Jimi Hendrix played guitar in Little Richard's band. Richard claimed correctly that he had a profound influence on the development of rock music. Throughout his second rock 'n' roll incarnation, Little Richard's songs seldom rose to the top of the charts, and he blamed racism in the recording industry. "The *Billboard* 'Hot 100,' " he charged, "is like a Ku Klux Klan meeting." The pressure of constant tours took its toll, and Little Richard turned to drugs. By 1975 he had a thousand-dollar-a-day cocaine habit and, for the first time in his career, was not giving audiences their money's worth. In the mid-1970s he again withdrew from the stage and became an evangelist. His career as a musician influenced millions, and unlike some performers, he turned from drugs in time to save himself. "Rock music may be just a bunch of noise to some people," he explained, "but to me it was the music of love. My music brought togetherness, happiness. My music broke barriers that had seemed unbreakable."

Meanwhile, with the capital earned from selling Elvis to RCA, Sam Phillips turned to other performers—Carl Perkins, Johnny Cash, Jerry Lee Lewis, Charlie Rich, and others. Phillips had a way of talking to these raw youth, giving them confidence, and then driving them to innovate. He was only a decade older than these restless young men, but he knew how to challenge them. When Jerry Lee Lewis, who personified the inner war between the music of God and the music of the Devil, hesitated to record "Great Balls of Fire," Phillips engaged him in a religious discussion and convinced him that rock 'n' roll was more revolutionary than the Bible. Lewis would fight the Devil many times, often looking to one of his cousins, Jimmy Swaggart, who was an evangelist, and wondering if that was the path he should have taken, or to another cousin, Mickey Gilley, to contemplate the money and ease that popular country music could provide. But Lewis usually sided with the Devil, and he picked up an outlaw nickname, "The Killer."

The most difficult task in approaching the 1950s is to make some sense out of the paradoxes that fill the decade. Robert Palmer, who has written several books on Southern music, saw in Jerry Lee Lewis the personification of the age. "I think I zeroed in on Jerry Lee in particular because I sensed that of all these first-generation rockers, he was the most resistant to the idea of limits. I was acutely aware of limits all around me—school, church, family, anti-communist righteousness, my own still-awkward body." To listen to and champion rock 'n' roll was, in effect, to slap polite and paranoid society in the face. In 1957 students at Wake Forest University disrupted compulsory chapel by setting off alarm clocks, walking out, and staging a dance-in to protest the Baptist State Convention's ban against dancing on campus. There was a new spirit upon the land.

What was relevant in Palmer's mind was the message of revolt that the eight million copies of Jerry Lee Lewis's "Whole Lotta Shakin' " contained. Palmer saw in the record "the most profoundly revolutionary statement an artist can make in the rock 'n' roll idiom. It bypasses language, obliterates social conditioning, fulfills a basic human need for rhythmic movement, arouses primal hungers, and suggests how one can go about gratifying them." Jerry Lee Lewis, of course, was not conscious of such a cosmic role, and neither was Sam Phillips.

After Phillips had made Carl Perkins a star with "Blue Suede Shoes," he flew from Memphis to Dallas to give Perkins a pair of blue suede shoes with blue sparkles on them to wear on stage. As Guralnick pointed out, none of these young men had many material goods until they turned to rock 'n' roll. "You got to remember that Elvis, Cash, none of us had anything," Perkins remembered. "We were very poor, came from poor people, and it was Sam—I know he did for me—bought me the first clothes I ever had to wear on stage." Phillips took Elvis, Cash, and Perkins at a formative stage, molded them, encouraged them, recorded them, and then they drifted on to larger labels and to fame. Phillips understood a lot more than money; he thought more of talent.

Sam Phillips eventually sold Sun in 1969; he has continued as a successful businessman. Yet he has never lost the spirit that made him gamble on black and white poor folks and their music. Something spiritual happened at Sun, something that Phillips could never forget. He watched big companies buy up his stars, watched some of them wilt, turn to commercial successes or spiritual failures, and believed that the large companies played it safe and drained out the performers' creativity. Something had been lost, he reiterated in his Guralnick interview. "All of us damn cats and people that appreciate not the fifties necessarily but that freedom are gonna forget about the feel. We gonna be in jail, and not even know it." Perhaps Sam Phillips, even as he recorded Elvis and Jerry Lee, could feel the chill around him.

Not only did rock 'n' roll emerge during the post-World War II years, but other musical forms also flourished. As music historian

Bill Malone observed, amid the proliferation of labels, "most of them specialized in grass roots music (country, rhythm and blues, gospel, Mexican, Bohemian, Cajun) and served local interests." The term "hillbilly" gave way to the more neutral designations of country, or country and Western. The Grand Ole Opry continued broadcasting to millions of Americans on WSM, the 50,000-watt clear-channel station in Nashville. People tuned in to hear Roy Acuff sing "The Wabash Cannon Ball," or "The Great Speckled Bird," and by the 1940s, Bill Monroe, Ernest Tubb, and Eddy Arnold. The rise of Hank Williams, an Alabama-born singer, brought modern superstar status to country music. Women had always shared in country music, and after the war Patsy Montana, Maybelle Carter, Kitty Wells, and a host of others rose to stardom. Later Patsy Cline, Loretta Lynn, and Dolly Parton followed.

By the late 1950s, country music began a comeback against rock 'n' roll. With the founding in 1958 of the Country Music Association, a trade organization that promoted country music on the radio and on records, and the emergence of Nashville as the center of country music, a new sound swept across the land. "The music that emerged from the recording studios of Nashville, called variously the 'Nashville Sound,' 'country-pop,' 'countrypolitan,' or 'middle-of-the-road music,'" Malone wrote, "de-emphasized or omitted the fiddle and steel guitar and introduced background voices and sedate instrumentation designed to reach new listeners while holding on to the older ones." Country singers were patriotic, and during the Vietnam War they reinforced the nation's commitment to the Asian conflict. Like the toning down of rock 'n' roll, the taming of country music made it more acceptable to a wider audience.

After the surge of rock 'n' roll had eased in the late 1950s, popular music changed. British musicians, including the Beatles, altered both the presentation and the content of music. Writing about the British influence at large, Malone charged that their "heavy electric instrumentation, their stage costuming, their sex-and-drugs-oriented repertories, and their brash performing styles suggested very little of the earlier rural-tinged music of the southern rockabillies." Instead, music became urbanized and nationalized and directed to a youth audience.

Janis Joplin, as much as any performer of the sixties, represented the culture of that decade. Born in Port Arthur, Texas, talented, insecure, nonconformist, and wild, she strove relentlessly to achieve stardom. She rebelled against the polite music and conventions of her day and patterned herself after black blues singer Bessie Smith. After a few years at the University of Texas, and singing in downtown Austin, she left, heading for the hippie kingdom by the sea, San Francisco. There she worked her way to popularity and in 1967, at the Monterey Pop Festival, became a nationally known performer. With her bottle of Southern Comfort onstage and drugs offstage, she led a life that revolved around unhappy love affairs and the desire to be accepted and secure. She claimed that all else except performing on stage was waiting. In 1970, while completing the album *Pearl*, she died of an overdose of heroin. One cut of that album, "Get It While You Can," typified her life.

Other Southerners spurn most kinds of popular music in favor of gospel. Both black and white gospel groups tour the country and play at school auditoriums, churches—wherever they can find a stage. In some instances such performances turn into revivals. The audience might hear a dozen talented groups perform, and after intermission it returns, in some cases, full of more than the Holy Spirit. The audience appears saved—but laid back. Gospel also plays on television and radio. In Tennessee, for example, the Reverend and Mrs. J. Bazzel Mull have become legendary.

After World War II, the South produced musicians out of all proportion to the rest of the country. In *Mississippi: Conflict and Change*, editors James W. Loewen and Charles Sallis include a map of the state showing the home towns of musicians. The list is staggering; it contains some ninety names of performers, among them Elvis Presley, Tammy Wynette, Conway Twitty, Robert Johnson, Charley Pride, John Lee Hooker, Ike Turner, Son House, Mose Allison, Bukka White, Big Bill Broonzy, Jimmy Reed, B. B. King, Muddy Waters, Elmore James, Otis Spann, Jimmie Rodgers, Leontyne Price, Bo Diddley, Bonnie and Delaney Bramlett, and William Grant Still. Other Southern states might not match Mississippi in producing musicians, but many grew bumper crops.

Country music strayed far from the mountain home. The old singers and their songs dealt with serious matters in circuitous ways, rarely confronting head-on the tough subjects of running around, broken families, and dependence on alcohol. Bluegrass has attempted to preserve the old Southern sound, but like all American music, it has been eclectic, and that was the key to its energy. In a way, country music, even the overdone Nashville sounds, reached back to values, conservative values. "Country music is a popular form of the American historical imagination," Robert Cantwell commented, "and bluegrass is a pure form of country music." Bill Monroe's pilgrimage from rural Kentucky to Whiting, Indiana, and back to his roots, typified the search for authenticity. It also showed the way Southerners moved about the country, carrying their culture with them. Along with Bill Monroe, North Carolinian Earl Scruggs helped popularize bluegrass music. First with the Blue Grass Boys and then with Lester Flatt, Scruggs, in the words of Bill Malone, "featured a style that revolutionized the sound of the banjo and did much to make bluegrass music nationally popular." Using a three-finger style, Scruggs can coolly coax an explosion of sounds from his instrument—in "Foggy Mountain Breakdown," for example. The Scruggs innovations and the steady career of Bill Monroe influenced a generation of musicians who sought to preserve the old music while generating something new. For many people, especially those self-exiled from rural areas of the South, the only way to return home was through music. The imagination supplied the magic carpet; there are worse ways to spend time.

Southern music has evolved from obscurity to be celebrated as a vital part of the country's cultural heritage. Many Southern musicians have graced the stage of the Smithsonian Institution's annual folk festival. People who would never have ventured into the densely packed bars of the Mississippi Delta hear on the Mall in Washington authentic blues, or in another year Cajun or Zydeco, or mountain music. On one level the different strains of music give a lesson on the Southern musical exchange. On another level the festival is patronizing, perhaps unavoidably so. The national musical heritage is pre-packaged for the middle class, and though many visitors to the festival are sensible and sensitive, there are invariably the wide-eyed, broad-smiling professional studiers of quaintness. To them, musicians are like circus sideshows. Such listeners marvel at the musicians' creativity but ignore the culture that produced them.

The South, what remains of it, seems more available in the backward-looking lyrics of country music and the imaginative world of fiction than in reality. Both music and fiction thrived even as the old society disintegrated. The number of festivals hearkening to the past increased in direct proportion to the abandoned farms and exiled people. The songs and novels provided for an alienated people, and for the writers and performers, a link with the past heritage, continually filtered and altered to suit the tastes of the present. There are always lost lovers and lost dreams, and for Southerners there is a lost way of life. The cultures that existed in the early years of the century endured to some extent, and in more recent days they have become celebrated in festival and in scholarship. "But in a sense," Bill Malone has written, "at the hour of their victory the southern-born musical forms also suffered defeat. Commercial acclaim, general popularity, and international recognition have been won at the price of the loss of distinctiveness and individuality."

Cockfighting

Stock-car racing and rebel music were but the most visible manifestations of the seething netherworld of Southern recreation and leisure. While rebellious youth copied James Dean hair styles and listened to rock 'n' roll music, other rebels hung out at country and Western bars and nightclubs, danced, fought, and went through the courtship ritual. There were also other pastimes.

Cockfighting is an ancient sport; the people who raise, train, and fight cocks are honorable people. They form one of the most intriguing underground networks in the country, for cockfighting is illegal in all but four states—Arizona, New Mexico, Oklahoma, and Louisiana. Several magazines, including *Grit and Steel* (founded in 1899), *Feathered Warrior*, and *The Gamecock*, inform enthusiasts about breeding and training and also carry advertisements for chickens, feed, and other items. Fights are held from September through June, when molting season begins. The sport is international, and the Southern variety, which has flourished since colonial days, has been fed by numerous streams of tradition, especially English and Spanish.

"There's as many different kinds of game chickens as they is different kinds of dogs," Joe Farmer told his *Foxfire* interviewers. As Vaughn Callenback observed, "You've got to breed chickens to fight, not for show birds. You've got to have a rooster that's got it all—speed, power, everything." Among the favorite breeds fought in the South are Roundheads, Arkansas Travelers, Clarets, Butchers, Kelsos, and Greys. Since cocks fight naturally, they are kept apart. Most breeders have a series of small chickenhouses and tether their roosters with a cord, one end attached to a leg and one end to the house.

Many people think that gamecocks are exploited, but breeders argue that they are the most coddled of animals. "There's nothing in the world treated better than them roosters," Duncan Long insisted. They are fed primarily proteins—cracked corn, oats, greens, sunflower seeds, vitamins, even dog food and table scraps. Breeders pet and pamper their birds. When time for a fight approaches, the breeder selects from among his stock the most alert birds weighing five pounds, plus or minus about half a pound. The birds are conditioned and put on special feed for several weeks.

Cockfights are highly formalized, and tradition rules the contests. Each bird is weighed, tagged, and then matched against a bird of the same weight, much as prizefighters. Just before the fight, handlers attach gaffs to the trimmed spurs on the cock's legs; they are narrow, curved, and very sharp. A pit usually measures about twenty feet in diameter, but they vary. Handlers enter the pit holding their birds. When the referee says, "Bill your birds," the handlers let the birds peck at each other, "so they will start getting mad." Then each handler retreats, bird in hand, behind lines some twelve feet apart. When the referee signals "Get ready," the handlers place the cocks at the lines; when he says "Pit," the handlers release the cocks and they run or fly toward each other and meet in the center of the pit. Novelist Harry Crews observed: "They powered toward each other in a great flapping of wings, both highfliers, each trying to get over the other. They met in the air nearly four feet off the ground and locked up in a fury that was awesome and beautiful and dreadful. A single sustained roar came from the throats of the men and women and children around the pit."

Once a fight starts, it goes on until one of the cocks is dead or refuses to fight. If neither bird kills the other, the last one pecking wins. A referee has complete control over the fight; there are no appeals. There are several types of fights—hack fights, mains, tournaments—but the most popular in the South recently has been the derby. Some dozen to three dozen owners enter from four to six roosters each and pay an entrance fee that makes up the pot. The owner whose birds win the most contests takes the entire pot. The derby, Harold A. Herzog, Jr., says in an essay in *Appalachian Journal*, "has been responsible for the 'democratization' of cockfighting, as it has allowed individuals with a fairly low number of roosters to compete at least several times a year."

There is as much activity among the spectators as in the pit. "The first fight I was ever at I watched guys shouting across the pit at one another, calling numbers, signaling to each other with upheld fingers, and it seemed to me that there was no way in the world they could keep track of the bets," Harry Crews marveled. These were just the side bets that spectators and owners make as the fight develops. Bets are settled at the end of each fight: the losers approach the winners and pay. Crews was amazed that anyone could keep up with the bets, and surmised that welching would be easy. But, someone informed him, "welching on a bet can buy you a lot of trouble real cheap. You could even git dead from it." Honor rules the betting, the same way it does all aspects of cockfighting. As Paul B. Stamey said, "most of the chicken people is a pretty good breed of people." They insist that game birds are born to fight, and that through the centuries cockfighting has been an honorable sport. Duncan Long defended the sport by describing it from the chicken's point of view. "If you put yourself in a chicken's place, which would you rather be? A hen put in a little pen and fed high-protein feed and forced to lay? She'll lay one year and then they take her and eat her," he complained. "Hadn't you rather have a chance for your life as a chicken as to go get your head cut off?"

Cockfighting flourishes in the absence of complaints, so fights are held away from populated areas. Law officers do not raid fights unless there have been complaints. "If your local sheriff tells you you can fight, it's all right. If he don't, you can't. It's up to the local sheriff," Clyde Gibson explained. "Now a few people aren't satisfied with nothing," Paul Stamey argued. "That kind of people has got to gripe. They say it's wrong for you to drive over fifty-five miles an hour; it's wrong for you to drink beer; it's wrong for you to fight a rooster; it's wrong for you to smoke a cigarette. You know, that kind of people has got to gripe." Crews has little patience with critics of the sport. "I've always been addicted to blood sports of all kinds," he wrote. "And I make no apology for it. We don't sleep with poodles or whisper baby talk to horses."

Perhaps nothing shows better the complicated legal position of cockfighting than a robbery staged early in the morning before a cockfight in, appropriately, Cocke County, Tennessee. In May 1979 some half-dozen bandits surprised early arrivals at a cockfight near Newport, and by 8:30 in the morning they had collected some quarter million dollars in loot and fled in a van. The suspects were arrested later in the day, and law officers recovered much of the stolen money and jewels. Fifty-seven of the victims visited the Cocke County Courthouse to claim their valuables. The press reported that people from "at least eight Southeastern states" were in attendance at the fight, that there were 330 cocks present, and the purse was $27,500. After the alleged robbers were behind bars, one of the cockers entered the courthouse with a wad of hundred-dollar bills and offered to post bond for the man who robbed him. "I've got a score to settle with him," he said. In this case, law and order sided with the cockfighters, who had been robbed, and no charges were brought against them. The man who organized the robbery was arraigned, but before his trial he committed suicide after being chased through Knoxville by the city police.

Cockfighting is intriguing because it defies stereotypes. People who raise cocks to fight love animals, love the very birds they are raising to pit in a deadly contest that could lead to their deaths. To an outsider, cockfighting is epitomized by gambling, by blood, and by the fight to the death. Yet trainers and breeders talk fondly of their birds, praise their fighting ability, mourn those who fought and lost, and kill those that refuse to fight. There are many people who love animals as animals, who pet and pamper them, who explore their limits, and who can develop their potential. Cockers keep alive a sport that has been outlawed but, like race drivers and early rock 'n' roll musicians, has not been completely tamed.

10 / A Second Chance
at Reconstruction

BY 1960, THERE WAS MORE INTEGRATION IN MUSIC AND IN THE
sports world than in schools or in society at large. The undercurrent
of rebellion in the South that unleashed rock 'n' roll, stock-car
racing, the Montgomery bus boycott, and a general revolt against
conformity reemerged in February 1960. Four young black men
entered Woolworth's in Greensboro, North Carolina, made a few
purchases, and then sat down at the segregated white lunch counter.
They were not served, but they continued to occupy seats at the
counter. Within days this simple defiant act not only had attracted
their fellow students at North Carolina Agricultural and Technical
College in Greensboro but had recruited white students from the
area. The phase of meeting only on the playing field and on the
dance floor ended; from that point on, the civil-rights movement
was energized by a coalition of blacks and whites. No longer would
the traditional white liberal formula of making timid suggestions,
condemning the system, and hoping for a new day prevail. Young
people took up the burden, the crusade; the waiting was over. By
April 1960, sit-ins had spread to nine states, convulsed fifty-four
cities, and captured the imagination of the nation. Young blacks
and whites banded together to erase the heritage of segregation and

discrimination; they insisted on equal rights. Given the history of Reconstruction, with its violence, and the heritage of resistance to any tear in the cotton curtain of segregation, the stage seemed set and the cast assembled for a massive and violent drama.

Yet blacks armed for battle not with the weapons of death but with the olive branch of love. The Student Non-Violent Coordinating Committee (SNCC), organized in Raleigh, became the youth arm of the Southern Christian Leadership Conference. Martin Luther King, Jr., challenged whites with his concept of love; he would outlove the whites and bear whatever violence they meted out, without fighting back. When television showed blacks being assaulted, beaten, driven back with fire hoses, and arrested, a numbed nation realized that segregation was an evil that could no longer be ignored. Southerners, watching their neighbors and leaders attack unarmed blacks, became confused and then ashamed, and many reconsidered their defiance. A new spirit moved across the South, and while most white adults still whispered their racist thoughts, many of their children were protesting segregation at lunch counters.

The sit-ins came during a Presidential election that pitted John F. Kennedy against Richard M. Nixon. To a young, rebellious, and idealistic generation, Kennedy personified liberalism and a future purged of racism and bigotry. His Catholicism made him even more attractive to a younger generation that had tired of religious and color tests for any purpose. The Democrats openly campaigned for black votes, and Kennedy won by a narrow margin. He had, meanwhile, attempted to keep the Southern power brokers at bay, much as had Woodrow Wilson and Franklin D. Roosevelt. Kennedy could champion civil rights and form links to Martin Luther King, Jr., and the emerging civil-rights leadership, but he could not ignore Southern political power in Congress. Still, he appointed blacks to high positions in his Administration and responded to pressure from black leaders.

The Streets

Meanwhile, civil-rights groups were in turmoil. The leadership of SCLC proved too cautious for the young radicals in SNCC, so they revolted. The NAACP, which had seldom advocated direct action, competed for the allegiance of militant youngsters. The Congress of Racial Equality (CORE) emerged from obscurity in 1961 by electing James Farmer as national director and then sponsoring a Freedom Ride into the Deep South to test integration on public transportation. The images of flaming buses and brutal beatings burned deeply into the consciousness of the nation. The NAACP continued its legal battles, SCLC deliberately sponsored direct-action programs, CORE challenged with its direct-action agenda, and SNCC moved to the vanguard with a membership dedicated to living on the edge, challenging restrictions, rallying working-class blacks, and going to jail when necessary.

By the time John F. Kennedy was assassinated in November 1963, the role of whites in the civil-rights movement was changing. Blacks had always been hampered, as well as helped, by white leadership and white liberal allies. In the early years of the century, under quite different circumstances, white liberals met with blacks and usually commiserated with them about the deteriorating state of race relations. The NAACP, founded by whites and blacks, became increasingly a black-led organization. By the 1960 sit-ins, a new sense of pride and confidence had swept through black organizations and communities. For one thing, white liberals and church groups were in some instances not ready to move as quickly or as radically as were most blacks, and there lingered the suspicion that whites would coopt or blunt the edge of militance. There was ambivalence on both sides. White youths who had grown up hearing their parents talk about the inferiority of blacks and who had rebelled against segregation and their parents discovered that their black counterparts sometimes refused to accept them as equal allies in the movement. It was a variation on the theme introduced by William Faulkner when he asked white Southerners to take the lead in changing the structure rather than having the federal government shape Southern destiny. "White," as a designation, and "white liberal," as a tag of opprobrium, were drummed into the sensitive ears of maturing white youngsters and confused them. Blacks, who had for years been forced to accept a long list of epithets, turned the name-calling upside down. Black was beautiful; black pride soon became black power.

Some of the leftward movement of civil rights in the early 1960s came from forces set in motion much earlier. When blacks migrated to the North to escape racism, mechanization, and other problems, many found jobs in factories. By the early 1950s, however, automation sent blacks onto the unemployment rolls. As Americans embraced the consumer society, watched TV ads that whetted their appetites for ever more gadgets, blacks fell into poverty. In the early 1950s, blacks earned about half the median income of whites, and a decade later the ratio had changed little. The country, by and large, ignored black Americans, for it was comfortable to assume that, if there was a race problem, it was to be found only in the South. In the South blacks suffered through the last stages of rural mechanization, and many could not find alternative employment. They marched for equal rights even as a few years later their Northern cousins would riot in frustration.

In the spring of 1963, the SCLC confronted Birmingham, Alabama, with a direct-action crusade. When the protest got off to a slow start, the leadership used schoolchildren in demonstrations; thousands were arrested. When the police reacted angrily with fire hoses, dogs, and brutality, outraged Americans (as well as the Birmingham business community) insisted that injustices be ended. President Kennedy went on television to turn civil rights into a moral crusade and call for a civil-rights bill.

With the civil-rights movement becoming the crucial issue of the decade, a group of black leaders and Protestant, Catholic, and Jewish religious leaders organized a march on Washington. Blacks and whites thronged to the Lincoln Memorial in the summer of 1963 to hear black and white leaders review the past and point toward the future. It was the high point of hope and expectation. In the end it was Martin Luther King, Jr., who took the many threads and wove them into his "I have a dream" speech. In some respects the gathering was like a revival, a great awakening, and it unleashed a tidal wave of emotions. When Kennedy died in November of that year, Lyndon Johnson took up the crusade and insisted on a civil-rights law. The Civil Rights Act of 1964 opened public accommodations to blacks nearly twenty years after Jackie and Rachel Robinson made their harrowing journey to spring training.

As the civil-rights movement has receded into memory, the consensus is that it achieved equal rights through direct action and enlightened legislation supported by the Supreme Court. The tenseness, ambivalence, and bitterness, all the feelings, including the bravery, spirit, and accomplishments of the two races, dims as time passes. Yet, in 1960, with confrontations all along the color line, there were staggering possibilities for violence. Compared with the potential, relatively little violence erupted in the South. One has only to read the history of the Reconstruction years to appreciate what might have happened in the sixties. The nightly TV news which showed meanness and violence directed toward blacks sickened the public at large and embarrassed many Southerners. Something was wrong with a people who could pose as gracious and easygoing hosts and God-fearing people and simultaneously appear as raging bigots. Were Southerners, white Southerners, both? Were they, who so often accused blacks of being fiends, guilty of what they feared in blacks?

In autobiographies, news reports, and scholarly studies, those who battled for equality and those who opposed it recorded their thoughts and actions. Among the many accounts, Anne Moody's *Coming of Age in Mississippi* remains a classic. She spent her first few years on a cotton plantation in southern Mississippi; then her mother moved to Centreville, a small town south of Natchez. During her youth, she witnessed cruelties—overt racial snubs and subvert slights and behavior that branded her, her family, and her friends as a sub-class. She wondered, as did many black youngsters, why so many blacks were killed and why there seemed to be no recourse. While she was in high school in the 1950s, a local member of the NAACP was gunned down near his home. "His death brought back memories of all the other killings, beatings, and abuses inflicted upon Negroes by whites." She wanted retribution and even fantasized that she would buy a machine gun and kill whites in Centreville.

She was an excellent basketball player and attended Natchez College on a scholarship. She resented the rigid discipline there, which rivaled that of Fisk and Hampton in the 1920s. After a year of being a loner, she began to change. She won a full scholarship to Tougaloo College, near Jackson; she admired the school's spirit, which encouraged academic excellence and self-expression. Soon she learned of the NAACP chapter on campus, and when the Jackson SNCC chapter in 1963 started a voter-registration drive in the Delta, she agreed to help.

Before long she was staying in Freedom Houses and taking an active part in voter registration. "I really got to like all of the SNCC workers," she remembered. "I had never known people so willing and determined to help others." She learned that many of them had been shot at and that some of the houses had been bombed. SNCC workers tried to help blacks in the Delta, but many blacks were fired from their jobs when they registered to vote. That summer, though, Anne Moody felt that something was going to change. "For the first time I began to think something would be done about whites killing, beating, and misusing Negroes. I knew I was going to be part of whatever happened."

Whites in Centreville, hoping to end her activism, intimidated her mother, but this made Anne even more determined. She joined in a sit-in at the Jackson Woolworth's lunch counter. Some local white boys took the rope that had been put across the other seats and tied it into a hangman's noose and tried to put it over the heads of the half-dozen demonstrators. A white man took out his knife and opened it; then he put it back in his pocket. Then the whites started slapping and beating the demonstrators. They grabbed Anne by the hair and pulled her across the floor, but she and the others returned to the counter and were joined by a white Tougaloo faculty member. "The mob started smearing us with ketchup, mustard, sugar, pies, and everything on the counter." They sat there, joined by other students, for three hours, before the president of Tougaloo College came for them. The police had not interfered.

Later, she and thirteen others, black and white, staged a pray-in at the Jackson post office and were arrested. From a paper smuggled in by a black trustee, they learned that four hundred high-school students had been arrested at another demonstration. "From the way everyone was describing the scene it sounded like Nazi Germany instead of Jackson, USA," she concluded. This was the summer of 1963.

On June 12 a sniper killed thirty-seven-year-old Medgar Evers, a black NAACP organizer, as he got out of his car at his house in Jackson. Evers had fought in World War II and at the time of his death was selling insurance while working for the NAACP. He had often told his friends, "Mississippi will end up being one of the best places to live." Outraged at this latest act of violence, Anne Moody and her friends demonstrated. The Jackson police arrested protesters, and Moody and twenty of her friends were packed into a paddy wagon and with the heater on (it was a hundred degrees that day) were taken to the fairgrounds and left to stew for two hours before the doors were opened. "It reminded me of a concentration camp," she observed. When released a few days later, she had lost fifteen pounds. Such experiences hardened an entire generation of activists. They believed, above all, that the South had to be changed, and they took up the burden so often neglected in the past. In this sense, Southerners, with help from Northern allies, were taking the lead in shaping the future of the South. That white politicians and other leaders were absent from the ranks of the freedom fighters in no way diminishes the fact that much of the energy of change came from the South. Without such dedicated activists, the federal government would have found it more difficult to integrate voting rolls, school districts, and public accommodations.

Evers's murder was intended to terrorize black organizers, just as violence had been used in the time of the Reconstruction. Some people did buckle under, but most young activists became more committed to carry on. While SNCC and CORE organized more demonstrations and the NAACP turned its energy to voter registration, Mississippi became the focus of the fight for equal rights. During the Freedom Summer of 1964, some thousand black and white volunteers from all over the country entered the state to help push the civil-rights movement by setting up freedom schools. Organized by the Council of Federated Organizations (COFO), the movement gained national attention. At the same time, the Mississippi Freedom Democratic Party (MFDP) challenged the regular Mississippi Democratic Party because it excluded blacks.

The summer had barely begun, however, when three civil-rights workers disappeared in Neshoba County. Michael Schwerner ran a community center in Meridian; Andrew Goodman had just arrived from New York the day before; and James Chaney, a young black man, was an activist in the movement. Forty days later, after a massive FBI investigation, the bodies of the young men were recovered from a dam in Neshoba County. Violence continued, and before the summer ended, thirty-seven churches were burned, thirty homes bombed, eighty civil-rights workers were beaten, and police arrested more than a thousand activists.

A new spirit emerged among blacks and their white allies. Young white men and women returned north from battle, only to discover inequalities there. They carried a message of hope, but they also carried a new consciousness of injustice that would ultimately help launch a reinvigorated women's movement and efforts to sweep away all forms of discrimination. Of course, along with the new spirit of indignation, a parallel militance grew among Southern whites to stop the movement.

Most discussions of the civil-rights movement fail to deal with the fears of whites. Most white adults had been reared on the belief that blacks were inferior, and the laws of the South since the turn of the century had segregated blacks. It was hard enough for many Southerners to watch baseball games on TV and become confounded by the performance of blacks. It was more difficult to accept the rulings of the courts that their system was unconstitutional. Yet, so long as they saw the movement only on TV, many whites still believed that it might disappear. When protests became local, however, whites reacted in various ways. Some remained quiet and refused to take a stand; others were hotheads and threatened violence. White society fractured even as black society mobilized into a broad movement dedicated to erasing discrimination.

During the summer of 1964, blacks from Mississippi visited Democratic National Convention delegates in other parts of the country to argue their case even as, in Mississippi, voter registration and political organizing progressed. Leslie B. McLemore recalled that he spoke to delegates in Minnesota, Wisconsin, and Illinois. Introduced by a Northerner as someone straight from Mississippi, McLemore recalled, "I would get up with my Mississippi accent and talk about Mississippi, and after they heard me for a while they'd say, 'Yes, he's from Mississippi. The genuine product. No question about it. This guy's legitimate.'" McLemore was vice-chairman of the Mississippi Freedom Democratic Party and attended the Democratic National Convention in Atlantic City. At the time he was still a college student, and it gave him "a different perspective on the world."

Freedom Summer culminated in August 1964 when the MFDP challenged the Mississippi regular Democrats at the party's convention in Atlantic City. The highlight of the convention came when Fannie Lou Hamer testified before the Credentials Committee. Born in Montgomery County, Mississippi, in 1917, she was the youngest of twenty children and had spent most of her life in Sunflower County as a sharecropper and timekeeper on the W. D. Marlowe plantation. When she tried to register in Indianola, Marlowe threw her family off the plantation. Then, in the early 1960s, she turned her energies to the civil-rights movement and quickly became first a leader and then a symbol of bravery. She moved to Ruleville, became active in SNCC, and in 1964 helped lobby for the MFDP.

Her testimony was one of the most gripping ever carried on TV. She told about her attempt to register and how she was treated after she attempted to use the facilities at the Winona bus station in 1963. "They carried me into a room and there were two Negro boys in this room. The state highway patrolman gave them a long, wide blackjack and he told one of the boys, 'Take this . . . and if you don't use it on her, you know what I'll use on you.'" The young man beat her till he gave out. "And I was trying to guard some of the licks with my hands and they just beat my hands till they turned blue," she testified.

The MFDP delegates argued that they were the true Democratic Party of the state; they had an integrated delegation. The committee suggested a compromise—seating the regular delegation and also two members of the MFDP as guests. The MFDP refused and started a demonstration; most of the regular party delegates left the convention floor.

Freedom Summer not only had an impact on students and other activists but also changed the hearts of some white Mississippians.

Mississippi State University, for example, decided to play in the NCAA basketball tournament, despite the fact that it and most Southern white schools had an unwritten rule not to participate in integrated events. The state legislature removed voting restrictions based on race. The Voting Rights Act of 1965 permitted federal registrars to police registration in thirty-one Mississippi counties. Businessmen also realized that the unfavorable publicity was harmful to their interests. Some no doubt realized that integration would be good for business, and applied pressure for changes in the state.

In 1967 a Meridian jury found seven men guilty of conspiring against James Chaney, Michael Schwerner, and Andrew Goodman. That same year another jury convicted eleven men for murder and arson in connection with the death of black leader Vernon Dahmer. Schools began token integration, and despite some violence and retaliation, the process continued. Because Mississippi was generally regarded as the most backward of the Southern states with regard to civil rights, the victories there marked a turning point in the movement. Whites throughout the South slowly realized that the hope for equal rights promised more than segregation could ever deliver. Gradually, the South turned inward and began to work out its own problems.

The bravery of civil-rights activists, facing armed police and snipers, became legendary, as well it should. Violence could, and often did, erupt suddenly. Marchers, registrars, and protesters throughout the South realized that at any moment they could die. Martin Luther King, Jr., continued to march and to speak throughout the South and the nation. He preached love, and that love was more powerful than hate. By 1968 he argued that the civil-rights movement had been hurt by the Vietnam War and that the anti-war protests sweeping the country robbed the civil-rights movement of its vitality. In the spring of 1968, he went to Memphis to aid in a strike by garbage workers. He was assassinated while talking to friends on the balcony of the Lorraine Motel. The next day, blacks rioted and burned property in several cities. The movement would never achieve the unity and publicity it had before King's death, but neither would the country be able to turn back the forces of freedom that he and his followers and friends initiated. The civil-rights movement was the South's finest moment.

The Schools

By the time school integration began—indeed, by the *Brown* decision in 1954—the old plantation system was disintegrating, and landlords were no longer dependent upon poor and illiterate laborers. In addition, many rural people had moved out of the country, and city schools presented a more complex problem in dealing with integration. Had children been ordered to integrate schools in 1954 on their own, no doubt the process would have been orderly. No white leader appeared to set a tone of moderation, so by the 1960s, when all efforts to evade the *Brown* ruling had been expended, both parents and children faced mixed schools with apprehension and fear.

Rural schools integrated with much less friction than urban schools. First of all, private schools provided the only alternative in such areas; there were no white suburbs to escape to. When rural schools consolidated, almost every child rode a bus to a central location. Moreover, many black and white families knew each other either through work or by being neighbors along rural roads. Children were not being mixed with strangers. Equally important, many parents warned their children not to cause trouble that would reflect poorly on their families. Families so long kept separate by law and custom attempted to make the new system work.

By the mid-1960s, federal courts started striking down the tuition grants that had allowed private schools to flourish. The federal government under the Johnson Administration asked for desegregation plans and withheld federal money from districts that did not cooperate. This federal intrusion provided incentives to implement integration. Despite such support, integration moved slowly, for as late as 1969 some eighty percent of black schoolchildren were still segregated. When the Supreme Court in 1969 struck down the freedom-of-choice plans, the last legal barrier to integration fell.

Such rulings did not end white evasions. Families in rural areas had only the option of private schools, but those in cities fled from the areas where blacks lived. Whites moved from inner cities to the suburbs. Federal agencies countered by pairing predominantly black and white schools and then busing students from one to the other to achieve a racial balance. Busing quickly became an emotional issue. Despite evasions, by 1975 over ninety percent of Southern black pupils were in integrated schools.

The Nixon Administration opposed busing, as did many Southern politicians and many black and white citizens. Busing served to harm community schools and undermine the pride that parents and children had in their neighborhoods and schools. Blacks as well as whites had reservations about busing children out of their communities, yet black schools needed white students to achieve equal status in the eyes of school administrators and funding agencies. The busing crusade received a setback in 1973 when the Supreme Court sustained a lower-court ruling in a Richmond case.

A decade or more passed after the *Brown* decision before most Southern whites faced school integration. In LaFayette High School in Chambers County, Alabama, Randall Williams remembered that it was in 1967 when he studied under his first black teacher. "I had a nigger schoolteacher in 1967, when I was a tenth-grader," he recalled , "and one of the things I remember best about it is that somehow in the course of that year the nigger stopped being a nigger and became just a teacher." During most of the year, however, Williams and his chums made life miserable for their teacher, Miss Oliver. "I don't think we meant it personally," he said later. "But she was black and this was a white school, regardless of what any judge said, and she wasn't supposed to be there." Yet Miss Oliver, Williams remembered, was a strong woman. "She won some of her students over with her patience and what came to be acknowledged as courage; she won others by absorbing them in the history she taught; mostly she won by simply holding on until her white students got to know her." White parents, claiming that integration lowered academic standards, founded an academy to preserve "quality" education. The high school gradually became ninety percent black, while the academy, Chambers Academy, took the name "Rebels," the color gray, and flew a Confederate flag as its symbols.

Rudolph Copeland was in the first class at LaFayette High that blacks were permitted to attend. He had not wanted to attend LaFayette High; his former school had upgraded its athletic program and he was looking forward to a good year. He was apprehensive and wondered if he could hold on to his starting-quarterback position. Years later he still rankled at the coach's refusal to play him as quarterback. When the white quarterback was injured in a game, Copeland went in and scored two touchdowns. To prevent blacks attaining class offices, white students held elections the spring before integration; and blacks were not invited to the prom that year. The white reaction, in Copeland's eyes, was not unexpected. In his opinion, there were few mediums for bringing blacks and whites together except school, and that opportunity was never fully realized after the academy was started. In that sense the reaction of the football coach was indicative. White parents and elders were afraid that school integration would work, so they took precautions to make it fail.

Private schools in the South emerged as an answer to integration, but parents also shifted their children because they were upset over other changes in society. Private schools, in the eyes of parents, were fortresses to protect children from temptation. They feared dwindling church attendance, sexually explicit movies, the acceptance of cursing, drugs, and permissiveness. Private schools sought to preserve traditional white values. Parents talked in hushed tones about public schools—declining standards, lack of discipline, drugs, fighting, and sexual looseness. In a sense they were correct, for public schools in the South were the caldrons of change, the laboratories in which two different cultures were working out a new way of life.

Christian schools also kept the faith, the old Fundamentalist faith that characterized the South. Children prayed in private schools. Even the theory of evolution, an explosive issue in the 1920s, again became important. The reconciliation that William Louis Poteat found in the 1920s seemed lost on a generation of parents who saw any departure from the Scriptures as a threat. To build new classrooms, athletic facilities, and libraries, provide lunches and transportation, and hire good teachers proved expensive. Private schools not only meant double taxation for parents but in many instances offered a mediocre education; both parents often had to work to pay the tuition. If public schools were the hope of the civil-rights movement, private schools perpetuated a way of life that was doomed.

Southern colleges and universities had a difficult time meeting federal guidelines. Formerly white institutions were eager to recruit black athletes, and many schools aggressively sought good black students. This jeopardized the position of predominantly black schools. In most Southern states, there were separate systems of black and white state-supported colleges, and black colleges were inadequately funded. Even after black schools were incorporated into the state system, they attracted few white students. Tradition-ally white schools dominated graduate and professional education, and in most states the graduate programs at black colleges were inferior. Thus, black graduates attended white graduate schools, and many black schools were left without a law school, a medical school, or graduate studies. Still, black graduate students were no longer denied admission to white institutions of higher learning. There were positive and negative elements at work, and despite advances in Southern education, both secondary and university ed-ucation lagged far behind the rest of the country.

Politics

Voter registration, the Civil Rights Act, the moral victory of the MFDP, and Lyndon Johnson's support of the movement repre-sented only one side of race relations in 1964. George Wallace, the governor of Alabama, entered the Presidential primaries and did well both in Southern and in Northern states. Barry Goldwater, the Republican candidate, had voted against the civil-rights bill and advocated that states, not the federal government, maintain power over matters of race. Most Southern states were controlled by whites, and to give them power meant basically to reverse civil-rights gains. More obvious, the Republican Party had come to epitomize what white Southerners believed in, and significantly, Senator J. Strom Thurmond switched to the Republican Party, finishing a journey begun with his Dixiecrat campaign sixteen years earlier.

Changes in Southern politics reflected how the region was reacting to the civil-rights movement. No longer could Democrats take the South for granted, and Republicans seized upon the unsettled South as a new area to organize and exploit. From 1960 to 1984, the Presidency had been shared by Democrats and Republicans, twelve years each, but Ronald Reagan's victory in 1984 pushed the GOP past the Democrats in national power. In many ways, Reagan's victory showed how radically the South had changed over those years. Republicans had captured many whites who had formerly voted Democratic, for they looked to the GOP to end the move toward civil rights and restore old values. The South, as the number and size of businesses increased, attracted middle-class professionals and businessmen, who were natural allies of the Republican Party. The Democrats, meanwhile, lost many white voters, gained most blacks, and kept much of the labor vote. The Democrats were becoming a minority party, at least on the national level. While they still controlled most state and local offices in the South, time seemed to be running out on a Democratic domination.

As long as blacks had no political power, whites could control the Democratic Party. In 1947 only some half million blacks were registered to vote, but after the registration drives of the early 1960s the number rose in 1966 to 2.3 million and by 1972 to 3.5 million. Gradually, blacks began to exert their political muscle, and by 1966 there were twenty blacks in Southern state houses. Throughout the South in 1972 there were 1,148 black elected officials, some 1.3 percent of the total officeholders.

Two strong currents ran through the South after the civil-rights movement started. Along with the traditional conservative Democrats, a new breed of politicians who favored civil rights emerged. In 1970, for example, Reubin Askew of Florida, Jimmy Carter of Georgia, John C. West of South Carolina, Dale Bumpers of Arkansas, and Edwin Edwards of Louisiana won governor's seats. Democrats discovered that to win a seat they had to favor black aspirations. At the same time, a new breed of Republicans emerged. In addition to Strom Thurmond's switch to the Republican Party in 1964, two years later two Southern states elected Republican governors, and Howard Baker won a Senate seat from Tennessee.

Four years later, veteran Tennessee senator Albert Gore lost his seat to Republican William E. Brock III. His son, Albert Gore, Jr., won the seat back in 1984.

While much of the political dialogue was conducted in the usual manner of campaign promises, a new language dominated Southern (and national) politics: code words, such as law and order (alarm at a rising crime rate and race riots), big government (federal intrusion in civil rights and other areas of life), busing (integrating schools by shifting students), school prayer (reversing the Supreme Court decision forbidding such prayers), and welfare cheating (abuses of various programs such as food stamps). When Thurmond made his Southern strategy bargain with newly elected President Richard Nixon in 1968, the Republican Party emerged as a vehicle for sidetracking the civil-rights movement. Without ever saying it explicitly, Nixon and his Administration began defusing what was left of the movement.

But neither Nixon nor any other Presidential candidate could match the innuendos of George Wallace and Jesse Helms. Wallace, who had once been defeated in Alabama politics because he did not address the race issue, vowed that it would never happen again. Helms, who saw integration as a liberal or at times a communist plot, wrote off the black vote while catering to the fears and frustrations of white voters. The two men, one a Democrat and one a Republican, personify the changes in Southern politics since the early 1960s. When George Wallace stood at a schoolhouse door to protest the admission of blacks, Jesse Helms was a television commentator in Raleigh. Helms attacked the civil-rights movement, speakers at the state universities, and unions, among other things. Their careers, while not always in the mainstream of Southern politics, remain instructive for an understanding of the fears of Southern whites.

George Corley Wallace came from a family of courthouse politicians in Barbour County, Alabama. Considering his small-town Black Belt roots, he did well, serving as a page in the state senate, winning the state's Golden Gloves boxing championship in the bantamweight class, graduating from the University of Alabama, and taking a law degree. He served in World War II and then began working his way up through a series of state offices. During those years, Wallace did not trade on the race issue. Indeed, when he was serving as a circuit judge in the early 1950s, he had the reputation for being impartial regarding race. "I've never been before a judge who was as cordial," a prominent black lawyer in Birmingham remembered.

The bantamweight Wallace fell under the influence of Governor James E. Folsom, a six-foot-eight giant who harbored a wide streak of Populism, the kind of class understanding that played down the race issue. In 1959, Wallace served as Big Jim Folsom's campaign manager in southern Alabama. When the state legislature passed an interposition ruling, Folsom branded it "hogwash" and set it aside. According to some accounts, Folsom listened patiently to Martin Luther King, Jr., and gave him paternalistic advice. When he entertained Harlem congressman Adam Clayton Powell in the governor's mansion, however, it caused an uproar in the state. Despite his moderation on the race issue, he did not halt the mob that drove Autherine Lucy, a black woman, from the University of Alabama in 1957.

Wallace watched his master fall in 1958 as a result of his moderation on the race issue. When George Wallace ran for governor in the Democratic primary that year, a hard-line segregationist, John Patterson, defeated him. It was then that Wallace vowed never to allow an opponent to out-segregation him. Four years later Wallace won the governor's seat, and at his inaugural he stated, "I draw the line in the dust and toss the gauntlet before the feet of tyranny, and I say: Segregation now—segregation tomorrow—segregation forever." In 1963, with a sense of timing and a dramatic flair, he stood in the university doorway to bar two black students from entering. Although President Kennedy federalized the state's National Guard and the black students entered the university, Wallace continued to confront any attempt at integration with a dramatic gesture. While other governors moderated their tone on race issues, Wallace became the champion of the forces that vowed to keep the South segregated. Indeed, at Ku Klux Klan rallies, Wallace literature was sprinkled generously with the racist tracts that circulated through the crowd. During his first term as governor, Alabama became the battleground of civil rights—and violence. A Birmingham church was bombed, and four young black girls were killed. Across the state, freedom riders and demonstrators were beaten, hosed, and jailed.

Wallace learned that he could deplore the violence and still keep his segregationist following. Southerners who watched events unfold on television either condemned the violence or cheered Wallace. Unable to succeed himself, Wallace persuaded his wife, Lurleen, to run. She handily defeated the Republican candidate, but died in office. Meanwhile, Wallace began testing the waters of national politics and in 1964 made respectable showings in Maryland, Indiana, and Wisconsin. Four years later he was on the ballot in all fifty states. In 1970 he won the governor's chair and girded for a national campaign in 1972.

Despite Wallace's Populist rhetoric, he did little for average Alabama citizens. The racial conflict in the state had stunted the drive for industrialization. The state's regressive tax code favored large corporations, and Alabama was next to the bottom in per-capita income. As the agricultural system moved from sharecropping to agribusiness, the dispossessed received little aid from the governor. Many residents moved from the state, and those who remained often lived in poor housing. Wallace sided with the Farm Bureau—not with sharecroppers.

Wallace gained national attention not only because he opposed the civil-rights movement but also because he attacked government bureaucrats, favored school prayer, condemned pornography, and articulated the frustrations of people facing abrupt change. In a sense he foreshadowed the issues that gave rise to Ronald Reagan a few years later. In 1972, Wallace entered national politics again and was a major threat to the Presidential campaign. On May 15, he was shot at a shopping center in Laurel, Maryland, and though he survived, he was partially paralyzed. Wallace's victories in Michigan and Maryland were only portents of what could have been a serious bid for the nomination.

George Wallace recovered, and from his wheelchair he again emerged as a state leader. His political platform, however, had changed dramatically. He built bridges to the black community, received both Senator Edward Kennedy and President Richard Nixon, got the backing of the AFL-CIO in 1974, crowned a black homecoming queen at the University of Alabama, spoke before a black mayor's conference at Tuskegee, and visited Martin Luther King, Jr.'s church and addressed the congregation. With Wallace still holding power in Alabama, the state's Republican Party had little chance on the state level. While much of the South tottered before Republican onslaughts, Alabama under Wallace kept the support of poor whites and gained black support as well. Evidently the racist factions remembered the old Wallace when he was the favorite of the Klan, while blacks saw the new Wallace who crowned black homecoming queens. While Jesse Helms garnered national attention for opposing issues, for fighting losing battles, Wallace kept support by growing and changing. Still, his national aspirations were over.

The career of U.S. Senator Jesse Helms, the North Carolina Republican, personifies the growing power of the Republican Party's right wing, the mixing of politics and religion, and the rise of the Republican Party as a challenge, if not a replacement, to the old Bourbon Democratic Party. Helms's childhood, as he remembered it, was idyllic. Monroe, North Carolina, had about three thousand inhabitants when Helms was a youngster, and his father was both police and fire chief. After a summer at Wingate College, a Baptist school, he enrolled at Baptist-sponsored Wake Forest College. Before completing his degree, he took a sports-reporting job at the Raleigh *News and Observer* and married Dorothy Coble when he turned twenty-one.

One can only surmise the trials of the awkward young bespectacled son of a town policeman and speculate on how his highly developed sense of cunning and strategy evolved from being so near the forces of law and order. Helms presented a deceptive appearance, for to many he seemed more like a small-town preacher or a second-generation Snopes out of a Faulkner novel than a U.S. senator. Indeed, Helms was a man of many contradictions; he could pose as a generous, humble, and affable man, but those who watched him closest pointed out that he was mean-spirited, vain, and retributive. The same man who taught Sunday School, adopted a child with cerebral palsy, and developed friendships with media pastors could lash out at enemies and label them communist sympathizers, radicals, or atheists simply for disagreeing with him. While piously disclaiming any political motivations and, Pilate-like, washing his hands of controversy, he angrily pointed an accusing finger at his opponents for harboring political instincts. There was much of the Pharisee in his actions.

After working as U.S. Senator Willis Smith's administrative assistant, serving as executive director of the North Carolina Bankers Association, and then sitting on the Raleigh city council, in 1960 he bought a small interest in WRAL television in Raleigh and began a career editorializing to the people of eastern North Carolina. By 1960 white Tarheels were upset at the sit-ins in Greensboro, the founding of SNCC, and the civil-rights movement.

For Helms the situation proved easy to manipulate. He castigated Martin Luther King, Jr., denounced media coverage of civil-rights efforts (which struck many white Southerners as unnecessarily one-sided), and condemned a long list of evils, including radical speakers on college campuses, the United Nations, welfare, Medicare, and food stamps. Helms rarely favored anything; rather, he condemned everything that might generate an emotional response, while alluding to the loss of vague and mystical values of the past. By 1972, he had switched registration from Democratic to Republican and ran successfully for the Senate, hanging on to the coattails of Richard Nixon, who also pulled Republican James Holhouser to the governorship. Even if the election was a fluke, Helms possessed a vision, an understanding of human nature, and the knack to turn people's frustrations into money, which led him to found the Congressional Club of North Carolina as a fund-raising front. He hired direct-mail expert Richard Viguerie, and by promising to lead the fight against black militants, labor organizers, bureaucrats, communists, and secular humanists, he amassed a campaign chest of $7 million for the 1978 election.

In the context of 1972, Helms was just another accidental senator from the South, and he earned a reputation for opposing bills and offering dilatory amendments, for forcing votes of record on controversial issues such as school busing, military preparedness, abortion, school prayer, and government spending. When examined critically, Helms's program embodied the very intrusive element that he purportedly opposed. He proposed bills and amendments that would bring the federal government into the schoolroom (to prescribe prayers and dictate that the biblical account of creation be taught) and into decisions that women made about their lives (whether or not to have an abortion). With such an agenda, Helms won few allies in the Senate, nor did he cultivate friendship. He remained the loner, the constant opponent, the obstructionist; his was not the world of new bills aimed at the nation's needs but of amendments that had no chance of passage. Some senators charged that Helms proposed amendments so that they could be defeated and make a martyr of him—all the better to raise funds.

By 1980, a year when Helms was not up for election, the Congressional Club spent over $7 million on the campaigns of others, including support of John East, who ran against North Carolina's other U.S. senator, Robert B. Morgan. East, a professor of political science at East Carolina University, distorted Morgan's respectable conservative voting record and portrayed him as an ally of liberals George McGovern and Edward Kennedy. The East campaign flooded TV with expensive advertisements, and riding on the coattails of Ronald Reagan, East won the seat in a very close election. By that time, Helms with his money had extended a line of political credit that he would call in. The Republican senators who took control of the Senate in 1981 realized, as did the new President, that Helms would become a force in politics. In September he graced the cover of *Time* magazine; two months later *People* magazine did a feature on him. Despite his position as chairman of the Committee on Agriculture, Helms had not become a leader. His strong support of the federal tobacco support program (mandatory for all North Carolina politicians) contradicted his opposition to most federal subsidies. In 1983 he vehemently opposed a holiday in honor of Martin Luther King, Jr., charging, as he filibustered, that King had been a communist agent and that unreleased FBI material would prove it. Even as he debated, Helms sent out fund-raising letters and ran advertisements denouncing the holiday. It was Helms at his worst—using the issue of communism as a front to attack a distinguished black leader and at the same time raising money and stirring up conflict.

His power derived from his awesome ability to raise money and avoid compromise. Helms moved to control the Republican platform in 1976, 1980, and 1984. The party had come to him; the issues that he had championed in the days when he was in the Senate wilderness had become national issues. Nearly all were the result of the country's moving from a rural, small-town environment into an urban age. Further, the unrest generated by the civil-rights movement and the Vietnam War created among some people a more conservative political outlook. Helms also established several tax-exempt foundations to press for his wider programs.

Helms rose to power largely on issues that had traditionally remained outside politics, issues that thoughtful people could disagree on but that Helms saw in moralistic terms. Most politicians refused to confront Helms, but Senator Robert Morgan attacked him and his pious allies. In March 1980, Morgan delivered a speech before the North Carolina Baptist State Convention on the separation of church and state. Morgan taught a Baptist Sunday School class and approved of officeholders subscribing to religious principles. "But what I am saying," he explained, "is that on matters upon which reasonable persons may differ, religion and church should not be used as justifications for dogmatic political positions propounded from the pulpit or condemnation of those who disagree." He went further. "Demagoguery from the pulpit, I think you would agree, is no different from demagoguery on the campaign trail, on the floor of a legislative body, or on the street corner." (He also had harsh words regarding direct-mail campaigns, the television ministry, and the Moral Majority.) Such pious and dogmatic appeals to emotion, he argued, hardly squared with Christ's compassion and tolerance. He also ruminated about the fate of the minority, for Baptists had suffered a long history of persecution. "If a state morality should prevail," he queried, "what would become of the dissenters?" Morgan's speech not only reviewed the history of Baptists but also issued a warning about the ultimate program of his fellow Tarheel, Jesse Helms.

Helms's insistence that the state should control the lives of citizens, that his concept of morality should be legislated, and his piousness, revealed a spirit of totalitarianism. Helms raised himself to a position of leadership, a pulpit where he has become the godfather of the forces of doom. Ignoring blacks, condemning liberals, denouncing humanists, and fighting windmills, Helms carved a career for himself that traded on negativism. While George Wallace moved from segregation and other emotional issues to a more balanced ideology, Helms refused to grow, except in power.

It would be difficult to imagine two political careers more different than those of Jesse Helms and Jimmy Carter. On the national level at least, Carter owed little to his Southernness. His ascendency to the Presidency came about primarily because of the repulsion many Americans felt toward the abuses of power under the Nixon Administration, especially the glimpses of Nixon privately cursing, conniving, and lying. Carter, an honest politician, a born-again Christian, a soft-spoken Southerner who shyly told people he would never lie to them, caught voters at a time when they were searching for old values. Despite the slave and plantation past and the sharecropping abuses, Southerners seemed somehow more perceptive of moral derailings.

Yet Jimmy Carter was not a typical Southerner, upper-class or lower. His rural roots were with the landed class, but his education at Annapolis and his tour with the navy created an engineer and technician, not a Southerner deeply informed by the peculiar history of the region. He championed the aspirations of black Americans, openly boasted of his private praying, brought Willie Nelson into the White House to entertain, and banned strong drink at state functions. Yet he often appeared unsure, tentative. He rarely utilized the Southern experience, the themes of defeat, guilt, and futility that characterized the history of his state and region.

The same people who thought they had found a pious and sensitive leader in Jimmy Carter turned on him in 1980 and elected a movie star. Carter had a rich tradition to call upon, but he lost himself in details, in trivia. His fall came not from his lack of ability or his good heart; it came from his inability to understand the past and relate it to the country's future. In that sense, he became a tragic figure, a man with the best intentions, gifted, hardworking, and sensitive, but the naval technician never emerged from briefing books and introversion to become a charismatic leader.

By the time Jimmy Carter left office in 1981, Southerners had weathered the worst strains of the post-war years. The potential for violence along the color line had largely disappeared, and blacks went about their lives with a new sense of dignity and security. Politicians such as Carter had been crucial in setting a new tone, an acceptance of integration and an awareness that the changing South would need factories to employ rural laborers who left the land. In part Martin Luther King, Jr.'s dream had come true, for black Southerners had attained goals that seemed impossible to an earlier generation. Equally important, many white Southerners, despite reactionary politicians, believed that harmony and equal opportunity should form the basis of Southern life.

11 / Consolidating
the Revolution

THE REVOLUTION THAT SWEPT THROUGH THE SOUTH SINCE 1950 has paused to consolidate. Farmers continue to work under the direction of federal planners, while those who left the land adjust to a nine-to-five routine, or unemployment. Communities that had been segregated are attuned to a more open society. Many Southerners have opted for suburban living, while others remain in urban slums or decaying rural housing. Most people have air-conditioning in their homes, workplaces, and automobiles, and this has dramatically reshaped Southern living. Blacks and whites seem comfortable with most aspects of integration, yet both realize that their cultures are in many ways still distinct. Although some people have adjusted to life away from farms and rural routines, others still look back with nostalgia to what they consider a more harmonious existence.

Southerners have always been churchgoing people, but the rise of TV evangelists and their political agenda have dramatically changed the tone of white Fundamentalism. Black churches were the center of community life and the staging area of the civil-rights movement, but white churches had only reluctantly embraced social issues—

until the Moral Majority stirred them to action. Even as Southerners have adjusted to drastic changes, novelists have created a body of literature that attempts to reconcile the past and the present, and historians have weeded out myths and clarified the South's heritage. The consolidation process has barely begun. Whether the South will attune itself to change or lapse into reaction is a question for the emerging generation.

Air-Conditioning

"Air-conditioning cannot be a grand success in the South," Clarence Cason wrote in 1935, "for the reason that the honest natives of the region recognize the natural summer heat as a welcome ally in that it makes the inside of houses and offices agreeably uninviting, if not actually prohibited territory." No doubt Cason and a whole generation of Southerners reared at the turn of the century would marvel at people rushing from air-conditioned home to air-conditioned car to air-conditioned office, as if pausing in the summer heat might melt them. The increased use of air-conditioning in the North followed parallel lines, but because the South has more oppressive summer heat (and thus unique ways of dealing with it), it forced greater changes south of the Potomac River.

Historian Raymond Arsenault has written of the significance of air-conditioning on Southern change, tracing its development and deployment in the South. Even as air-conditioning and mechanization in agriculture increased, mules and sharecroppers died out. Before air-conditioned homes, offices, and cars, people made their accommodations to the heat as best they could—with high ceilings, with floors raised above the earth so that air circulated under them, and with ample windows. More prosperous homes boasted ceiling and portable electric fans.

In 1906 the first Southerners to have air-conditioning in their lives were Belmont, North Carolina, textile workers. The controlled humidity prevented fibers from breaking. In 1909 tobacco factories used air-conditioning to control humidity, thus standardizing weight. In both cases factory owners were more interested in the health of the commodity than in that of the worker. By the 1930s department stores introduced air-conditioning, as had government buildings in the nation's capital a few years earlier. Prior to World War II, most Southern air-conditioning was in movie theaters, business establishments, and factories. Only in the early 1950s, after the agricultural revolution had made progress, did window units become available to average people. Then, in the space of a decade, air-conditioning became a necessity, and people wondered how Southerners had managed all those years without it. In 1960, 18.2 percent of households in the eleven "census" South states had air-conditioning; ten years later the figure was 50.1 percent, and in 1980 it was 73.2 percent. Blacks did not share cool air proportionately; figures for the same years were 3.9 percent, 20.8 percent, and 52.1 percent, respectively. Only about 40 percent of black households in both Mississippi and South Carolina in 1980 had air-conditioning, while the figure for all households in the states was near 70 percent. Even as it became imperative to air-condition homes, automobile dealers advertised "factory air," and salesmen quickly added "air" to other options. By the mid-1970s some 80 percent of cars sold in the South had "air."

Air-conditioning had a profound influence on Southern culture. Not only did buildings move skyward; they also came to resemble a refrigerator, if not an upturned casket. Windows for ventilation were no longer necessary, so architects sealed up buildings. It was not just that air-conditioning kept people comfortable; it also added status and changed the way people related to natural air. Southerners kept their windows closed from spring to autumn, as if a natural breeze would be untoward. The hum of a compressor, a sealed house, and a boringly stable temperature set off no danger signals of entropy. Because it was modern, because it was there, people turned it on, much as they turned on the television, the radio, and appliances. So Southerners moved indoors, at least middle-class people did, out of the sun, and many put on white collars in the morning. The old culture of sweat ("Horses sweat, men perspire, women glisten," Blanche McCrary Boyd reminded us) has been purged from most cities and towns and only lurks in the hinterland, or in the blue-collar world. Sweat, sharecroppers, and mules, all memories.

The Last Sharecroppers

With mechanization and the use of weed-killing chemicals, the need for rural laborers declined rapidly. Millions of Southerners, first tenants and sharecroppers and then small-farm owners, left rural areas to make way for large, mechanized, centralized neo-plantations. After 1950 the number of Southern farms declined rapidly, falling from 2.1 million to 722,000 by 1975. The number of sharecropper-run farms during those twenty-five years fell from roughly 50 percent to under 10 percent. Black farmers, the mainstay of the old system, declined from about 900,000 in 1920 to 540,000 in 1950 and 55,995 in 1978. The number of Southerners making a living by farming, 43 percent in 1940, fell to only 6.9 percent by 1970. Southern life had been epitomized by farming, but that standard has largely disappeared.

No longer did people move in seasonal harmony and consult the almanac for signs of planting, cultivating, and harvesting, nor did hog killing in the autumn or winter break up the routine of watching TV soap operas or the steady grind of a nine-to-five job. The old routines were gone, and with them went many of the milestones of young people moving through incidental chores to full man- or woman-sized jobs. Being old enough to watch *Dallas* was not exactly a rite of passage that rivaled a bear hunt or plowing a field for the first time.

The white South's acceptance of civil rights came partly from the restructuring of agriculture. By adopting machines, landlords no longer needed a large colony of compliant sharecroppers. The federal government subsidized farmers the same way it aided many refugees from agriculture with welfare. The burgeoning factory system took advantage of black laborers as it had not during earlier years when segregated cotton mills typified Southern industry. Still, in rural areas the impact of the civil-rights movement was profound, for consolidated public schools were thoroughly integrated—despite a number of private schools catering to whites. Had the rural revolution not come about, the history of the equal-rights movement may have been quite different.

No single family could typify the disruption of the old order, but the Gudger family in *Let Us Now Praise Famous Men* is representative. In 1976, forty years after James Agee wrote that book, Bradford L. Jenkins looked up the remnants of the Gudger family and interviewed them. George Gudger had continued to farm on shares until his death in 1959. "George didn't live to enjoy some of the things we have now," his wife remembered. "We never had nothin' the whole time he was alive." Annie Mae Gudger bore three more children and continued to live in the same area of Alabama. Louise, the oldest child, married at fourteen after dropping out of school and at age forty-one committed suicide. Junior continued to farm, working for wages as a tractor driver on a five-hundred acre farm. "Out of my whole family, I'm the only one that farms today," he admitted. "All of the rest of them do public work, but working on a farm now is like public work. You're hired for one thing and that's what you do." Burt moved away from Hale County and remembered it with distaste. He attended a trade school, learned how to weld, and then helped unionize his shop, boasting that wages rose from $2.25 to $6 or $7 per hour. The glare of the torch and the fumes affected his eyes and sinuses, so he became a supervisor. Squeaky, the youngest, worked in a meat-packing plant in Tuscaloosa. Three of the families lived in mobile homes, the option that many Southern families took as the price of homes rose. Roughly half of the new homes purchased in the South are mobile homes. Many are comfortable and sit on several acres, while others are crowded into trailer parks.

Emma McCloud caught the attention of James Agee, and in *Let Us Now Praise Famous Men* he described an attractive and talented young woman who was leaving Hale County to join her husband, Lutie, twenty years her senior, in Mississippi. Agee felt an immediate attraction "for this girl who was so soon going on out of my existence into so hopeless a one of hers." By that time Emma had escaped from the cotton farm her father and his three remaining children tended. "We just worked hard from year to year—them three years until Daddy married again," she recalled. "We never had any more Christmas. We didn't have anything but one another. We was a pitiful three." She married Lutie when she was sixteen years old; she wanted a home of her own. Instead, she lived in his mother's house till her nerves frayed (Lutie's mother would not allow her to sing in the house), left briefly to stay with George and Annie Mae, and then Lutie got a job in Cherokee County. She was staying with George and Annie Mae again while Lutie got settled in Lee, Mississippi, before sending for her.

She bore children while Lutie moved from job to job, never making enough for a comfortable living. Eventually, Lutie registered with a government rehabilitation program, and Emma praised Roosevelt as "the only President I ever knew that done anything." After they lost everything despite the government's aid, Lutie went to Mobile to work as a guard and then took a job in Alabama. "He dressed like a million dollars, and my children went to school barefooted," Emma complained. Once he sent her a check for thirty dollars. "The rest of the time he always got robbed. He was always getting robbed," she remembered. She continued to work in the fields and, much to her distress, left her children in the house, even when they were sick. "I have shed enough tears to do a washing."

She had asthma, went to hospitals, but found no relief. Then a government man offered her a job at a nursing home. As a girl she had dreamed of becoming a nurse. Despite Lutie's opposition, she held the job and did well at it. The marriage broke up, and she eventually got a divorce. She took other jobs and managed to survive on her own. "This life has been kindly rugged here," she concluded. "I have never seen too much happiness. My road has been pretty bumpy. The happiest part was when I was trying to bring my children up and I thought I done the best I could."

In many respects the fate of the Gudger family and Emma McCloud typify the changes in Southern life. These people stayed in the area where they grew up, they visited, and they remained a close family. They were much better off in 1976 than forty years before when they were eking out a semblance of a living on the Hale County farm. Their lives were filled with hard work, and despite their hardships, they held on to their pride. Their dreams were not of mansions or possessions but of moving up one more step. "I looked for something real good to happen to me like a little home, a pretty yard of flowers, and a garden, even some chickens," Emma said in 1976. "And a good someone to be with, to laugh and talk with."

The New Fundamentalism _____

Because of the upheaval in Southern life in the past thirty years, many Southerners have turned to religion in what resembles another Great Awakening. The reconversion of the Bible Belt has many causes, but the popularity of TV preachers has certainly been the driving force. A surprising percentage of those who watch evangelists attack evil, offer platitudes, and ask for contributions to aid their ministry are the same people who watch wrestling and soap operas, go to stock-car races, cockfights, and rock 'n' roll concerts. Southerners have always liked good entertainment and reveled in contradictions. Many evangelists have succeeded primarily because their converts fear that a crucial aspect of society is collapsing around them. They are searching for eternal values in a changing world.

Many evangelists, starting with Billy Graham and Oral Roberts, have discovered the power of TV to attract both converts and funds. Jerry Falwell, pastor of the Thomas Road Baptist Church in Lynchburg, Virginia, has emerged as one of the most influential TV evangelists, bringing in $200,000 million a year from his various enterprises. His church has 21,000 members, his Old-Time Gospel Hour has some 6.5 million viewers, and through the Moral Majority, his political crusade, he reaches millions more. The Moral Majority has attached itself to the Republican Party, and with support from such powerful politicians as Jesse Helms, it has influenced the party's agenda. Christians have always been influential in American politics, but the Moral Majority links church and state in a way that is untraditional.

The religious crusade personified by Southerners Falwell, Pat Robertson, James Bakker, Jimmy Swaggart, and a host of TV preachers is based on a fear that Christian values are endangered. White men, especially, have seen their status crumble as blacks gained equal rights, as women revolted against their subservient place in society, and as unemployment threatened their livelihoods. Women shared with men a sense of decay and insecurity, intensified by a rising divorce rate and the widespread acceptance of abortion. To escape from the reality of a changing world, many Christians have become involved in sports, prayer groups, conferences, movies, and concerts, and many believers patronize only Christian-owned businesses. In addition, Falwell, as well as Bob Jones and Oral Roberts, have established colleges that restrict curriculums and course content.

The religious right is riddled with contradictions. While Falwell reversed his earlier opposition to civil rights (and his congregation now has high praise for civil disobedience), much of the voter registration among white Christians in recent elections has been in direct response to increased voter registration among blacks. Participation by organized religion in political issues violates a strong tradition among Fundamentalists, for the strictures against mixing church and state evolved in response to religious persecutions. The Moral Majority, by insisting on a set of controversial issues as a test of faith, shuts off debate and condemns those who disagree, no matter how rationally, as ungodly. The Moral Majority seeks to gain its religious objectives through politics, which is a radical departure from Protestant tradition.

Not only have Fundamentalists moved into national politics, but the religious right has become dominant in the Southern Baptist Convention. Moderate opponents charge that the right has packed the major committees of the convention and dominates it. Unless the heavy-handed purge ends, the convention could split into two wings (Northern and Southern Baptists split before the Civil War over the issue of slavery and have never reunited). The issue of evolution has also reappeared. Many right-wing believers insist that Creationism (the belief that the world was created in six days as recorded in the first chapter of Genesis) be taught in public and private schools. Courts have struck down such laws, the last one falling in Louisiana in the summer of 1985.

The religious right is a curious mixture of a Great Awakening and a retrenchment from the modern world. It is cut off from history, for it looks neither to secular nor to religious lessons but leapfrogs from the present to biblical times. Many of the converted have hitched their wagon to Jerry Falwell and Jesse Helms, two media stars, but there are, as the Bible warns, dangerous pitfalls along the road to righteousness.

Modern Southern Literature _____

While Fundamentalists cut themselves off from the flow of history and sought to build a heaven on earth, Southern writers explored tradition and history and attempted to reconcile past and present. They set about explaining an absurd world that had grown out of the oppressive past. The trails cut by William Faulkner, Ellen Glasgow, Thomas Wolfe, Richard Wright, and others opened new visions for the succeeding generation. Much of this fiction depicts people in crisis, traditional people concerned with civil rights, urbanization, failing farms, sexism, unions, and salvation. The memory of the past lingers, but modern Southern writers are also exploring the resilience of their heritage to incorporate new challenges.

Robert Penn Warren's career has been rich and complex and bridges the period from the Great Depression to the present. He contributed an essay to *I'll Take My Stand*, wrote about tobacco farmers rebelling against low prices in *Night Rider* (1939), explored the career of Willie Stark (in many respects, a fictional Huey Long) in *All the King's Men* (1946), probed the racial conflicts of Thomas Jefferson in *Brother to Dragons* (1953), and won the Pulitzer Prize for both literature and poetry. His contributions to literary criticism, along with those of Cleanth Brooks, shaped the direction of English courses for years. Most of his work reflects Southern history and the conflicts of people dealing with tradition and change.

In many ways novelist Eudora Welty personifies the post-World War II Southern novelist. She grew up in a middle-class family in Jackson, Mississippi. In her autobiographical work *One Writer's Beginnings*, she revealed some of the ingredients that shaped her view of the South—a morbid streak in her mother, her own aversion to organized religion, and her gratitude at not being deprived of the King James Version of the Bible. Her short stories and novels, usually set in rural and small-town Mississippi, have deservedly earned critical acclaim and a large readership. In *Losing Battles* (1970), she depicts the humor and crisis surrounding a family reunion. With her grasp of idiom, sense of plot, and ability to show both the dignity and the foolishness of people, she has created a sensitive catalogue of Southerners going about their lives.

Virginian William Styron's early novels explored crumbling Southern institutions and questioned whether the emotions attached to them could endure. *The Confessions of Nat Turner* (1966) is a fictional account of the 1831 slave revolt in Southampton County, Virginia. After initial praise, a group of ten black writers attacked Styron, faulting him for his interpretation of Turner's revolutionary role and his relationship to blacks and whites. *Sophie's Choice* (1979) explores the interrelations of a young Southern writer (living in Brooklyn) and his two friends—Sophie, a Polish refugee, and Nathan, her emotionally disturbed lover. Styron includes musings on the parallels between concentration camps and slavery in the South, as well as other aspects of Southern guilt.

Flannery O'Connor of Georgia wrote fiction dealing with both the tragic and the comic aspects of Southern life. "The two circumstances that have given character to my writing," she said, "have been those of being Southern and being Catholic." Her religion gave her a world view, and her Southern background supplied the literary ammunition for her pen. She portrayed Southerners as grotesque and bizarre and too unrepentant and wayward to merit salvation. Her two novels, *Wise Blood* (1952) and *The Violent Bear It Away* (1960), and her collected short stories, *A Good Man Is Hard to Find* (1955) and *Everything That Rises Must Converge* (1965), detail the foibles of Southerners so far into depravity that it would be a test of God's grace to save them. Haze Motes, in *Wise Blood*, is a victim of Fundamentalist religion, which can warp and destroy a person. According to literary critic Lewis Lawson, O'Connor was "perhaps the writer of the modern southern school most conscious of the chaotic world caused by the declining belief in older religious institutions. Thus her satire was the most desperate, for to her it was most obvious that the old order was crumbling." Her brilliant career ended in 1964 when she died of lupus; she was only thirty-nine years old.

Alice Walker, born in Georgia in 1944, won the Pulitzer Prize for fiction for *The Color Purple* (1982). It is a story of triumph, a Cinderella tale that explores the cruelty of life and ultimate salvation in the rural South. Her literary vision, she explains, comes from seeing the world through the lenses of blacks, women, poor people, and Southerners in general. In addition to her poetry, her other novels include *The Third Life of Grange Copeland* (1970) and *Meridian* (1976).

Walker Percy has emerged as a preeminent Southern writer. He studied medicine, but an illness prevented him from practicing. Instead, he turned to fiction and philosophy; *The Message in the Bottle* reveals the philosophical underpinnings of his fiction. *The Moviegoer* (1961) shows his keen insight into the middle-class search for meaning in a changing society. If his characters sometimes seem like Southern Woody Allens, his attempt to make sense out of alienation and absurdity is remarkable. His works treat Southerners caught in transition, casting about for anchors to hold them fast from the tides of change. His is an important Southern voice, which has moved far beyond old institutions to question the direction and possibilities of the emerging Southern society.

In 1980, with little fanfare, Louisiana State University Press brought out John Kennedy Toole's *A Confederacy of Dunces*. Within weeks, it had attained cult status among Southerners and prompted a sharpened vocabulary of outrage. Every Southerner, it seemed, had known some "character" who resembled Toole's four-hundred-pound weakling, Ignatius Jacques Reilly. Self-indulgent, hypochondriacal, lazy, and bizarre, Reilly believes his fate is linked to Boethius's *rota Fortunae*, the wheel of fortune spun by a blind goddess. His outrage at the century's failings ("I am at the moment writing a lengthy indictment against our century," he announces to a policeman) extends, among other subjects, to TV, movies, fashion, the police, capitalism, buses, and moderation. He keeps his encyclopedic narratives in Big Chief notebooks strewn around his bed. Reilly's mother, Patrolman Mancusco, and Burma Jones, a black man with a perpetual pillar of smoke circling just beyond his sunglasses, have joined Miss Trixie, Gus Levy, and a host of other New Orleans characters.

Toole was obviously a genius, and slowly his personal story has emerged. One day when Walker Percy was holding office hours at Loyola University in 1976, Thelma D. Toole asked if he would read some chapters of a book written during the sixties by her son, who had committed suicide in 1969. Toole had sent the manuscript to a commercial publisher in New York, but it had been rejected. Ever the gentleman, Percy promised to read it.

Percy immediately recognized the worth of the manuscript, and ultimately the book became a best seller and won the Pulitzer Prize for literature, a sad commentary on the literary establishment that had passed it by in the sixties. Toole's experience with the publishing world and his death reflect the downward swing of Fortuna's wheel. Toole chose his title from a work by Jonathan Swift, and the epigraph to the book is a comment on Toole's fate and on the fate of all creative people who labor in obscurity, undiscovered and unappreciated. "When a true genius appears in the world, you may know him by this sign, that the dunces are all in confederacy against him."

These writers, only a sampling of the five hundred or so who have produced novels since 1940, are bonded both by their Southern origins and by the focus of their subject matter. Southern writers have always been aware of their heritage. One generation was mired in the Lost Cause; the next was preoccupied with the revolt against defeat and stasis; and the present is fascinated by the collapse of institutions that carried the South through almost a century. Instead of avoiding the travail of the past, modern Southern novelists build on it, use it, and then pose questions about its significance and the new values that challenge tradition. Defeat, race, and poverty are never far from their thoughts. Most have looked not to wealthy and aristocratic people for themes but to the preterites. If untamed Southerners seldom write their own history or literature, they generously supply the raw material. It has been the poor, the despised, the sinners, and the sinned against who have given the South its special character and its literature.

The End of the South?

It was a century of lasts and firsts, of cemented segregation and then abrupt fractures, of sharecroppers drifting farther from their communities, of lynch first and ask questions later, of prohibition and bootlegging, of creative forces in music and literature and reactionary demagogues damming up inquiry, of white religion resisting change and black religion militantly pressing for human dignity, of the federal government aiding commercial farmers and condemning sharecroppers, of reaction and revolution. In the end the forces of the twentieth century reconfigured the South, and though in some respects the region remains distinct, it is no longer the South of slavery and racial violence, of poor farmers and rich merchants, or even of isolated, distinct cultures.

For one thing, millions of people born in the South or descended from Southerners live elsewhere. Even as outward migration continued, Northern whites filled part of the vacuum, but these neo-carpetbaggers came not to challenge Southern ways but to retire or to work as managers in the burgeoning Southern factory system. For many the move south was a pilgrimage from the lower middle class to the upper, a shift from Democrat to Republican, from inner-city or Northern rural life to Southern small-town or city life. They settled on the suburban Southern frontier beside Southerners escaping from the inner city or the hinterland and moving up the social ladder to respectability; both groups discovered they had much in common. They detested the acrimonious Klan, but they resisted busing their children to predominantly black schools. They wanted clean streets, regular garbage pickups, and schools that would prepare their children for college. They had joined the great American middle class and turned their sights to the accumulation of furniture, gadgets, automobiles, and status. No cars up on blocks and no whitewashed tires marred their front yards, although the ever popular jockey (with his face and hands painted white) holding up a lantern stood guard at the driveway to remind callers that the residents indeed knew their heritage. They laughed at the sitcoms, told racist jokes, belched through football games, sent their children to soccer practice, worried about drugs, read *Southern Living* and *Sports Illustrated*, attended a nearby church (or watched one of the evangelists on television), and lived or died by the victories and defeats of their college alma maters. In other words, they were thoroughly American.

They tried to buy off their children's rebellion with toys, with permissiveness, with a personal TV and telephone, and later with a video recorder, and at last with a personal computer. There was little left of the rural South that depended on children for chores, then for small tasks, and finally for a day's work in the fields and kitchens. Without work, without milestones, without purpose, many young black and white Southerners drifted toward complacency, loathing at once the present and the yearning of their parents for the old values left behind. Yet materially most Southerners were far better off than had been the case before the agricultural revolution banished them from the countryside. In retrospect, Southerners looked back to that life with mixed emotions, with feelings of nostalgia and bitterness, with a chilling memory of poverty and a quite different view of social relations and a unity with nature.

The coming of television in the 1950s presented Americans with an object that in one sense was company—they kept it on no matter who was visiting—and in another sense was an annoyance. White Southerners were comfortable with laugh tracks, with cowboy shows, and with the classic Andy Griffith series, but the civil-rights movement, integrated baseball in the 1950s and 1960s, and even the more ludicrous depictions of Southerners as in *The Beverly Hillbillies* and *The Dukes of Hazzard* gave them pause. Southerners on TV seemed eternally caught up in racial strife or making fools of themselves in cars or in courthouses. The message was clear; the idiotic Southerner, the militant Southerner, should change and become part of the mainstream. Just as school textbooks watered down literature and history to meet some censor's pencil, Southerners should become respectable and shuck their accents and distinctiveness. With few exceptions, blacks fared no better than whites on TV, for few programs allowed dignity to overcome caricature.

As the evidence of rural life dwindled, nearly every county had its festival to keep alive the memory of earlier (and, of course, idyllic) times, and folklorists and antique dealers hunted for something genuine. The more Southern society drifted from the old ways, the more people tried to recapture it, either by surrounding themselves with objects from the past or by listening to country music that, despite its smoothness and blandness, still echoed a heritage of hardships and lost loves.

What Southerners—all Americans, for that matter—realized was that a revolution had moved through the land. The twentieth century had been a time of great adjustment. The new work routines left many people unfulfilled. No longer did spring mean plowing and planting, or summer sweat and hoeing and more plowing, or both seasons combined mean renewal of life, nor did fall mean harvest and money. Checks arrived monthly, work continued with no break, and status became measured by payment books that represented a house, a boat, and a car. And the question, muted to be sure, arose: Was this life better than the former one? Had the rush to become respectable and middle class left them too far from their history? In the thirties many Southerners worried about their next meal; in the eighties they worried about their next payment.

Rural blacks and whites still know each other and mix at work, at crossroads stores, and at supermarkets, and they still ask about each other's health, about family, about how they are getting along. The tension and potential for racial violence that attended segregation have disappeared, and though schools, restaurants, and jobs have been integrated, blacks and whites customarily attend separate churches and social gatherings. Since laws assure equal opportunity, blacks and whites are free to work at creating a new Southern way of life. Blacks vote Democratic; whites increasingly vote Republican. Although vestiges of racism linger and some politicians still encourage racism through code words, many rural Southerners take pride in their ability to adjust. Confederate flags still decorate bumpers and wave over outlaws at stock-car races, but they are statements of nonconformity rather than of racism or nostalgia. Local newspapers carry black and white news, and even publish photographs of prospective brides regardless of race. Even gossip columns carry the weekly visits of blacks and whites. Thus, it has been rural Southerners who have most easily adjusted to the changing way of life and, ironically, most stubbornly clung to their distinct accents and folkways. But rural areas are shrinking, accents are becoming less distinct, and Southerners are being tamed.

Bibliographical Essay

General Works

A student of twentieth-century Southern history should start with C. Vann Woodward's works, especially *Origins of the New South, 1877–1913* (Baton Rouge, 1951), an important historiographical milestone which outlined the "Redeemer" thesis and laid the groundwork for all subsequent interpretations that emphasize change amid continuity in Southern history. George B. Tindall, *The Emergence of the New South, 1913–1945* (Baton Rouge, 1967), another monumental work, is often seen as a companion to Woodward; it argues that the 1930s and 1940s forced the South to break the bonds of tradition. Also see Charles P. Roland, *The Improbable Era: The South Since World War II* (Lexington, 1976), which continues Tindall's story, but more superficially. For general works on Southern agriculture, see Gilbert C. Fite, *Cotton Fields No More: Southern Agriculture, 1865–1980* (Lexington, 1984); Jack Temple Kirby, *Southern Worlds Lost: Agriculture, Rural Life, Folks, 1920–1960* (Baton Rouge, 1986); and Pete Daniel, *Breaking the Land: The Transformation of Cotton, Tobacco, and Rice Cultures Since*

1880 (Urbana, 1985). These three works give special emphasis to poor and outcast Southerners, a long-neglected topic. An excellent but dated bibliography of Southern history can be found in Arthur S. Link and Rembert W. Patrick, eds., *Writing Southern History: Essays in Historiography in Honor of Fletcher M. Green* (Baton Rouge, 1972). General histories of the South include William B. Hesseltine and David L. Smiley, *The South in American History*, 2nd ed. (Englewood Cliffs, 1960); John S. Ezell, *The South Since 1865* (New York, 1963); Thomas D. Clark and Albert D. Billington, *The American South: A Brief History* (New York, 1971); and Francis Butler Simkins and Charles P. Roland, *A History of the South* (New York, 1972). These works, however, are textbook in nature and less interpretive than the works of Woodward and Tindall. Wilbur J. Cash's eccentric but telling portrait, *The Mind of the South* (New York, 1941), raises serious questions about Southern individualism and peculiarity; and Michael O'Brien's *The Idea of the American South, 1920–1941* (Baltimore, 1979) is an imaginative intellectual history. Albert E. Cowdrey's *This Land, This South: An Environmental History* (Lexington, 1983) traces the diversity of landscape, soil, and vegetation in the South and how resources were used and abused.

1: Southern Cultures in Conflict _____

There are several excellent analyses of the Populist Party and the farmer movements of the 1890s. The best overview of the Populists is Lawrence Goodwyn, *Democratic Promise: The Populist Moment in America* (New York, 1976), also available in an abbreviated version entitled *The Populist Moment*. Robert C. McMath, Jr., *A History of the Southern Farmers' Alliance* (Chapel Hill, 1975) is excellent, especially describing the way Populism functioned as a religious movement. The most informative works on Southern agriculture, in addition to the general works mentioned above, are Nannie May Tilley, *The Bright-Tobacco Industry, 1860–1929* (Chapel Hill, 1948); Douglas Helms, "Just Lookin' for a Home: The Cotton Boll Weevil and the South" (Ph.D. dissertation, Florida State University, 1977); Joseph Cannon Bailey, *Seaman A. Knapp:*

Schoolmaster of American Agriculture (New York, 1971); Roy V. Scott, *The Reluctant Farmer: The Rise of Agricultural Extension to 1914* (Urbana, 1970); J. Carlyle Sitterson, *Sugar Country: The Cane Sugar Industry in the South, 1753–1958* (Lexington, 1953); and John Norman Efferson, *The Production and Marketing of Rice* (New Orleans, 1952). By far the best description of the seasonal routine and the trials of a black farmer is Theodore Rosengarten, *All God's Dangers: The Life of Nate Shaw* (New York, 1974), a firsthand account that is very human, sometimes humorous, and always moving.

Ronald D. Eller's *Miners, Millhands, and Mountaineers* (Knoxville, 1982) gives a sensitive overview of changes in mountain culture; and David E. Whisnant's *All That Is Native and Fine: The Politics of Culture in an American Region* (Chapel Hill, 1983) is a brilliant study of cultural intrusion into the mountains. On mining life, see David Corbin, *Life, Work, and Rebellion in the Coal Fields: Southern West Virginia Miners, 1880–1922* (Urbana, 1981), and John Faventa, *Power and Powerlessness: Quiescence and Rebellion in an Appalachian Valley* (Urbana, 1980).

The best overview of Southern music can be found in Bill C. Malone, *Southern Music / American Music* (Lexington, 1979), a book that reminds readers that much work remains to be done on this topic. On the development of black music, see Dena Epstein, *Sinful Tunes and Spirituals: Black Folk Music to the Civil War* (Urbana, 1971), and Lawrence Levine, *Black Culture and Black Consciousness* (New York, 1977), a work primarily concerned with slave culture but having wider implications. Henry Shapiro's excellent thoughts on mountain culture, *Appalachia on Our Mind: The Southern Mountains and Mountaineers in the American Consciousness, 1890–1920* (Chapel Hill, 1978), also discusses mountain music and should be consulted for other topics in Southern intellectual and literary history. There are many books that deal with the development of the blues, and among the best are Robert Palmer, *Deep Blues* (New York, 1981); Samuel Charters, *The Country Blues* (New York, 1959) and *The Bluesmen* (New York, 1967); William Ferris, Jr., *Blues from the Delta* (Garden City, 1978); and Jeff Tilton, *Early Downhome Blues: A Musical and Cultural Anal-*

ysis (Urbana, 1977). For an introduction to the prolific literature on jazz, consult Rudi Blesh, *Shining Trumpets: A History of Jazz*, 4th ed. (London, 1958); Barry Ulanov, *A History of Jazz in America* (New York, 1955); Rex Harris, *Jazz*, 5th ed. (Harmondsworth, 1957); and Marshall Stearns, *The Story of Jazz* (New York, 1970). The best accounts of Cajun culture are James H. Dorman, *The People Called Cajuns: An Introduction to an Ethnohistory* (Lafayette, 1983), and Glen R. Conrad, ed., *The Cajuns: Essays on Their History and Culture* (Lafayette, 1978).

2: Politics and Urban Growth _____

Dewey Grantham's *Southern Progressivism: The Reconciliation of Progress and Tradition* (Knoxville, 1983) provides a thorough synthesis of the Progressive movement in the South, as do his numerous other books and essays. Jack Temple Kirby's *Darkness at the Dawning: Race and Reform in the Progressive South* (Philadelphia, 1972) is perhaps the most compelling interpretation of the race issue and the movement, including a brilliant analysis of Edgar Gardner Murphy which clearly shows the problems of Southern liberalism. Two other works, Morton Sosna, *In Search of the Silent South: Southern Liberals and the Race Issue* (New York, 1977), and H. Shelton Smith, *In His Image, But . . . : Racism in Southern Religion* (Durham, 1972), also treat the topic in an absorbing manner. J. Morgan Kousser provides a careful analysis of disenfranchisement, the impact of the poll tax, and the importance of planters in the disenfranchisement of blacks and poor whites, in *The Shaping of Southern Politics: Suffrage Restrictions and the Establishment of the One-Party South, 1880–1910* (New Haven, 1974). Albert D. Kirwan, *Revolt of the Rednecks: Mississippi Politics, 1876–1925* (Lexington, 1951), a pioneering study, and Lester A. Lamon, *Black Tennesseans, 1900–1930* (Knoxville, 1973), offer model state studies of the social strains during the era. There are biographies of many politicians of the time, two of the most important being William F. Holmes, *The White Chief: James Kimble Vardaman* (Baton Rouge, 1970), and Dewey W. Grantham, *Hoke Smith and the Politics of the New South* (Baton Rouge, 1958). Joel Williamson in *The Crucible of Race: Black–White Relations in the American South Since Emancipation* (New York, 1984) analyzes the causes for the abrupt change in Southern politics, especially racial radicalism, and also provides a brilliant analysis of the problem of racism in the South. John W. Cell's carefully argued and imaginative comparison of racism in South Africa and the American South, *The Highest Stage of White Supremacy: The Origins of Segregation in South Africa and the American South* (Cambridge, 1982), is a model of comparative history, a topic which is receiving growing attention. Louis R. Harlan in *Booker T. Washington: The Wizard of Tuskegee, 1901–1915* (New York, 1983), the second volume of his biography, deals with Washington's political power as well as his links with black and white businessmen. Lewis Baker in *The Percys of Mississippi: Politics and Literature of the New South* (Baton Rouge, 1983) supplies new material on the Percy family, but he fails to put them into the context of Southern history. William A. Percy's *Lanterns on the Levee* (New York, 1941) gives the upper-class perspective, with its advantages and limitations, and is a classic of Southern literature. Louis R. Harlan in *Separate and Unequal: Public School Campaigns and Racism in the Southern Seaboard States, 1901–1915* (Chapel Hill, 1958) sets the educational debate in the political context as well as convincingly showing how blacks were discriminated against in education.

The best overviews of Southern women are Anne Firor Scott, *The Southern Lady: From Pedestal to Politics, 1830–1930* (Chicago, 1970), and the essays in Joanne V. Hawks and Sheila L. Skemp, eds., *Sex, Race, and the Role of Women in the South* (Jackson, 1983). Paul E. Fuller's narrowly focused study, *Laura Clay and the Women's Rights Movement* (Lexington, 1975), describes the role of one of the most important women in the movement for equal rights. A. Elizabeth Taylor has written *The Women Suffrage Movement in Tennessee* (New York, 1957) and articles on the role of women in most Southern states; and Marjorie Spruill Wheeler has delivered several papers from her dissertation in progress, "New Women of the New South: Leaders of the Woman Suffrage Movement in the South" (University of Virginia).

There is no general overview of urbanization during the progressive years, but the subject is covered in larger works and in articles. David Goldfield, *Cotton Fields and Skyscrapers: Southern City and Region, 1607–1980* (Baton Rouge, 1982) gives a thorough discussion of the rise of Southern cities, as do essays in Blaine A. Brownell and David A. Goldfield, eds., *The City in Southern History: The Growth of Urban Civilization in the South* (Port Washington, 1977). There are a number of works that concentrate on urban subjects, such as Bradley Robert Rice, *Progressive Cities: The Commission Government Movement in America, 1901–1920* (Austin, 1977), and specialized studies such as Carl V. Harris, *Political Power in Birmingham, 1871–1921* (Knoxville, 1977), and William D. Miller, *Memphis During the Progressive Era, 1900–1917* (Memphis, 1957). There are several essays in August Meier and Elliott Rudwick, *Along the Color Line: Explorations in the Black Experience* (Urbana, 1976) that bear on this era, including "The Boycott Movement against Jim Crow Streetcars in the South, 1900–1906." Automobile racing through the streets is covered in Julian K. Quattlebaum, *The Great Savannah Races* (Athens, 1983). Many topics concerning both segregation and Charleston city life are given thoughtful consideration in Mamie Garvin Fields and Karen Fields, *Lemon Swamp and Other Places: A Carolina Memoir* (New York, 1983).

For a background of Southern thought regarding business, its promotion, and its place in society, see Paul M. Gaston, *The New South Creed: A Study in Southern Mythmaking* (New York, 1970), a work that neatly categorizes Southern thinking during the period. The rise of tobacco manufacturing is covered in Nannie May Tilley, *The R. J. Reynolds Tobacco Company* (Chapel Hill, 1985), and Robert Durden, *The Dukes of Durham, 1865–1929* (Durham, 1975), which contains an excellent account of the Bassett affair and the presidency of John Carlisle Kilgo. David Carlton in *Mill and Town in South Carolina, 1880–1920* (Baton Rouge, 1982) argues that the South's first cotton mills were owned not by the old planter class but by an emerging business class with ties to capitalists in Charleston and the North. Melton A. McLaurin's *Paternalism and Protest: Southern Cotton Mill Workers and Organized Labor, 1875–1905* (Westport, 1971) describes the role of organized labor in early textile mills. Walter B. Weare's *Black Business in the New South: A Social History of the North Carolina Mutual Life Insurance Company* (Urbana, 1973) is a model business history.

3: The Grid of Violence

There is no definitive work on Southern violence, although the theme emerges frequently both in fiction and in history. A good general account is Hugh Davis Graham and Ted Robert Gurr, eds., *Violence in America: Historical and Comparative Perspectives* (New York, 1969). Whitecapping is discussed in William F. Holmes's biography of James K. Vardaman and in "Whitecapping: Agrarian Violence in Mississippi, 1902–1906," *Journal of Southern History* 35 (May 1969). On Kentucky night riders, see John G. Miller, *The Black Patch War* (Chapel Hill, 1936). The best overview of the campaign against lynching is Robert L. Zangrando, *The NAACP Crusade Against Lynching, 1909–1950* (Philadelphia, 1980). There have been a host of books on lynching, including Walter F. White, *Rope and Faggot: A Biography of Judge Lynch* (New York, 1929); Arthur Raper, *The Tragedy of Lynching* (Chapel Hill, 1933); Frank Shay, *Judge Lynch, His First Hundred Years* (New York, 1905); and NAACP, *Thirty Years of Lynching in the United States, 1889–1918* (New York, 1919), each of which contains rather graphic accounts of lynchings. Jacquelyn Dowd Hall's *Revolt Against Chivalry: Jesse Daniel Ames and the Women's Campaign Against Lynching* (New York, 1979) not only treats Ames's career but relates her protest against lynching to the larger themes of race and sex. *Crisis*, the magazine of the NAACP, carried articles on lynching and other forms of violence.

Walter White described his experiences in the Atlanta riot in his autobiography, *A Man Called White: The Autobiography of Walter White* (New York, 1948), and there is a thorough account in John Dittmer, *Black Georgia in the Progressive Era, 1900–1920* (Urbana, 1980), a work that also sheds important light on Southern Progressivism. John D. Weaver in *The Brownsville Raid* (New York, 1973) shows how racial prejudice helped frame the black troops accused of rioting; and Robert V. Haynes has written a definitive account of the Houston riot in *A Night of Violence: The Houston Riot of 1917* (Baton Rouge, 1976). The best treatment of the intellectual intimidation of this era is in Joel Williamson, *The Crucible of Race*, mentioned above. David M. Chalmers's *Hooded Americanism: The History of the Ku Klux Klan* (Garden City, 1965) offers the best overview of that organization. The Percys' struggle with the Klan is discussed in William A. Percy's *Lanterns on the Levee* and in Lewis Baker, *The Percys of Mississippi*, mentioned above. Violence is discussed in Pete Daniel, *The Shadow of Slavery: Peonage in the South, 1901–1969* (Urbana, 1972), which tells how agricultural laborers as well as turpentine workers and others were held involuntarily, constantly intimidated, beaten, and occasionally murdered. The Scottsboro case has been studied by Dan T. Carter in *Scottsboro: A Tragedy of the American South* (Baton Rouge, 1969).

4: Tolling of a Bell

The role of Woodrow Wilson as a Southern politician is discussed in Woodward, *Origins of the New South*, and Tindall, *The Emergence of the New South*, mentioned above. For the definitive account of black thought in the era, see August Meier, *Negro Thought in America, 1880–1915: Racial Ideologies in the Age of Booker T. Washington* (Ann Arbor, 1964), a monumental work that deals with both Southern and national themes. Arthur S. Link provides a general view of the President in *Wilson: The New Freedom* (Princeton, 1956). Stephen R. Fox describes Trotter's confrontation with Wilson and the editor's fascinating career in *The Guardian of Boston: William Monroe Trotter* (New York, 1970). D. W. Griffith's career, as well as an imaginative overview of how the South has been portrayed in the media, is discussed in Jack Temple Kirby, *Media-Made Dixie: The South in the American Imagination* (Baton Rouge, 1978). Also see Edward D. C. Campbell, Jr., *The Celluloid South: Hollywood and the Southern Myth* (Knoxville, 1981), a more narrowly focused study than Kirby's.

There is no definitive history of the migration of blacks or whites from the South, and according to Jack Temple Kirby in "The Southern Exodus, 1910–1960: A Primer for Historians," *Journal of Southern History* 54 (Nov. 1983), there probably never will be, for lack of documentation. Among the most useful books on the subject are Louise V. Kennedy, *The Negro Peasant Turns Cityward: Effects of Recent Migrations to Northern Centers* (New York, 1930); Daniel M. Johnson and Rex R. Campbell, *Black Migration in America: A Social Demographic History* (Durham, 1981); Florette Henri, *Black Migration: Movement North, 1900–1920* (Garden City, 1975); Flora Gill, *Economics and the Black Exodus: An Analysis of Negro Emigration from the Southern United States, 1910–1970* (New York, 1979); Neil Fligstein, *Going North: Migration of Blacks and Whites from the South, 1900–1950* (New York, 1981); Robert Coles, *The South Goes North* (Boston, 1971); and Arna Bontemps and Jack Conroy, *Anyplace but Here* (New York, 1966). On the role of Robert Abbott, see Roi Ottley, *The Lonely Warrior: The Life and Times of Robert S. Abbott* (Chicago, 1955).

The role of white Southerners in the First World War is discussed in varying degrees in most general histories. For black participation in the war effort, the contemporary account by Emmett J. Scott, *Scott's Official History of the American Negro in the World War* (Chicago, 1919), remains a good starting place. Robert R. Moton describes his investigation of rape and conditions among black troops in *Finding a Way Out* (London, 1920); and the career of Charles Young is covered by Abraham Chew, *A Biography of Colonel Charles Young* (Washington, 1923).

James Weldon Johnson gives an exciting account of his life as a teacher, musician, leader in the NAACP, and of the Red Summer, in *Along This Way: The Autobiography of James Weldon Johnson* (New York, 1933). The riots of 1919 are covered in Arthur I. Waskow, *From Race Riot to Sit-in, 1919 and the 1960s: A Study in the Connection Between Conflict and Violence* (Garden City, 1966).

Most of the material relating to Southern rural life during this era can be found in the general works by Kirby, Fite, and Daniel. Margaret Jarman Hagood's study of farm women, *Mothers of the South: Portraiture of the White Tenant Farm Woman* (New York, 1939), is a thorough exploration of rural life. There are excellent studies of diseases that ravaged Southerners, such as Elizabeth W. Etheridge, *The Butterfly Caste: A Social History of Pellagra in the South* (Westport, 1972), and John Ettling, *The Germ of Laziness: Rockefeller Philanthropy and Public Health in the New South* (Cambridge, 1981).

5: The Coat of Many Colors _____

The events surrounding the staffing of the veterans' hospital are covered in Pete Daniel, "Black Power in the 1920s: The Case of Tuskegee Veterans Hospital," *Journal of Southern History* 36 (Aug. 1970). The crises on black campuses are chronicled by Raymond Wolters in *The New Negro on Campus: Black College Rebellions of the 1920s* (Princeton, 1975). Ray Ginger provides a popular account of the Scopes trial in *Six Days or Forever? Tennessee v. John Thomas Scopes* (New York, 1958), a book that sees Bryan as a figure to be pitied rather than admired. The life of William Louis Poteat is sympathetically treated in Suzanne Cameron Linder, *William Louis Poteat: Prophet of Progress* (Chapel Hill, 1966); and James J. Thompson, Jr., in *Tried as by Fire: Southern Baptists and the Religious Controversies of the 1920s* (Macon, 1982), analyzes the conflicts that tested Baptist doctrine.

For an overview of Southern writers during the romantic period, see Wayne Mixon, *Southern Writers and the New South Movement, 1865–1913* (Chapel Hill, 1980). On Ellen Glasgow, see E. Stanley Godbold, Jr., *Ellen Glasgow and the Woman Within* (Baton Rouge, 1972), and Frederick P. McDowell, *Ellen Glasgow and the Ironic Art of Fiction* (Madison, 1960). On Cable, see Arlin Turner, *George W. Cable: A Biography* (Baton Rouge, 1966). For a general account of fiction in the 1920s, see Frederick J. Hoffman, *The Twenties: American Writing in the Postwar Decade* (New York, 1962).

The best general account of country music is Bill C. Malone, *Country Music, USA* (Austin, 1968); and Malone and Judith McCulloh, eds., *Stars of Country Music* (Urbana, 1975) offers biographies of some of the most important country artists. Jimmie Rodgers's life is carefully analyzed in Nolan Porterfield, *Jimmie Rodgers: The Life and Times of America's Blue Yodeler* (Urbana,

1979). Linnell Gentry, *A History and Encyclopedia of Country, Western, and Gospel Music* (Nashville, 1961) is a treasury of articles and sketches. Archie Green in *Only a Miner: Studies in Recorded Coal-Mining Songs* (Urbana, 1972) gives accounts not only of songs but of life and culture in Southern mining regions. The story of the Grand Ole Opry is related in Charles Wolfe, *Grand Ole Opry: The Early Years, 1925–1935* (London, 1975). The best summary of Southern music in general is Bill C. Malone, *Southern Music / American Music*, mentioned above.

On the labor strife of 1929 in the South, see Tom Tippett, *When Southern Labor Stirs* (New York, 1931); Irving Bernstein, *The Lean Years: A History of the American Worker, 1920–1933* (Boston, 1960); and Liston Pope, *Millhands and Preachers: A Study of Gastonia* (New Haven, 1942), one of the first modern sociological studies of the South. For a reinterpretation of mill life and home environment, see Jacquelyn Dowd Hall, Robert Korstad, Christopher Daly, Lu Ann Jones, James Leloudis, and Mary Murphy, *"Like a Family": An Oral History of the Textile South, 1880–1940* (Chapel Hill, 1986).

6: *The Conservative Revolution* _____

The 1927 flood is treated in Pete Daniel, *Deep'n as It Come: The 1927 Mississippi River Flood* (New York, 1977); and the drought, in Nan Elizabeth Woodruff, *As Rare as Rain: Federal Relief in the Great Southern Drought of 1930–31* (Urbana, 1985). Both works stress the ambivalent role of the federal government in dealing with these disasters.

T. Harry Williams has placed Huey Long in a clear perspective in *Huey Long* (New York, 1969). Williams's biography relies on traditional documentation as well as interviews and shows that Long was a complex man who was on his way to national power before his assassination. The book is also excellent on Depression era Southern politics. In *Voices of Protest: Huey Long and Father Coughlin, and the Great Depression* (New York, 1982), Alan Brinkley analyzes both Long's career and his masterful use of the radio in getting his message across to the nation. On the President's role in the South, see Frank Freidel, *FDR and the South* (Baton Rouge, 1965), a small but highly intriguing volume.

The essays in James C. Cobb and Michael V. Namorato, eds., *The New Deal and the South* (Jackson, 1984) provide a good introduction to Southern history in the 1930s, and outline trends of contemporary historiography on this subject. The essays in Erwin C. Hargrove and Paul K. Conkin, eds., *TVA: Fifty Years of Grassroots Bureaucracy* (Urbana, 1984) provide an overview of the role of TVA. Michael J. McDonald and John Muldowny give an excellent narrative and quantitative account of the human costs of TVA in their analysis of the people removed from the Norris Basin in *TVA and the Dispossessed: The Resettlement of Population in the Norris Dam Area* (Knoxville, 1982). On the impact of electricity on rural areas, see D. Clayton Brown, *Electricity for Rural America: The Fight for REA* (Westport, 1980).

Nearly every government agency has received the attention of historians. A good starting place to understand agricultural policy is Paul E. Mertz, *New Deal Policy and Southern Rural Poverty* (Baton Rouge, 1978). The Southern Tenant Farmers Union is discussed in David Eugene Conrad, *The Forgotten Farmers: The Story of Sharecroppers in the New Deal* (Urbana, 1965), and Donald H. Grubbs, *Cry from the Cotton: The Southern Tenant Farmers' Union and the New Deal* (Chapel Hill, 1971). H. L. Mitchell in *Mean Things Happening in This Land: The Life and Times of H. L. Mitchell, Co-Founder of the Southern Tenant Farmers' Union* (Montclair, 1979) offers a firsthand account of union activism during the 1930s and beyond. Anthony P. Dunbar looks at Mitchell and other Southern radicals in *Against the Grain: Southern Radicals and Prophets, 1929–1959* (Charlottesville, 1981), and shows, with perhaps some overemphasis, the role of preachers in the movement for Southern justice. On resettlement, see Paul K. Conkin, *Tomorrow a New World: The New Deal Community Program* (Ithaca, 1959), and Donald Holley, *Uncle Sam's Farmers: The New Deal Communities in the Lower Mississippi Valley* (Urbana, 1975).

The best account of the NRA and the New Deal's attitude toward business is Ellis W. Hawley, *The New Deal and the Problem of Monopoly, 1933–39* (Princeton, 1965). Other agencies are covered in John A. Salmond, *The Civilian Conservation Corps, 1933–1942*

(Durham, 1967), and his biography of Aubrey Williams, *A Southern Rebel: The Life and Times of Aubrey Willis Williams, 1890–1965* (Chapel Hill, 1983).

Irving Bernstein's *Turbulent Years: A History of the American Worker, 1933–1941* (Boston, 1969) treats laborers and related issues. Southern topics are covered in Gary Fink and Merl Reed, eds., *Essays in Southern Labor History* (Westport, 1976), and in John W. Hevener, *Which Side Are You On: The Harlan County Coal Miners, 1931–1939* (Urbana, 1978). The rise of the CIO is traced in Walter Galenson, *The CIO Challenge to the AFL: The History of the American Labor Movement, 1935–1941* (Urbana, 1978). For an overview of the growth of Southern industry, see James C. Cobb, *Industrialization and Southern Society, 1877–1984* (Lexington, 1984).

There are several excellent accounts of the literary renaissance in the South, including Daniel Joseph Singal, *The War Within: From Victorian to Modernist Thought in the South, 1919–1945* (Chapel Hill, 1982), and Richard H. King, *A Southern Renaissance: The Cultural Awakening of the American South, 1930–1955* (New York, 1980). William Faulkner's historical consciousness is explored in Walter Taylor, *Faulkner's Search for a South* (Urbana, 1983); and a comprehensive treatment is David Minter, *William Faulkner: His Life and Work* (Baltimore, 1980). The definitive biographical work is Joseph Blotner, *Faulkner: A Biography*, 2 vols. (New York, 1974). For the best sampling of Faulkner's writing, see Malcolm Cowley, ed., *The Portable Faulkner* (New York, 1946).

On women writers in the South, see Anne Goodwyn Jones, *Tomorrow Is Another Day: The Woman Writer in the South, 1859–1936* (Baton Rouge, 1981); and on Carson McCullers, Virginia Spencer Carr, *The Lonely Hunter: A Biography of Carson McCullers* (Garden City, 1975). A good survey of black women writers in the South is Barbara Christian, *Black Women Novelists: The Development of a Tradition, 1892–1976* (Westport, 1980).

7: The Two-Front War

There is no definitive work dealing with the South during World War II. For changes in rural areas, consult the general works mentioned above on agriculture. The best account of desegregation in the armed forces is Richard M. Dalfiume, *Fighting on Two Fronts: Desegregation of the U.S. Armed Forces, 1939–1953* (Columbia, Mo., 1969). On the March on Washington Movement, see Herbert R. Garfinkel, *When Negroes March: The March on Washington Movement in the Organizational Politics for FEPC* (Glencoe, Ill., 1959). The definitive account of black troops is Ulysses Lee, *The Employment of Negro Troops* (Washington, 1966); and Charles E. Francis chronicles black pilots in *The Tuskegee Airmen: The Story of the Negro in the U.S. Air Force* (Boston, 1955). On the demise of the Farm Security Administration, see Sidney Baldwin, *Poverty and Politics: The Rise and Decline of the Farm Security Administration* (Chapel Hill, 1968). Southern racial violence during World War II is covered in James A. Burran, "Racial Violence in the South During World War II" (Ph.D. dissertation, University of Tennessee, 1977).

8: *The Movement for Civil Rights* _____

The literature on the civil-rights movement is vast and uneven. Jules Tygiel's *Baseball's Great Experiment: Jackie Robinson and the Integration of Major League Baseball* (New York, 1983) is not only a revealing biography of Robinson, an intriguing chapter in American sports, but also an excellent overview of the early civil-rights movement. Richard Kluger in *Simple Justice: The History of Brown v. Board of Education and Black America's Struggle for Equality* (New York, 1975) follows the principals in the case through the Supreme Court decision, providing excellent social background. The best accounts of Southern white reaction to challenges from the courts are Numan V. Bartley, *The Rise of Massive Resistance: Race and Politics in the South During the 1950s* (Baton Rouge, 1969), and Neil R. McMillen, *The Citizen's Council: A History of Organized Resistance to the Second Reconstruction* (Urbana, 1971). August Meier and Elliott Rudwick explore the origins of black protest as well as the development of the legal arm of the NAACP, in several essays in *Along the Color Line*. President Harry S. Truman's Committee on Civil Rights reported in *To Secure These Rights*

(Washington, 1947); and the best account of Truman's civil-rights record is William C. Berman, *The Politics of Civil Rights in the Truman Administration* (Columbus, 1970). Robert F. Burk traces Eisenhower's conservative stance on civil rights in *The Eisenhower Administration and Black Civil Rights* (Knoxville, 1985). Milton Viorst, *Fire in the Streets: America in the 1960s* (New York, 1980) contains a fascinating biographical essay on E. D. Nixon and a good account of Rosa Parks's role in the Montgomery bus boycott.

Anthony Lewis provided an excellent overview of the years immediately after the *Brown* decision in *Portrait of a Decade: The Second American Revolution* (New York, 1964). For early attempts at integrating Southern schools, see Don Shoemaker, ed., *With All Deliberate Speed: Segregation-Desegration in Southern Schools* (New York, 1957), and Benjamin Muse, *Ten Years of Prelude: The Story of Integration Since the Supreme Court's 1954 Decision* (New York, 1964), two works that are especially valuable since they were written during the central phase of the civil-rights movement.

Martin Luther King, Jr., described the crisis in Montgomery in *Stride Toward Freedom: The Montgomery Story* (New York, 1958); and King's career is discussed in detail in David L. Lewis, *King: A Critical Biography* (New York, 1970). Hanes Walton, Jr., in *The Political Philosophy of Martin Luther King, Jr.* (Westport, 1971), explores King's ideas on politics. The most comprehensive recent biography is Stephen Oates, *Let the Trumpet Sound: The Life of Martin Luther King, Jr.* (New York, 1982). On Prince Edward County, Virginia, and its efforts to fight the *Brown* decision, see Robert C. Smith, *They Closed Their Schools* (Chapel Hill, 1965).

9: Domesticated Violence

Two good introductions to Grand National stock-car racing are Jerry Bledsoe, *The World's Number One, Flat-Out, All-Time Great, Stock Car Racing Book* (Garden City, 1975), and Kim Chapin, *Fast as White Lightning: The Story of Stock Car Racing* (New York, 1981).

There is a library of excellent books dealing with rock 'n' roll music. Nick Tosches traces the origins of rock 'n' roll before Elvis

Presley in *Unsung Heroes of Rock 'n' Roll* (New York, 1984); Peter Guralnick in *Lost Highway: Journeys and Arrivals of American Musicians* (Boston, 1979) discusses the interrelation of country, blues, and rock 'n' roll by means of biographical essays on a diverse group of musicians. Greil Marcus's interpretation of several groups of musicians and how their search for music is part of the search for the American dream in *Mystery Train: Images of America in Rock 'n' Roll Music*, rev. ed. (New York, 1982), is one of the most thoughtful explorations of the meaning of rock 'n' roll. The essay on Elvis Presley places him in historical perspective and, like Peter Guralnick, sees him as a tragic figure incapable of living up to his godlike image. Marcus's bibliographical notes sort through the pile of books on Elvis with excellent recommendations. Little Richard and his friends tell his story in vivid detail in Charles White, *The Life and Times of Little Richard: The Quasar of Rock* (New York, 1984). Nick Tosches explains the conflicts that raged in Jerry Lee Lewis in *Hellfire: The Jerry Lee Lewis Story* (New York, 1982); Robert Palmer provides a fascinating interpretive essay and rare photographs in *Jerry Lee Lewis Rocks!* (New York, 1981).

Bill C. Malone's *Southern Music / American Music*, previously mentioned, traces the history of rock music after the classic years, and his bibliography provides valuable guidance for further reading. The career of Janis Joplin is thoroughly analyzed in Myra Friedman, *Buried Alive* (New York, 1973). On white gospel music, see Lois Blackwell, *The Wings of the Dove: The Story of Gospel Music in America* (Norfolk, 1978). A good introduction to black gospel music is Tony Heilbut, *The Gospel Sound: Good News and Bad Times* (New York, 1971). Robert Cantwell explores the origins and continued popularity of one strain of country music, in *Bluegrass Breakdown: The Making of the Old Southern Sound* (Urbana, 1984). The most thoughtful—and disturbing—account of this genre is Nick Tosches, *Country: Living Legends and Dying Metaphors in America's Biggest Music*, rev. ed. (New York, 1985).

The illegal status of cockfighting shields it from publicity, but several accounts have emerged. The best discussion of the people who raise and fight cocks is Eliot Wigginton and Margie Bennett, eds., *Foxfire 8* (Garden City, 1984). Harry Crews's essay is in

Florida Frenzy (Gainesville, 1984); and a technical discussion can be found in Harold A. Herzog, Jr., "Hackfights and Derbies," *Appalachian Journal* 12 (Winter, 1985).

10: A Second Chance at Reconstruction _____

The best account of the sit-ins in Greensboro and the climate of race relations in North Carolina is William H. Chafe, *Civilities and Civil Rights: Greensboro, North Carolina, and the Black Struggle for Freedom* (New York, 1980). The emergence of the Student Nonviolent Coordinating Committee is covered by Clayborne Carson, *In Struggle: SNCC and the Black Awakening of the 1960s* (Cambridge, 1981). Howard Zinn, *SNCC: The New Abolitionists* (Boston, 1964) reflects the revisionist phase of American historiography so prevalent in the 1960s. The role of John F. Kennedy in the civil-rights movement is treated in Carl M. Brauer, *John F. Kennedy and the Second Reconstruction* (New York, 1977). August Meier and Eliott Rudwick wrote the definitive account of the Congress of Racial Equality in *CORE: A Study in the Civil Rights Movement, 1942–1968* (New York, 1973). There are several treatments of the summer of 1964 in Mississippi, and a good introduction is Mary Aickin Rothschild, *A Case of Black and White: Northern Volunteers and the Southern Freedom Summers, 1964–1965* (Westport, 1982), and Elizabeth Sutherland, ed., *Letters from Mississippi* (New York, 1965). The best study of the Mississippi Freedom Democratic Party is Leslie Burl McLemore, "The Mississippi Freedom Democratic Party: A Case Study of Grass Roots Politics" (Ph.D. dissertation, University of Massachusetts, Amherst, 1971).

Historians and political scientists are still grappling with the effects of Southern political change as the region undergoes realignment. Numan V. Bartley and Hugh Davis Graham, *Southern Politics and the Second Reconstruction* (Baltimore, 1975), and Jack Bass and Walter DeVries, *The Transformation of Southern Politics: Social Change and Political Consequences Since 1945* (New York, 1976), offer good analyses of issues and personalities. For a recent update of Southern politics, consult Alexander P. Lamis, *The Two-Party South* (New York, 1984). A good but eccentric account of

Wallace is Marshall Frady, *Wallace* (New York, 1968). But there is no definitive account of Wallace's or Helms's career or their place in Southern politics, or that of Jerry Falwell. In addition to periodical literature on both men, there is William D. Snider's unanalytical but informative account of the Helms–Hunt Senate campaign of 1984, in *Helms and Hunt: The North Carolina Senate Race, 1984* (Chapel Hill, 1985).

11: Consolidating the Revolution

There has been no overall synthesis of Southern society since 1954, so Charles P. Roland's *The Improbable Era*, mentioned previously, remains the starting place for students of the period. Raymond Arsenault's analysis of air-conditioning, "The End of the Long Hot Summer: The Air Conditioner and Southern Culture," *Journal of Southern History* 50 (Nov. 1984), is an introduction to the impact of cool air in the South. The works on agriculture by Fite, Kirby, and Daniel deal with the impact of machines and government programs on farm life, and several articles have traced the sharecroppers discussed by James Agee and photographed by Walker Evans in *Let Us Now Praise Famous Men* (Boston, 1941). John Egerton's *The Americanization of Dixie: The Southernization of America* (New York, 1974) is an excellent and reflective synthesis of changes and their significance.

Southern and national TV evangelists have not received the scholarly treatment they deserve. Susan Friend Harding is working on a study of Jerry Falwell's congregation that promises to be a major reinterpretation of the religious right.

Lewis A. Lawson, *Another Generation: Southern Fiction Since World War II* (Jackson, 1984) is the best introduction to Southern literature; and Louis D. Rubin, Jr., has written extensively of Southern literature in *The Faraway Country: Writers of the Modern South* (Seattle, 1963), *A Gallery of Southerners* (Baton Rouge, 1982), and, with Robert Jacobs, eds., *Southern Renascence: The Literature of the Modern South* (Baltimore, 1953).

In Peggy Whitman Prenshaw, ed., *Women Writers of the Contemporary South* (Jackson, 1984), a number of women writers' careers and works are discussed; and Richard J. Gray, *The Literature of Memory: Modern Writers of the American South* (Baltimore, 1977) gives insights into the obsession with the past in Southern writing.

Louis D. Rubin, Jr., ed., *The American South: Portrait of a Culture* (Baton Rouge, 1980) is an excellent collection of essays on contemporary Southern culture. In addition to Kirby's *Media-Made Dixie* and Campbell's *The Celluloid South*, two excellent overviews of how the Southerner has been stereotyped in the media, see Richard Kelly's *The Andy Griffith Show* (Winston-Salem, 1982; rev. ed., 1985), a superb study of perhaps the most famous television image of the South—Mayberry, home of Sheriff Andy Taylor and his deputy, Barney Fife. The magazine *Southern Exposure* is a treasury of contemporary Southern life.

Index

253